EDUCATION AND SOCIAL CHANGE

To the AARC,

October, 1985

Steve Walker.

Education and Social Change

Edited by
Len Barton and
Stephen Walker

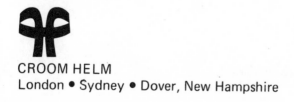

CROOM HELM
London • Sydney • Dover, New Hampshire

©1985 Len Barton and Stephen Walker
Croom Helm Ltd, Provident House, Burrell Row,
Beckenham, Kent BR3 1AT

Croom Helm Australia Pty Ltd, Suite 4, 6th Floor,
64-76 Kippax Street, Surry Hills, NSW 2010, Australia

British Library Cataloguing in Publication Data

Education and social change.
    1. Electronic digital computers – Study and
teaching – United States
I. Barton, Len II. Walker, Stephen, 1944-
370.19   QA76.27

   ISBN 0-7099-3904-3

Croom Helm, 51 Washington Street, Dover,
New Hampshire 03820, USA

Library of Congress Cataloging in Publication Data
Main entry under title:

Education and social change.

   Includes indexes.
    1. Education and State – Great Britain – Congresses.
2. School Management and organization – Great Britain –
Congresses. 3. Schools – Centralization – Great Britain –
Congresses. 4. Teachers – Great Britain – Rating of –
Congresses. 5. Great Britain – Social conditions –
Congresses. I. Barton, Len. II. Walker, Stephen F.
LC93.G7E37   1985   379.41   85-19020
ISBN 0-7099-3904-3

Printed and bound in Great Britain by
Biddles Ltd, Guildford and King's Lynn

CONTENTS

ACKNOWLEDGEMENTS

We would like to express our thanks to Peter Sowden, to Kathryn Phillips, to Margaret Christie and to Sarah Chiumento for their help in the preparation of the manuscript for this book. Thanks also to Roger Osborn-King and to Carfax Publishing Company for their generous support of the International Sociology of Education Conference at which the papers in this volume were originally presented.

The paper by Gerald Grace in this book, 'Judging teachers; the social and political contexts of teacher evaluation', has also appeared as an article in the British Journal of Sociology of Education, Vol. 6, No. 1.

As always, our thanks to Joan Barton and to Sandra Walker for their patience and understanding.

LIST OF CONTRIBUTORS

Stephen Ball   Education Area, University of
                    Sussex, England.

Len Barton   Education Department, Bristol
                    Polytechnic

Heather Cathcart   Faculty of Educational Studies,
                    The Open University, England.

Geoff Esland   Faculty of Educational Studies,
                    The Open University, England.

Gerald Grace   Department of Education, Univer-
                    sity of Cambridge, England.

Ronald King   University of Exeter, England.

Gertrude McPherson Department of Sociology, Univer-
                    sity of Saskatchewan, Canada.

Henry Miller   Faculty of Management and Policy
                    Studies, Aston University,
                    England.

Jennifer Nias   Cambridge Institute of
                    Education, England.

Jenny Shaw   University of Sussex, England.

Stephen Walker   Newman College, Birmingham,
                    England.

Philip Wexler   Rochester University, U.S.A.

Ann Marie Wolpe   Department of Sociology, Middle-
                    sex Polytechnic, England.

EDUCATION AND SOCIAL CHANGE

Len Barton and Stephen Walker

It is probably easier to begin this
introduction by saying what this book isn't about
rather than what it is. We start in this way
because we are conscious that our title,
Education and Social Change, may well have a
depressingly familiar ring to it. It echoes
certain headlines which often appear in
undergraduate sociology of education syllabuses
and, in these contexts, the title usually betokens
courses about the construction of models of how
education systems operate or about the study of
grand theories on the general characteristics and
mechanisms of social and educational change.
Certainly, the emphasis in this book is not upon
this kind of work. Whilst much of the argument
developed in the collection does challenge the
theoretical frameworks we use to explain and to
monitor the processes by which societies and
education systems change, such a critique is not
the primary objective here. Instead, most of the
discussion in the collection centres upon attempts
to catch the here and the now, on some of the real
and recent instances of change, either inside or
outside education, which are having such dramatic
impact on both educational and social life. This
being the case, that the focus is upon the present
and upon contemporary educational affairs, the
selection of issues for examination in the papers
here is varied and represents personal evaluations
of exactly how and where current social changes are
exerting most pressure on the education system.
Discussion in the book ranges through consideration
of such pressing educational matters as the
survival strategies teachers adopt, developments in

teacher assessment policy, changes in the control
of educational policy, planning and provision, the
significance of new vocational initiatives and the
impact of changes in the internal organisation of
schools - particularly, the consequences of
comprehensive re-organisation; discussion also
includes exploration of how these educational
issues are related to wider social changes such as
new directions in the management of the economy, of
class relations and of the political system. If
this range seems to promise a too extensive or even
a fragmented agenda, we hasten to explain that,
notwithstanding the breadth of interest represented
in this book, we believe one can also find certain
common and interrelated themes which run through
the different papers and which link both the
analyses and the commentaries to be found in the
separate contributions. In this introduction, we
intend to make a brief statement of what we take to
be the major unifying elements.

The papers in this collection are all edited
versions of presentations made at the VIIth
International Sociology of Education Conference,
held at Westhill College in January, 1984. The
choice of theme for this conference, 'Social
Change, Teachers and Education', was not a casual
decision. In fact, to put this selection in
context, our choice was a deliberate attempt to
find a theme which reflected a mood amongst
speakers and participants which we detected at
previous conferences. This mood can best be
described as one of growing frustration and anxiety
and seemed to have a number of sources. It
certainly arose from a feeling shared by many
teachers and educationalists that they were being
displaced from their positions as valued and
influential consultants and advisers on educational
practice and thinking by political policy-makers
with largely doctrinaire or reactionary interests.
But, the mood was also related, we think, to a
sense of bewilderment, a certain confusion about
the kind of strategies teachers and educationalists
should employ to achieve a more effective response
to the regressive educational policies being
pursued in the 1980s. It was not just the savagery
of short-term education cuts and spending policy of
the crudity of 'new' educational ideas like
privatisation, vocationalism and increased
monitoring of pupils and teachers which caused
concern. The real source of anxiety was that the
apparent deconstruction and reconstruction of

education essential to the educational programmes incorporated in Conservative policy for the 1980s was being implemented quickly, comprehensively and relentlessly. The conference was intended to provide, therefore, a forum in which instances of current educational and social change could be documented and in which participants could analyse the consequences of these developments and consider the different principles and possibilities on which responses to such changes might be based. It seemed appropriate to insist that, given the crucial position teachers occupy as 'gate-keepers' of educational policy, that their experience of the changes debated should receive special emphasis - and this emphasis is marked throughout this book.

If theorising about social change is hard, documenting its occurrence and impact is desperately difficult. Probably this is because, as a concept, 'social change' has such panoramic reference as to defy precise definition and to force selectivity in usage. Given the climate in which the 1984 Sociology of Education Conference took place, it is not surprising that a particularly distinctive view of social change received prominence and is one which acts as a starting-point for analysis in all the articles that follow. This view of change, social and educationally specific, is most concisely expressed by Margaret Archer in the introduction to her important work, 'Social Origins of Educational Systems'. In this introduction, Archer identifies and answers two fundamental questions about the nature and the development of education systems. She writes,

> . . . why does education have the particular inputs, processes and outputs which characterize it at any given time? The basic answer is very simple. Education has the characteristics it does because of the goals pursued by those who control it. The second question asks why these particular inputs, processes and outputs change over time. The basic answer given here is equally simple. Change occurs because new educational goals are pursued by those who have the power to modify previous practice. As we shall see, these answers are deceptively simple. They are insisted upon now, at the beginning, because . . . education is fundamentally about what people have wanted of it and have been

able to do to it.

The usefulness of these assertions, we feel, lies in the fact that they draw attention to several issues about the way the concept 'change' is used in this book. Our attention is drawn to the centrality of goals and interests as the bed-rock which analysis of social movements and trends must reveal; we are reminded of the complex interrelation between educational policy, practice and outcomes; and, most importantly, we are given a clear directive on the need to incorporate an analysis of the politics of education control in any study of specific instances of shifts in educational thinking and provision.

A key dimension, then, of the perspective of change which keeps appearing in this book, and against which we would want to set the discussions which are developed in the collection, is that particular educational innovations in society are directly related to changes in the control mechanisms used at the political centre. But it is not a simple as that. It is not just that recent educational developments are seen as consequences of revisions in the politics of educational control. It is the view of the nature of these revisions of control that counts - and this involves seeing them as not merely superficial changes in how educational control is achieved and defended, but as fundamental changes in what those in control wish to achieve through education, goals which are inevitably related to their overall social vision and ambitions.

To provide some framework in which we can explore some aspects of how this interpretation applies to a study of the changes in the control of education we are presently experiencing, we would like to remind readers of a view we put forward in the previous Sociology of Education Conference collection to this one, 'Social Crisis and Educational Research'. In an attempt to reach a more secure understanding of certain critical events like successive rounds of cuts of educational expenditure, school closures, teacher redeployment and redundancy programmes and evidence of curriculum contraction and redefinition, we suggested that these had to be seen as part of a more global Conservative social policy being pressed in many advanced industrial nations in the 1980s, which we described as an attempt to redefine the relationship between the individual and the social formation.

We saw the dogmatism with which monetarist-inspired economic enterprises were being presented and advanced as the key characteristic of this redefinition. The radicalism of this policy, we argued, was to do with the absolute supremacy being accorded to the economic project. This project has, as its main goal, the removal or careful control of any social barriers - be they administrative structures, legal routines or everyday customs and cultural practices - which might act as obstacles to the establishment of the quintessential requirement for economic rejuvenation and social stability - an efficient market-based economy in which market forces are allowed unimpeded and uninterrupted free play. In practical terms, however, pursuit of this policy has transformed the relationship between government and electorate, between the state and the individual in a particular way. Roger Dale has put his finger on what we have in mind here in his description of the goal of Tory policy in Britain as "the restoring of the hegemony of the market by removing the obstacle of the social democratic welfare state". The basis for settling conflicts over the allocation of resources or the definition and satisfaction of people's material and welfare needs or even over the question of individual rights has changed. It has changed from a settlement based on conciliation and the tolerance of diversity to one based on confrontation and coercion. In the peculiar logic of the monetarist inspiration this change is inevitable - the firm commitment to allowing market forces to regulate economic and social development not only ruling out the possibility of mounting programmes which might act as a barrier or a brake on these forces but also calling into question the rights of individuals or groups to advance such schemes.

Since we first expressed the ideas summarised above, we have seen, in Britain at least, three broad changes in educational control and management which appear to arise from the more basic social policies we have outlined.

The first of these, and the most obvious, has been the enormous increase in the direct use of economic principles, instrumentalism and the business ethic as a basis of educational planning and policy-making. This operates at various levels. Decisions about the future of schools and courses are being made increasingly on the basis of financial pay-off; expenditure on resources and aids which have obvious commercial possibilities is being given priority over those with less mercenary educational promise; control groups with mainly industrial interests, like the Manpower Services Commission, the Department of Industry, and private enterprises are being encouraged to get involved in the administration and development of educational services and programmes; and, at the level of the curriculum, vocationalism is being pushed to the fore as a central ideology through both special projects and through manipulation of new examination modes and syllabuses.

The second broad change in managerial strategy is a change in the way oppositional groups, real or imagined, are represented and treated by those controlling education through a policy of exclusion. This is evidenced in the crude rhetoric used to characterise critics as 'trendy egalitarians' (or, paradoxically, as 'incompetent subversives') or, more seriously, through devices like replacing elected representative forums such as the Schools Council with bodies made up of members nominated by politicians or through the practice of pushing a notion of efficiency (in cost terms, of course) as the standard for educational evaluation.

The third change in the balance of educational management policy, and arguably the most visible and most vigorously pursued change, is, quite simply, the massive increase in the centralisation of control. It is difficult to find an area of education life in Britain today which has been left untouched by this recent movement. Central financial control has been increased by measures like exerting pressure on bodies such as the University Grants Commission or like curbing both the amount and the target of local authority spending. Central curriculum control has been increased through the establishment of national curriculum criteria and new modes of public examinations, both monitored by centrally-directed HMI and the APU. Central control of 'performance' in education has been achieved through an increase in the amount and extent of official surveillance of the work of teachers and teacher trainers.

Although each of the main trends listed above deserves separate exploration, it is the cumulative impact of these changes which emerges as the major consideration in this book. Cumulatively, these changes in the politics of control can be seen to be exerting a profound influence on two areas of educational practice and research, areas which receive special attention in this collection. The first is an influence upon the image teachers have of themselves and that which others have of them. The second is an influence on the ideological processes which operate within schools. And we hve grouped the papers in this collection into two parts reflecting these particular areas of influence.

The examination made of social change and teachers' identity, in the first part of the book, is conducted through investigations of the concept of teacher identity and how identity changes (Nias), of the effects of changes in the internal organisation of schools upon teachers' views of themselves and their work (Ball), of the response teachers collectively make and might make to changes in local educational conditions (Miller), through an historical analysis of the images of teachers andof the source of these images (McPherson), and of the changing social and political contexts in which the evaluation of teachers take place (Grace).

From a reading of the papers in this first section, we can identify three aspects of the formation and development of teacher identity which are influenced by current changes in the strategies of educational control. The first is that increased standardisation and centralisation is likely to undermine an important source on which teachers draw to establish personal identities and to cope with identity crises, that is - the existence of ideological and value diversity within different schools and areas which permits teachers to find different kinds of fulfillment and different kinds of satisfaction in their work. Secondly, the increase in the overt politicisation of educational management seems, especially in cases like the Liverpool experience described by Miller, to lead to a corresponding increase in the appreciation teachers have of the effectiveness of collective action and of the benefits of closer association with other groups of workers. Thirdly, and in some ways working in an opposite direction to the second trend, changes in control strategies, in the direction we have described, inevitably moves the assessment of teachers from inside to outside of the realm of professional influence and promises an increase in the use of untested and uncritical assumptions about teaching of the kind revealed in the papers by McPherson and by Grace.

The second part of this book, which contains the discussion of the impact of social change on the ideological basis of schools and schooling, falls into two sub-sections - a discussion of how recent changes have influenced crucial ideas used in schools to construct certain categories of pupils and a discussion, in the last two papers, of the theories we employ to debate the relationship between education and the political and social order. In the discussion of substantive topics, the effect of social change on how social relationships are formed and used in schools is explored in relation to gender divisions by Shaw, to the modes of punishment and control used <u>within</u> schools by Wolpe and in relation to pedagogic practice which reflect a 'new' vision of the needs of school-leavers by Cathcart and Esland. All three of these papers testify to the increased divisiveness of current social policy which is matched by the decreased opportunity for teachers to promote critical understanding through the curriculum, through pedagogy or through assessment practices. However, the book ends on a slightly optimistic note. Although, as Cathcart and Esland caution, we should be aware of the danger of "being over-sanguine about the capacity of teachers and educational administrators to debate and confront the implications of these new developments", this collection concludes with a paper by King in which he argues the case for looking for the spaces created by the 'degrees of autonomy' which exist in the education system and with an article by Wexler in which he outlines the transformative potential of educational analysis which aims at a collective production of creative, critical interpretations and at the appropriation by educational analysts and actors of meanings, principles and ideologies.

Throughout this book, the value of criticism is stressed. Critique of processes, of events, of ideologies and, without doubt, of the principles we ourselves use to debate and explore education and social change. We hope that this book can make some small contribution to the development of this kind of critique.

REFERENCES

Margaret S. Archer (1979), Social Origins of Education tion Systems, London, Sage.
L. Barton and S. Walker (eds.) (1984), Social Crisis and Educational Research, London, Croom Helm.
R. Dale (1983) 'You ain't seen nothing yet: the prospects for education' in Wolpe, A.M. and Donald, J., Is there Anyone here from Education? London, Pluto Press.

PART I

TEACHERS AND SOCIAL CHANGE

A MORE DISTANT DRUMMER:
TEACHER DEVELOPMENT AS THE DEVELOPMENT OF SELF

Jennifer Nias

As every pupil knows, teachers are not people. Yet people become teachers. Evidently therefore teaching as a profession robs men and women of their individuality, even their identity. Much research into both adult and teacher development and most teacher education has been tacitly posited on this belief. This paper suggests that the separation of person from occupation is theoretically as well as practically unsound, since both personal and teacher behaviour are determined by the individual's concept of him/herself. Apparent changes in the group of teachers who are the subject of this study can be tentatively explained as a continuing search for a match between their view of themselves as people and as workers.

PERSONAL DEVELOPMENT AND PROFESSIONAL DEVELOPMENT

To put the notion of personal identity in the forefront of an understanding of teachers implies a need to examine theories of both adult and professional change, and the links that have been made between them. Adult development has been conceptualized in a number of ways. The first is as a process of maturation. According to writers such as Allport and Gessell neither training, education nor experience affects the age at which particular behaviours will be exhibited. While there are some teacher attributes, for instance the physiological effects of ageing, to which theories of maturation might apply, they do not appear to have much explanatory force in the context of teacher development and hence will not be considered further in this paper. A related notion is that of Willie and Howey (1981) who, according

3

to Smyth (1983), argue that certain themes (search for intimacy, interaction with life's work, quest for meaning) run through adult development and constantly recur as adults mature.

A third approach implies for the adult learner a much more active role in his/her own development. Theorists such as Piaget and Kohlberg and their successors (e.g. Hunt, 1975; Loevinger, 1976; Gilligan, 1982) point to a sequence of hierarchical, invariant stages of development in the cognitive and conceptual systems of human beings. Each stage is held to signal qualitative changes in cognitive structures resulting from the learner's need to accommodate to environmental dissonance. Each progressively fits the individual more and more adequately for life in a complex society, since, it is claimed, at the higher stages he/she will function more comprehensively and empathically. A similar stance is suggested by the developmental tone of some American advisory programmes (notably Bussis et al, 1976) even though their growth reflects a philosophical rather than a psychological impetus.

Closely resembling these ideas are those life-cycle theorists (e.g. Erikson, 1950; Havinghurst, 1953; Huberman, 1974) who have examined the stages of psycho-social growth in humans. Movement from one stage to another results from successful resolution of the successive tasks or crises faced by each man or woman in the normal course of life. Like the cognitive-developmental theorists these writers assume that development is through an invariant sequence of hierarchical stages, that it is interactional and that each stage is qualitatively better than previous ones. Life-age theorists (e.g. Sheehy, 1976; Levinson, 1978) on the other hand examine the roles and coping behaviours faced or adopted by the majority of adults at particular ages. Like the life-cycle theorists, they argue that these behaviours are evoked by environmental concerns, but they do not take an evaluative stance towards them nor claim that they signal or result from qualitative psycho-social changes in the individual.

Recently there have been attempts to apply some of these theories to teacher education. Among others, McNergney and Carrier (1981), Oja (1981), Sprinthall and Sprinthall (1983) have reported programmes, based on cognitive-developmental theories, which were designed to promote the ego, moral and conceptual developmental of teachers and

4

student teachers. Others (e.g. Knowles, 1978; Howey and Garner, 1982; Smyth, 1983) cite research into adult learning in support of differing views on staff development programmes. A very useful, critical review of these attempts is Feiman and Floden (1980).

There have also been developmental studies of the professional socialization of teachers. Coulter and Taft (1973) see the teacher's 'social assimilation' proceeding from satisfaction through identification and acculturation. Raggett (1975) speaks of initiation, internalization and evolution (a relatively stable state of occupational acceptance which will change only slowly over the years). Katz (1972) uses similar terminology. These papers tacitly view the individual as a relatively passive recipient of an established occupational culture and none of them satisfactorily explains movement between stages.

A more fruitful approach takes cognizance of possible interactions between the personal and professional lives of teachers, particularly since teachers themselves make the distinction between teacher-as-person and teacher-as-teacher (Nias, 1984b). Sutton and Peters (1983) go further than this, arguing that it is sometimes necessary to think of the teacher-as-person-as-teacher (when, for example, career aspirations are affected by ill-health, or domestic responsibilities) and sometimes of the teacher-as-teacher-as-person (for instance, in explaining the home lives of many teachers. See, in particular, Spencer Hall, 1982). Fessler, Burke and Christensen (1983) have developed a hypothetical 'career cycle model' from an extensive review by Christensen, Burke and Fessler (1983) of American studies of teachers' concerns, ambitions, perceptions and capabilities at different points in their careers. Its components are: pre-service, induction, competency-building, enthusiastic and growing, career frustration, stable and stagnant, career wind-down, career exit. Many of these studies were initiated by Ryan (1979) and most, though they speak of 'stages', derive from the life-age tradition. They are generally of student teachers or of teachers with up to five years' experience. Only two (Peterson, 1979; Newman et al, 1980) focus on retired teachers or on those nearing the end of their careers. Each uses different criteria to characterize development; indeed, some do not make these criteria explicit. Thus, though the labels attached to different 'stages of career development' are often similar, it is hard to judge what distinguishes one 'stage' from another, to make comparisons between them or to see what causes movement between 'stages'. Evidence for the later career development of teachers is particularly lacking in differentiation and is often presented in terms which are open to subjective interpretation. The 'career cycle model' which is derived from these studies is therefore appropriately tentative. Moreover, it is not conceived by its authors as a linear model, but as one in which individuals will move in and out of particular phases in response to personal and/or organizational influences. Likely examples of these influences are listed and the authors present several 'typical scenarios' as examples of the interaction between personal situation, organizational context and career development.

For all their weaknesses, these pioneer attempts to present the dynamic interaction between teachers' lives and careers are a move in a promising direction. A similar impetus underlies recent biographical studies (e.g. Ingvarson, 1980; Woods, 1981; Ebbutt, 1982; Holly, 1983; Sikes, 1983a and b and Smith and Kleine, 1983). These have begun to probe the possible origins of teacher identities, careers and behaviours, and to suggest ways in which teacher-as-person may interact with teacher-as-teacher. Only Smith and Kleine use longitudinal evidence. Otherwise, these studies fall into two overlapping categories. Most are descriptive, presenting biographical facts which appear to have, or have had, an effect upon the way in which teachers behave and/or define themselves and their careers. In addition, a few (notably Woods and Smith and Kleine) have elicited from the evidence theoretical insights into the nature and extent of the reciprocality between self and situation which is displayed in their subjects' lives.

Fuller (1969), replicated in the UK with PGCE students by Taylor (1975), uses a different approach of considerable potential. Taking an implicitly Maslowian perspective, she studies the personal concerns of teachers-at-work. She does not suggest that these concerns are related to individual life-changes, but her research emphasizes the importance of considering what needs are met through their work for teachers-as-persons (see also Nias, 1981b). In later studies (Fuller,

Parsons and Watkins 1974; Fuller and Brown, 1975),
she refined her early conceptualization (non-
concern, concern with self, concern with pupils)
into concern with self, with task and with impact.
The first stage is one of survival. It is
characterized by anxiety about one's adequacy and
survival as a teacher, about class control and the
evaluative opinions of both pupils and supervisors.
The second stage is one of mastery; teachers are
trying to perform well. It is marked by concern
over features of the teaching situation (e.g. too
many pupils, time pressures, lack of resources).
In the third stage, the teacher may either become
resistant to change in his/her routines or become
concerned about the impact of his/her actions upon
pupils. Impact concerns relate to the social and
learning needs of individuals, discipline methods
and classroom climate, the choice and teaching of
particular curricula.

The fact that Fuller's formulation was, for
the most part, taken up by researchers in search of
'stages of career development' has tended to
distract attention from her emphasis upon the
teacher-as-person. There have, however, been a
number of recent studies which have recognized that
professional development is inseparable from
personal education (Taylor, 1980) or re-emphasized
the resistance of the individual to the
socialization pressures of the school and the
profession (Lacey, 1977; Woods, 1981; Tabachnik
et al, 1983; Nias, 1984a).

We can now see that three lines of argument
begin to converge. The first derives from work on
adult learning and development: adults develop
(although there is no consensus as to exactly how,
why or when), teachers are adults, therefore
teachers develop. The second springs from research
into professional socialization and the lives of
teachers: teachers alter, as teachers (although,
again, there is little precise knowledge about the
nature or reasons for these changes). The third
also stems from studies of teachers: teaching is a
personal activity. Therefore changes in teachers
need to be conceptualized not just as adult or
teacher development but as changes in the person.
Developmental studies, whether personal or
professional, will be incomplete unless they can
capture the individual's sense of 'personhood' and
examine it as it changes. This is, of course, a
formidable undertaking and one which, from a
symbolic interactionist viewpoint, would require

prior consideration of concepts as complex and slippery as ego and alter, identity and self-image, 'real' and 'ideal', 'substantial' and 'situational', multiple and context-specific selves. Elsewhere (Nias, 1984b) I have claimed that many people choose teaching because they believe that, as teachers, they can propagate or live consistently with the values, beliefs and attitudes which are incorporated into their 'substantial' (as opposed to 'situational') selves. Thus the individual's sense of personal identity is intimately bound up with his/her work and for this reason is protected from institutional pressures by the use of various social strategies. Here, I accept the distinction between 'situational' and 'substantial' selves which I elaborated in that paper and treat the 'substantial' selves revealed by my interviewees as if they were 'real'.

My argument is a modification of Fuller's notion of personal concerns. I suggest that the personal concerns of teachers are those preoccupations and interests which relate to the definition and maintenance of their 'substantial' selves, that apparent changes in these concerns reflect a long drawn out search for congruence between their view of themselves as persons and as teachers and that in default of such a match, they pursue sequential or parallel careers. These developments are accompanied and supported by changes in significant others.

Most of the teachers in my enquiry had made a conscious career choice. In addition, they tended to see themselves as both persistent and successful. Their main preoccupation was therefore to survive, in the eyes of pupils and validating superiors, their early encounters with teaching in a manner which was consistent with these aspects of their self-image. Survival did not however mean self-identification as a teacher. Before this was possible individuals apparently needed to satisfy themselves that they could become, somewhere within the profession, 'the sort of teacher I would like to be'. A period of search, often involving movement, followed that of survival. It had the same main aim - confirmation that the decision to teach was the right one - but its purpose was to achieve a match between the deeply held values and attitudes of the 'substantial' self and the behaviour expected by significant others of the 'situational' self. Those who achieved this match were able to consolidate their sense of

identification with teaching by becoming successful
at it, a process in which the reaction of pupils
was highly significant. Proving one's mastery of
the task was normally accompanied or followed by a
search for personal growth within it. In
particular, the conditions of primary teaching did
not always satisfy the individual's sense of
him/herself as someone with intellectual interests
and the need for self-expression. Finally (in the
time-span covered by my data) a few teachers began
consciously to consider their impact upon the
educational system as well as on their pupils.
They saw themselves as leaders and looked to
significant others who would validate them in this
view of themselves. Meanwhile, others had left
teaching to pursue different careers (notably
parenthood) or, constrained by personal
circumstances, had become 'privatized' workers
within it. In each case their concern was for the
preservation of their sense of personal identity
which, contrary to their expectations, they felt to
be threatened by the alienating or stultifying
effects of their work. In short, I too found
development over time in the concerns of teachers.
I would, however, argue that these changes were
more apparent than real since the individual's
continuing concern was for the preservation of
his/her self image. Self, task and impact concerns
are, in fact, different manifestations of teachers'
desire to preserve and realize their 'substantial'
selves in and through their work.

DATA COLLECTION

Full details of the methodology are available
in Nias (1981b and 1984b). My enquiry relied
heavily upon the personal accounts of ninety-nine
graduates who trained in one year Post Graduate
Certificate in Education (PGCE) courses for work in
infant and junior schools and who had, at the time
of interview, taught for between two and nine
years. Two-thirds of them had attended, over five
years, a course of which I was tutor; indeed, it
was personal interest in their careers which
stimulated this enquiry. The remainder, chosen as
a rudimentary control against subjectivity, were a
random sample who had between them attended similar
courses at seven universities, polytechnics or
colleges of education. Altogether there were
thirty men and sixty-nine women. In the first
group there were seventeen mature students (seven

9

men, ten women); in the second, three (one man, two women).

I knew all the members of the first group very well, and three-quarters of them had been in touch with me between the time that their course ended and my enquiry began. Few of the second group knew me previously. To my surprise I found that members of both groups were not only equally keen to talk to a neutral but interested outsider about their professional experience, but that all of them were free (sometimes to the point of indiscretion) in their comments. Twenty-two members drawn from both groups also kept a diary for one day a week for one term, and the perspectives revealed in these accounts were very similar across groups.

I contacted all the members of each group by telephone or letter. Six of the first group did not wish to be included in the project. With their prior consent, I visited in their schools (in many different parts of England), fifty-three of the remainder and all the second group. I spent roughly half a day with each of them in their classes, making unstructured observations which I subsequently noted down before each interview. I also visited in their own homes twenty of the first group who had left teaching and were bringing up families. I had long telephone conversations with a further eight from the first group (six were at home, two teaching outside England).

The purpose of the school visit was to provide a background against which I could interpret subsequent interview data and not to undertake any formal observation. Afterwards I conducted semi-structured interviews taking rapid notes in a personal shorthand. Respondents were encouraged to give long and if necessary discursive replies and I often used supplementary questions. Thus the shortest of the interviews took one and a half hours, the longest five hours. Most took about three hours. Many interviews of those in the first group were completed in the pub or members' homes. All of those in the second group took place at school. Respondents talked equally freely both in and outside their places of work. The data used in this paper are drawn from responses to questions used throughout the interview. The diaries were chiefly used to triangulate individual accounts of perspective and practice.

When I visited a teacher in his/her school, I also briefly (about half an hour) interviewed the headteacher, having said in advance that I intended to do this. In addition, I corresponded with, or interviewed by telephone, about 70% of the head-teachers of any school in which any of the sample had taught during the previous ten years. The purpose of these interviews was to cross-check factual information and sometimes statements of opinion, and to provide an institutional context for teacher replies. They have not been a primary source of data for this paper.

SURVIVAL

Most of my interviewees had chosen to become primary school teachers; many in making the decision to take a PGCE course had overcome resistance from friends, family, spouses and/or university lecturers. Seven had 'always' wanted to teach, four had made the decision several years before applying for training, four had left other jobs in order to teach. Yet whether or not they had made a conscious career decision, they found their first experience of the work very hard. They recalled, for periods varying between three months and two years, being 'permanently tired', 'lurching from one infection to another', 'never feeling well after the first two weeks of term'. Often exhausted or even ill, working very long hours, they found it hard to sustain a social life 'apart from the weekly moan in the pub with (other teachers)'. Locked into a cycle of sleep and work, they felt they were becoming boring, narrow-minded, petty. They told familiar stories - of large classes, children with acute learning difficulties and behaviour problems, unattractive buildings, colleagues lacking interest or even sympathy, heads who gave no support. Allowing for a natural tendency to overstate difficulties in retrospect and for the felt-need to experience an occupational rite de passage, their recollection of their early years in teaching made consistent and depressing listening.

Researchers have agreed in describing the first experience of teaching as 'initiation' or 'survival'. Moreover, many teachers perceive this period as a status passage, necessarily marked by suffering. Nevertheless, all but six of the total number of these teachers worked for at least one year, eighty-two for more than two. Indeed some of them endured three or four years when 'most days I didn't want to go to work . . . yes, of course, there were the good bits, but if you'd asked me

11

A More Distant Drummer

then if I was enjoying it, I'd have said "No - I
hate it"'.

I asked them the obvious question: why didn't
you give up? I have presented elsewhere (Nias,
1984b) detailed evidence to support the view that
the answer lay in their sense of personal identity.
Many were not used to failing, a few had for many
years defined themselves as teachers. Since their
chief concern was to preserve the self-image with
which they had entered teaching they could not
afford too early to abandon their chosen career.
To be sure, they were also concerned with survival.
They mentioned as characteristic of those early
months or years the same preoccupations which had
filled their minds on teaching practice. Could
they cope with class control? Were their pupils
learning as they should? Would the head or the
adviser judge them fit to pass their probationary
year? How could they teach all the subjects on the
curriculum in an appropriate and interesting
manner? In short, were they up to the job? These
anxieties are, almost to the word, those cited by
Fuller (1969) as typical of 'early concerns', and,
as she argued, they reveal a massive concern with
self-adequacy. Indeed, typical significant adult
others at this period were those perceived as
having validating capabilities - heads, advisers,
very visible and successful colleagues.

Yet one can interpret this overwhelming
preoccupation with survival and validation in
another way too. Becker et al (1961) and Gibson
(1976), in two very different studies, have both
suggested that students rediscover their initial
idealism at the end of their courses, when they are
about to enter the 'real world'. Part of the
expressed commitment of this group was a sense of
moral responsibility for pupils (Nias, 1981a).
When I asked, 'How did you know whether you were
being successful?' the invariable answer was 'the
children's response', even from those who also
admitted their need for recognition by a
sanctioning figure. 'The look on the children's
faces', 'If a child learns something because I've
taught it', 'The way their faces light up', 'When
they come in early to go on with something I've
started' - these are the characteristic touchstones
which my interviewees employed in judging their
classroom successes in their early years. Their
failures were determined in the same way: 'It only
needs one child not to learn . . .'; 'If the
children don't like it, it doesn't matter how good

12

anyone else thinks it is'; 'I used to judge by whether or not I'd had to send Kevin to the head . . .'. Pupils' potency as significant others evidently relates to their unsolicited ability to validate not just the technical competence but also the self-respect of their teachers.

For teachers who feel that they are not surviving, failure is, it seems, an ethical reproach. As Lewis (1979, 17) argues, in our culture failure 'threatens our self-esteem by causing us to doubt our character, our competence, or quite possibly both. To the extent . . . that our aspirations go unrealized (whatever the reason) we are threatened or troubled by personal guilt. Fearing that we have done less than we should, we are all too frequently haunted by the sense that we have done ill.' Indeed, some of my interviewees saw this themselves. More than one said, 'I blame myself when things don't go well' or, 'You always ask yourself "What did I do?"' One summed it up: 'If you haven't taught you don't have any idea how much it matters when you have a bad day. You can't go home and forget it, it nags away all evening, all night too if you're really low. It hurts – in a way you can't explain to people who aren't teachers'.

Altogether, it is not surprising that teachers are obsessed, during their early encounters with pupils, by the self-imposed need, as one put it, 'to get through today, never mind tomorrow or next week'. The costs of not surviving are high – loss of self-esteem and/or of a long-established sense of identification by self and others as a teacher, hurt pride, feelings of moral inadequacy and guilt. They are evidently so high that some of these teachers were prepared to put up with two or more years of 'hell – that's all I can say about it' rather than admit they had not succeeded in their chosen career.

IDENTIFICATION

By the start of their second year (though often sooner and sometimes later) interviewees generally seemed confident that they could fulfil the occupational obligations of 'being a teacher'. Validating colleagues, superiors and/or pupils had confirmed their survival for them; they felt technically competent. This did not, however, mean that they wanted to identify as teachers or that they knew 'what sort of teacher I want to be'. For a period which often lasted two to four years they proceeded to test their career choice against their experience of the profession.

In any case, most of them were not at this point at all sure they wanted to go on teaching. This was not because they felt unskilled – many had already begun to earn the golden opinion of their headteachers – but because they were not ready to see themselves as teachers. During interviews I did not explore with them what they meant when they said that they did not 'feel like a teacher' but in retrospect it seems a crucial question. As I have described in detail in Nias (1984b), at the time of interview only a third made a positive identification with their occupation. The rest were prepared to teach, often with considerable satisfaction, but did not wish to 'become teachers'. There have been very few studies of what 'becoming a teacher' means to those who take up the work (Eddy, 1969; Fuller and Brown, 1975; Lortie, 1975; Blase and Greenfield 1982). My evidence suggests that it means, in part, identifying as one of an occupational group, and in particular with those colleagues who are visible. Although assured of survival, many of my interviewees held this identification in suspense (typically, 'I love children but I hate schools' or, 'I like teaching but I don't want to be a teacher'). They also seemed unwilling to foreclose on a particular occupational identity (e.g. 'It isn't that I don't like teaching – I do, especially in this school. It's just that there are other things I'd like to do', and, 'I'd like to have a go before it's too late at some of the other things I'm good at').

Willingness to identify as a teacher depended in part for the individual on finding a school or sector of education which would enable him/her to 'be myself'. Often this meant searching for a match between personal beliefs and attitudes and the values of the school. Two-thirds of my sample were motivated by 'the pursuit of principle', as they described it, that is, by political or humanitarian concerns (though, it should be noted, their ideals encompassed a wide range of political and educational solutions). In pursuit of these ends they began to change jobs, several of them moving three or four times in as many years. They went not just from one primary school to another, but also to different sectors of the educational system. Within the nine year span covered by their experience almost one third (27) had taught in fifteen different types of school, other than mainstream state schools for children of 5 to 12 years. They took jobs in further education, home teaching, remedial and subject departments in secondary schools, four types of denominational school, private, nursery, hospital and special schools (of five different sorts). They also tried working in schools with large numbers of Asian, Caribbean, or Italian children, and in inner city, suburban and rural areas. In short, they seem to have been reluctant to give up teaching until they had satisfied themselves, through a careful search, that they could not 'be themselves', in value terms, anywhere in the profession.

Some were evidently seeking to realise a different aspect of their identities through their work. In Nias (1984b) I argued that many of my interviewees believed that primary teaching would offer them scope for self-expression; they saw themselves as people seeking self-actualization through employment. Thus the teacher (one of seven to move to special schools) who applied for a job in a hospital school said, 'As a teacher in an ordinary job, I cannot give children the attention I feel they need. With smaller numbers I can care more, and that's what I want to do'; and the infant teacher who moved to the remedial department of a secondary school explained, 'I knew that in that department, children came first, as I believe they should'. By contrast, two teachers with clearly stated conservative views had deliberately changed from schools on re-settlement estates to suburban areas. As one said, 'I don't believe that teachers should be social workers, I want to teach'. At a different level, some moved because they could not 'use my art in that school' or 'there was no scope for my sort of English teaching'. There are many more such examples.

Identification also appeared to depend upon contextual reinforcement. One argued, 'I need to move . . . I don't believe you can behave for very long in a particular way without becoming that sort of person . . . and I don't want to be like that', while another said, 'It's so difficult trying to act one way if everyone else behaves in another. You begin to wonder what sort of teacher you really are'. In Nias (1985) I described the way in which many of my interviewees seemed to use reference groups outside their places of employment to support a 'substantial' self which did not include the notion of self-as-teacher. At the same time they, and others, sustained an active quest for school-based reference groups which would confirm for them some congruence between 'situational' and 'substantial' selves. I interviewed thirteen teachers in their fourth or fifth year of service who were very positive about the ways in which they did or did not like to teach and about their short and long-term aims. All were actively seeking a change of schools and all gave reasons which suggested a felt-need for professional comradeship. All located their main sources of support outside their schools but deplored this fact. 'I want', as one said, 'a school where other people share my goals'; several pleaded for 'just one other person who feels the way I do. I could manage if I had just one other.' Eight other interviewees claimed that they had decided not to move at the point that a like-minded colleague had joined the staff of their schools or when the head had changed, altering the dominant ethos of the school. In each case the desire for a move was accompanied by feelings of personal threat: typically, 'You begin to feel it must be you who's wrong - I knew I wasn't but I needed somebody else to tell me . . . My father-in-law was marvellously supportive but we only saw him in the holidays and I'd got to the point of giving up when (a new head arrived) . . . You do need someone on the spot, someone who knows the same kids you do and is interested in what you're doing. Otherwise you begin to lose confidence in yourself, not just in what you're doing, but in your aims, in why you're doing something this way rather than that.'

As teachers search for positive identification with their work, pupils become increasingly important as significant others, emerging for many teachers as the critical 'reality-definers'. Riseborough (1985) has vividly described the power of career definition individual pupils have for particular teachers. As learners, they retain their capacity to undermine the self-esteem of teachers, to engender feelings of guilt and worthlessness and to cast doubt upon the soundness of the latter's career choice. By contrast they can confirm them in their own eyes as teachers, make them feel loved, needed and successful. Their power to shape, confirm or destroy the future careers of teachers by moulding the latter's view of their own characteristics, capabilities and aspirations has probably so far been underestimated.

CONSOLIDATION AND EXTENSION WITHIN TEACHING

At the end of this phase, both men and women appeared to reach a decision about their immediate careers. Those who had achieved a match between 'substantial' self and the 'situational' self confirmed by a potent school-based reference group, settled into a period of consolidation. Their concerns, as Fuller found, were with task, but with their performance of that task. They sought out courses of a practical nature, experimented with different types of classroom organization and teaching method, worried about the quality of resource provision and the size of their classes. They expressed relatively high levels of job-satisfaction, especially in terms of a sense of competency, and talked of feeling 'extended', 'purposeful', even 'fulfilled'. Their discontent was generally caused more by the features of school life which appeared to reduce their effectiveness (e.g. inefficient administration, lack of whole-school aims) than by teaching itself (Nias, 1981b). They wanted to teach well and resented it when apparent thoughtlessness or weakness on the part of the head prevented them from doing so (Nias, 1980). In short, having decided that they were teachers, they pursued the highest professional standards of which they were capable and expected others to do the same.

At the same time, however, many attempted to alter the role, rather than accepting other people's conception of it. They used their own definitions of good practice in learning from the behaviours and attitudes of others (Nias, 1984a) and took on those professional responsibilities beyond the classroom which they found personally extending. They learnt extra skills, undertook curriculum development or administrative tasks, began to specialize in curriculum areas or aspects of learning difficulty. Men, in particular, became very involved with extra-curricular activities. Indeed it is possible to identify a sub-group of eight men who thoroughly enjoyed working with children, especially in the context of games, environmental studies, field trips and the like, who admitted to finding classroom work rather boring, but who went on teaching because it offered them more of a chance to do more of the things they enjoyed than any other job would apparently do.

Men and women also sought confirmation that, as teachers, they could continue to be intelligent adults with a lively interest in ideas. They began to express a desire for more intellectual challenge in their work, applied for advanced courses, began reading again and enthusiastically discussed educational ideas whenever they could. They expressed dissatisfaction at the level of staffroom debate, deplored the 'pettiness' of many aspects of school life and the 'unthinking' quality of much classroom work and drew heavily upon intellectually-oriented reference groups (usually outside school).

Yet though many of them maintained contact with a reference group which confirmed that they were not 'merely' teachers, their significant others at school were those with whom they worked most closely: pupils and like-minded colleagues (occasionally, therefore, the whole staff). Indeed spouses to whom I spoke during or after individual interviews would say things like: 'It's a good job I feel that way about my work too, otherwise I'd be feeling left out'; 'I never go to school but I must know as much about her class as she does. She's always talking about them'; 'Sometimes I get fed up with the amount she puts into school, but she wouldn't be happy if she didn't, I suppose . . . anyway I'm away quite a bit, so it's just as well.'

It is difficult to relate this phase of task-concerned fulfilment and extension to particular ages or lengths of service. If an individual, whether late or normal entrant to teaching, had a strong sense of personal identity, easily found a congruent context and favourable working conditions then he/she was likely to pass rapidly through earlier phases and be confidently established by the start of the second year. On the other hand, a handful of those who had been teaching eight or more years were still exhibiting these kinds of task concerns. One said, 'I was a late starter - I hated my first four years and it's only since I came here that I've been able to teach at all properly.' Another claimed, 'You can always go on getting better at this job. I'm nowhere near the end of it yet - anyway, I've been lucky, I've had promotion (to a scale 2) within the school, and new responsibilities almost every year. I always feel stretched . . . I suppose I might start looking soon for a deputy's job, but I don't really want to . . . I'm happy here.'

INCREASED INFLUENCE

Eight of my sample, five with between seven and nine years' experience and three who were older but had been less long in teaching, expressed concerns which were different from those voiced by less experienced teachers. They were beginning to look for wider responsibilities within the educational service, to fulfil their view of themselves as persons of leadership potential and/or educational vision. Six were talking of deputy headships or headships, two had become active in their professional associations. Two were teacher-governors, several were closely involved in parent associations. In each case they expressed a desire to influence or change other people in the direction of their own ideas. One man and one woman felt that 'if you care about your religion you have to do something about it'. The rest spoke of their secular educational ideals and of their frustration in 'not being able to get anything done because I'm not at the top.' One woman said, 'I used to think I didn't want promotion, but recently I've begun to realise my ideas are better than most other people's that I meet. Why shouldn't I try to do something about them? Other people do . . .' The two who had turned to union affairs expressed similar views, but argued for the power of direct action rather than the influence of bureaucratic position. All of them showed what Fuller has described as 'impact concerns' but aspired to have a direct effect not, as she suggests, upon pupils' learning but upon some aspect of the educational system.

This change towards a wider view of education was accompanied by a broadening of reference groups and, to a lesser extent, a change in significant others. This group were likely not only to air their own educational philosophies and ideas, but also to quote the opinions of educationalists as widely disparate as A.S. Neill, Chris Searle and Rhodes Boyson. Several harked back, in interview, to one particularly inspiring teacher or headteacher whom they had known or read about, according this person almost the status of a personal guru. To be sure, they were not indifferent to the financial gains of promotion, but their main aim in seeking it seems to have been to acquire a base from which to put their own ideas into action.

Pupils remained important to them, but in slightly different ways. Whereas their younger or junior colleagues gained a keen satisfaction from meeting children's classroom needs and organizing their learning effectively, this group appeared to enjoy nurturing them in a broader sense. One deputy claimed, 'I love these children . . .', another argued, 'If I leave teaching at this point, I shall feel I have let the children down. I know enough now to help them - I must go on and try.' A man put it this way: 'I've always liked children . . . but as you go further up the ladder, you begin to think about all of them, not just your class. It may sound trite, but I have always felt I have a responsibility beyond my own teaching. Now I feel ready to try.'

At the same time, teachers with specific career aspirations took note of the opinions of their headteachers, of advisers, of colleagues with influence in the system - in short, of those with validating capabilities at the next hierarchical level. Promotion, after all, depends on the recommendation of one's superiors. Teachers who want to leave their footprints on the sands of time cannot afford to ignore those who act as gatekeepers to the beach.

CONSOLIDATION AND EXTENSION OUTSIDE TEACHING

Meanwhile, twenty-two had left the profession at the time of interview. All gave similar reasons. Some (including the four men who had always intended to become educational psychologists at the earliest opportunity) did not see themselves as teachers. As one woman said, 'It's no good; I've tried and I'm not a teacher'. A larger group (all women except for one man who had chosen to exchange roles with his wife) had chosen an alternative career in parenthood. Some had done so because they had felt unable to identify as teachers, some had been unsuccessful in finding a congruent setting, some had come to the end of the personal growth which seemed possible in particular schools. Whatever their reasons they saw parenthood as a positive step in another, but related direction. They liked children, they and their husbands wanted a family at some time; at the point when they had made this decision, sooner had seemed more personally satisfying than later. Few wanted to go back to being primary teachers, though most spoke of an eventual return to the profession in another sector or capacity.

I also interviewed three women who were hoping
very soon to become pregnant, or, in one case, to
adopt a baby. In each case, they admitted to
'having lost interest in the job'. 'I feel I'm
getting in a rut, I need something new . . . My
centre of interest seems increasingly to be at
home . . .'. Their significant others were clearly
pressing them, or colluding with them in their
desire to take on another occupation. By contrast,
I spoke to one woman who said 'I want to go on
teaching, I'm not bored yet, in fact I love it, but
I'm under so much pressure at home . . . my
parents, my husband, my mother-in-law. They all
want me to have a family . . . I feel trapped.'

I also include in this category one man and
two women who went to jobs abroad at the end of
four to six years' teaching and two men and one
woman who moved to jobs in secondary schools or
further education at the end of six years. In each
case they made the decision for reasons which
closely resemble those taken by future parents.
They were looking for 'new challenges', 'something
fresh to tackle', 'a job which was a bit different;
I had started to find (my last one) too easy'.
Like their peers who stayed in teaching their goal
was personal extension and to achieve it they were
prepared to pursue sequential careers. As Bethell
(1980) points out, one of the limiting features of
teaching is the difficulties it presents to anyone
who wants to opt in and out at different points, in
accordance with the dictates of felt-needs for
personal growth or refreshment.

'PRIVATIZED WORKERS'

There was also a small group of three women
who had, at the time of interview, exhausted the
possibilities, in terms of personal satisfaction
and extension, which teaching appeared to offer
them. All were described by their heads as competent teachers, yet all wanted to give the job up.
Each had domestic circumstances which made this
difficult. During the previous three to six years
two had tried various schools in an attempt to find
one in which they felt that they 'fitted'. One had
succeeded but confessed to 'stagnating' after four
years in that school. All talked in negative terms
about their lack of involvement with the job and
their dissatisfaction with it. However, they saw
the latter as resulting in part from the former,

which was itself due to their domestic commitments. They all saw themselves as 'being rather 9-to-4, I'm afraid', or 'getting very lazy', a stance for which there was referential support in their schools. It was also clear that the important part of their lives went on at home and that it was in the lateral roles of mother and daughter that they found significance. They had, in short, become 'privatized workers' (Goldthorpe, 1968).

A slightly different case was that of a man who had been an enthusiastic teacher but who had not long before married a widow with three children. He said, 'I know I'm not teaching as well as I could at the moment but the important thing for me just now is to make a success of being a step-father . . . Everything else is second to that . . . I find it immensely satisfying. What I need to do is find a balance between the two.' This man hoped, like Bennett's (1983) and Woods' (1984) art teachers, to seek self-fulfilment through the pursuit of a parallel career.

Teaching, after all, has to take its place alongside other life-age commitments. All but a few of my interviewees were very involved in their jobs for as long as they found them personally satisfying and/or extending or could realize their values through them. When this was no longer the case they tended to look for other career outlets, or, where this was not possible, to invest significance in their lateral roles (see also Fiske, 1980). One can predict, I would argue, that over a life-span an individual's involvement with teaching will fluctuate as a factor of his/her satisfaction with it (however caused), of the satisfactions and obligations attached to other roles and of the extent to which he/she can preserve his/her identity at work as opposed to in other settings. One cannot expect that the career-involvement of any teacher will proceed in a linear form.

CONCLUSION

Studies conducted from various theoretical standpoints have suggested ways in which we can conceptualize and investigate adult development. Other studies, though often with a weaker theoretical framework, have attempted to describe and explain the professional development of teachers. Within the tentative efforts which have been made to bring the two together, we can

distinguish two main thrusts: cognitive-
development theorists have used later developmental
stages as a goal in the planning of teacher-
education programmes and life-age theorists have
explored the lives of teachers with the aim of
increasing our understanding of teachers as people.
The former address the development of teachers as
teachers but ignore teachers' personal lives. In
addition they are open to all the criticisms which
can be levelled at developmental theories
generally. The latter suggest reasons for various
career patterns and occupational characteristics,
but do not explain changes in teachers as
professionals. Neither is therefore very
satisfactory, theoretically or as a guide to
action.

Yet teachers remain, irreducibly, people. We
cannot separate their personal and occupational
lives, conceptually or practically. Any
satisfactory theories of change or development in
teachers must take cognizance of this fact. Now
teachers, as adults, enter the profession with
closely-defined values, beliefs and attitudes
which, in the tradition of symbolic interactionism,
form the closely-defended core of their personal
identities. One possible way, therefore, to
unravel the relationship between professional and
personal development is to examine what influence
the individual's 'substantial' self has upon
his/her career development.

Interviews and journal material from primary
school teachers with between two and nine years'
experience confirmed this as a fruitful approach.
They appeared to move through career phases which
were dominated and determined by personal concerns
which were, as Fuller suggested, in turn for self,
task and impact. However, on closer examination,
these concerns were all expressions of the
individual's need to preserve his/her identity.
The decision to teach, and the consequent need to
survive the first experiences of the classroom
raised urgent questions for a group of people
unused to failing about personal adequacy, guilt
and career identification. Survival assured, many
then set about establishing whether or not they
wished fully to identify as teachers. For most of
them this was dependent upon finding a school or
sector of education in which they could experience
a reinforcing match between their 'situational' and
'substantial' selves. Those that succeeded took on
the next challenge - that of consolidating and

extending their identities as teachers through their mastery over the task. Those who did not moved on to other careers (notably parenthood) in which they believed they would find it easier to live consistently with their values and/or to encounter opportunities for personal growth. Similarly, a few who did not wish to see themselves as teachers but who were trapped by personal circumstances into the job, also located their 'substantial' selves mainly in their lateral roles. Finally, a number of the longest-serving teachers, assured by their job-satisfaction and proven competence of the match between self and occupation, turned for further self-development to impact concerns; in particular they sought for hierarchical positions which would enable them to influence and spread their ideas to others.

It could be argued, therefore, that the personal concerns of teachers do develop but that, in a fundamental sense they remain the same. The heart of this paradox is the notion that the 'substantial self' is the core of both person and teacher. In other words, there can be no change in a teacher unless the person who is that teacher also changes. To be sure, teaching met different needs for all of my interviewees at different times, often as a result of changing circumstances in their personal lives. Yet, throughout, their main professional concern was to find and carry out work which was consistent with their view of themselves as people. The evidence in this study must be interpreted tentatively, but to me it suggests that teachers march to the sound of a more distant drummer than legislators or administrators may think or teacher educators hope.

This need not however be seen as a depressing conclusion. First, there are many instances when it is educationally beneficial for the individual to resist the values or attitudes imposed by his/her colleagues or superiors. Second, there are lessons to be learnt by administrators and educators from the likelihood that teachers seek, as a priority, to preserve their sense of identity; and from the fact that involvement with teaching will vary over a career-span according to the extent to which personal needs are vested in school or elsewhere. Thirdly, the enduring importance to each teacher of his/her 'substantial' self throws teacher education back from peripheral concerns to where it rightly belongs - the personal education of individuals and the consideration of values.

REFERENCES

Becker, H. et al., 91961) Boys in White: Student Culture in Medical School University of Chicago Press.

Bennett, C. (1983) 'Paints, pots or promotion: art teachers' attitudes towards their careers', mimeo, Oxford University.

Bethell, P. (1980) 'Getting away from it all' Times Ed. Supp., 21 March.

Blase, J. and Greenfield, W. (1982) 'On the meaning of being a high school teacher: the beginning years' High Sch. J. May, pp. 266-271.

Bussis, A., Chittenden, E. and Amarel M. (1976) Beyond Surface Curriculum: an interview study of teachers' understandings, Westview Press, Boulder, Col.

Christensen, J., Burke, P. and Fessler, R (1983) 'Teacher life-span development: a summary and synthesis of the literature', Paper presented at AERA, Montreal.

Coulter, F. and Taft, R. (1973) 'Professional socialization of teachers as social assimilation' Human Relations, Vol. 26, pp. 681-93.

Ebbutt, D. (1982) 'Teacher as researcher: how teachers coordinate action research in their respective schools' TIQL Project, Working Paper 10, Cambridge Institute of Education.

Eddy, E. (1969) Becoming a Teacher, Teachers' College Press, Columbia.

Erikson, E. (1950) Childhood and Society, Norton, New York.

Feiman, S. and Floden, R. (1980) 'A consumer's guide to teacher development' Journal of Staff Development, Vol. 1, pp. 126-147.

Fessler, R., Burke, P. and Christensen, J. (1983) 'Teacher career cycle model: a framework for viewing teacher growth needs', Paper presented at AERA, Montreal.

Fiske, M. (1980) 'Changing hierarchies of commitment in adulthood', in (eds.) Smelser, N. and Erikson, E. Themes of Work and Love in Adulthood, Harvard University Press.

Fuller, F. (1969) 'Concerns of teachers: a developmental characterisation', Am. Ed. Res. J., Vol. 6, pp. 207-226.

Fuller, F., Parsons, J. and Watkins, J. (1974) Concerns of teachers: research and conceptualisation, Austin, R. & D.C. for Teacher Education, University of Texas.

Fuller, F., and Brown, O. (1975) 'Becoming a teacher', in (ed.) Ryan, K. Teacher Education: the seventy-fourth yearbook of the NatSSE, Part II, University of Chicago Press.

Gibson, R. (1976) 'The effect of school practice: the development of student perspectives', B. J. Teacher Ed. Vol. 2, pp. 241-250.

Gilligan, C. (1982) In a Different Voice: Psychological Theory and Women's Development, Harvard University Press.

Goldthorpe, J. et al. (1968) The Affluent Worker: Industrial Attitudes and Behaviour, Vol. 1, Cambridge University Press.

Havinghurst, R. (1953) Human Development and Education, Longmans, New York.

Holly, M.L. (1983) 'Two case studies of personal, professional development', Paper presented at AERA, Montreal.

Howey, K. and Garner W. (1982) The Education of Teachers: a look ahead, Longmans, New York.

Huberman, M. (1974) 'Looking at adult education from the perspective of the adult life-cycle', Int. Review Educ., Vol. 20, pp. 117-137.

Hunt, O. (1975) 'Person-environment interaction: a challenge found wanting before it was tried', Rev. Ed. Res., Vol. 45, pp. 209-230.

Ingvarson, L.(1980) 'Portrayals of teacher development', mimeo, Monash University, Melbourne.

Katz, L. (1972) 'Developmental stages of preschool teachers', Elem. Sch. J., Vol. 73, pp. 50-54.

Knowles, M. (1978) The Adult Learner: A Neglected Species, Gulf Publishing, Houston.

Lacey, C. (1977) The Socialization of Teachers, Methuen, London.

Levinson, D. et al., (1978) The Seasons of a Man's Life, Alfred Knopf, New York.

Lewis, M. (1979) The Culture of Inequality, New American Library, New York.

Loevinger, J. (1976) Ego Development, Jossey Bass, San Francisco.

Lortie, D. (1975) School Teacher, University of Chicago Press.

McNergney, R. and Carrier, C. (1981) Teacher Development, Macmillan, New York.

Newman, K., Burden, P. and Applegate, J. (1980) 'Helping teachers examine their long-range development', mimeo, Kent State University.

Nias, J. (1980) 'Leadership styles and job-satisfaction in primary schools', in (eds.) Bush, T. et al., Approaches to School Management, Harper & Row, London.

Nias, J. (1981a) 'Commitment and motivation in primary school teachers', Educational Review, Vol. 33, pp. 181-190.

Nias, J. (1981b) 'Teacher satisfaction and dissatisfaction: Herzberg's 'two-factor' hypothesis revisited', British Journal of Sociology of Education, Vol. 2, pp. 235-246.

Nias, J. (1984a) 'Learning and acting the role: in-school support support for primary teachers', Educational Review, Vol. 36, pp. 3-15.

Nias, J. (1984b) 'The definition and maintenance of self in primary teaching', British Journal of Sociology of Education, Vol. 5, pp. 267-280.

Nias, J. (1985) 'Reference groups in primary teaching: talking, listening and identity', forthcoming in (eds.) Ball, S.J. and Goodson, I., Teachers' Lives and Careers, Falmer Press, Barcombe.

Oja, S. and Sprinthall, M. (1978) 'Psychological and moral development for teachers: Can you teach old dogs?' in (eds.) Sprinthall, M. and Mosner, R. Value Development . . . as the Aim of Education, Character Research Press, New York.

Oja, S. (1981) 'Deriving teacher educational objectives from cognitive-developmental theories and applying them to the practice of teacher education', Paper presented at AERA, Los Angeles.

Peterson, A. (1979) 'Teachers' changing perceptions of self and others throughout the teaching career', Paper presented at Southwest ERA, San Francisco.

Raggett, M. (1975) 'Teachers' professional socialization', London Education Review, Vol. 4, pp. 10-18.

Riseborough, G. (1985) 'Pupils, teachers' careers and schooling: an empirical study', forthcoming in (eds.) Ball, S. and Grodson, I. Teachers' Lives and Careers, Falmer Press, Barcombe.

Ryan, K. (1979) 'The stages of teaching and staff development: some tentative suggestions', Paper presented at AERA, San Francisco.

Sheehy, G. (1976) Passages: Predictable Crises of Adult Life, Dutton, New York.

Sikes, P. (1983a) 'The life cycle of the teacher',

mimeo, Open University.

Sikes, P. (1983b) 'Teacher careers in the comprehensive school', mimeo, Open University.

Smith, L. and Kleine, P. (1982) 'Educational innovation: a life history research perspective', mimeo, Washington University, St. Louis.

Smyth, J. (1983) 'Teachers as collaborative learners in clinical supervision: a state of the art review', Paper presented at AERA, Montreal.

Spencer Hall, D. (1982) 'Teachers as persons: case studies of home lives and the implications for staff development', Paper presented at AERA, New York.

Sprinthall, N. and Sprinthall, L.T. (1982) 'The need for theoretical frameworks in educating teachers: a cognitive-development perspective', in (eds.) Howey, K. and Garner, W. The Education of Teachers: a look ahead, Longmans, New York.

Sutton, R. and Peters, D. (1983) 'Implications for research of a life-span approach to teacher development', Paper presented at AERA, Montreal.

Tabachnik, B., Zeichner, K., Densmore, K. and Hudak, G. (1983) 'The development of teacher perspectives', Paper presented at AERA, Montreal.

Taylor, P. (1975) 'A study of the concerns of PGCE students', British Journal of Teacher Education, Vol. 1, pp. 151-161.

Taylor, W. (1980) 'Professional development or personal development' in (eds.) Hoyle, E. and Megarry, J. Professional Development of Teachers, World Yearbook of Education, Kogan Page.

Willie, R. and Howey, K. (1981) Reflections on adult development: implications for in-service teacher education, University of Minnesota, Minneapolis.

Woods, P. (1981) 'Strategies, commitment and identity: making and breaking the teacher role', in (eds.) Barton, L. and Walker, S. Schools, Teachers and Teaching, Falmer Press, Barcombe.

Woods, P. (1984) 'Teacher, self and curriculum', in (eds.) Goodson, I. and Ball, S.J. Defining the Curriculum: Histories and Ethnographies of School Subjects, Falmer Press, Barcombe.

SCHOOL POLITICS, TEACHERS' CAREERS AND EDUCATIONAL
CHANGE: A CASE STUDY OF BECOMING A COMPREHENSIVE
SCHOOL

Stephen J. Ball

Comprehensive schools differ one from another
across a wide variety of forms of organization,
teaching practices and institutional philosophies.
Both Countesthorpe College and Highbury Grove are
in terms of minimum characteristics comprehensive
schools and yet in their working methods and
educational philosophies they have little in
common. Of course between such extremes of
difference there is a massive range of intermediate
positions as well as mixed-types.
It is usual to consider significant
differences between schools as arising from either
the particular characteristics of the catchment
area and community they serve or the particular
ideological commitments of those responsible for
the setting up and running of them. In either case
we are usually fairly safe in assuming that, in the
short term at least, these sources of definition
are fixed or change fairly slowly. However,
neither is totally immune to outside interference
or manipulation. Local authority or government
policy can and have affected school recruitment and
school-community relationships. And there have
been some notorious examples of conflict between
local authorities and teachers over the
philosophies and concomitant working practices of
particular schools (e.g. Risinghill and Madley
Court). But here I want to consider and explore a
third and less obvious aspect of definition and
change in schools, that is the micropolitics of the
institution. Hoyle (1982, p.88) defines micropolitics

    . . . as embracing those strategies by which
    individuals and groups in organizational
    contexts seek to use their resources of power

29

and influence to further their interests . . .
It is characterized more by coalitions than by
departments, by strategies rather than enacted
rules, by influence rather than by power, and
by knowledge rather than by status.

I take schools (Musgrove 1971) as all other
social organizations (Cyert and March 1963) to be
normally characterized by endemic and often
conspicuous conflicts.[1]   And the most significant
area of conflict in schools is that which arises
over who controls the definition of the school and
therefore which definition is enacted.   Most case-
studies of comprehensive education have tended to
concentrate, with some success, on the technical
aspects of schooling - grouping practices, pastoral
care, the curriculum - or have been focussed on
conflict between pupils and teachers in the
classroom.   There have been only a few sidelights
onto the conflicts between teachers, (see Woods
1979, Hammersley 1981, Hunter 1981, Riseborough
1981 and Bailey 1982a).   But these internal
conflicts and the competing definitions of the
school from which they derive are not merely side
issues in the business of analysing and
understanding policy-making in schools or in making
sense of the implementation and effectiveness of
comprehensive schooling.   For example, in my own
study of Beachside Comprehensive (Ball, 1981) the
processes of change from streaming to mixed-ability
grouping and the subsequent implementation of mixed
ability teaching could only be sensibly interpreted
in terms of the micropolitics of the school. The
innovation brought to the surface major differences
over the goals and purposes of the school which
were normally reconciled but which remained 'as
subterranean issues' (Lacey, 1977, p.137).
The micropolitics of the school are the
processes whereby particular definitions of the
school are maintained and through which alternative
definitions are contained or are asserted.   As was
the case at Beachside these processes and the
conflicts with which they are invested are probably
most visible during periods of major change or
stress within the institution.   In the case to be
considered here competing definitions were revealed
in the most dramatic way, through the setting up
and early existence of a new comprehensive school
created by the amalgamation of two secondary
moderns and a grammar school.   In general terms the
case study material presented is addressed to the

process of becoming a comprehensive school, and the alternative views and interests revealed by the teachers involved.[2] One of the primary vehicles for the analysis is an examination of the effects of the amalgamation on the careers of the teachers from the different schools involved. Hargreaves (1980, p.145) argues that:

> It is simply not enough to study the impact of the comprehensive school on pupils; we must study its impact on teachers, for it is in part through its impact on them and their culture that it has effects on pupils.

In the final section of the paper I pay particular attention to the career of the Headmaster of the case study school and question his role as 'critical reality definer' (Riseborough 1981) in the new institution.

CASTERBRIDGE HIGH SCHOOL

Casterbridge High School, in the town of Melchester, was opened as a comprehensive in September 1979, the product of the amalgamation of three existing schools – Melchester Grammar School for Boys, Egdon Heath Secondary Modern School for Boys, and Shottsford Road Mixed Secondary Modern.

The new school opened on the site of the boys' grammar school and Shottsford Road Mixed Secondary Modern which, conveniently enough, were based in adjacent buildings not more than 100 yards apart. The grammar school building (the East Block) was used to house the upper school (years 4-7) and the Secondary Modern (the West Block) years 1-3. The Egdon Heath site was closed.

As is the case with most amalgamations the appointment of staff to Casterbridge High was made in the first instance from the existing staff of the existing schools. The teachers in all the Melchester schools were invited to apply for posts at Casterbridge with the guarantee that their existing salaries would be protected. Obviously, despite the larger size of the new comprehensive the competition for many of the posts of responsibility (e.g. Heads of Department and Heads of Year) involved a number of incumbents being effectively demoted. For example, all three of the Heads of the English departments in the existing schools applied for and were interviewed for the Casterbridge post. Both the disappointed

31

applicants, from the grammar school and Egdon
Boys', in this case, remain as teachers in the
Casterbridge English Department at the time of
writing (Autumn 1983). In other words many staff
found themselves quite suddenly, as a result of the
amalgamation, 'in a situation where career
aspirations outstripped career realities'
(Riseborough, p.27).

The Head of Casterbridge was a new external
appointment. He was appointed prior to the
amalgamation and spent one year as Head of
Shottsford Mixed School in order to prepare for
comprehensivization.

If we examine the distribution of the
appointments made to the major posts of
responsibility at Casterbridge, in relation to the
proportion of teachers appointed overall from the
existing schools, an interesting and significant
pattern emerges (see Table 2.1).

<u>Table 2.1</u>

<u>Senior Posts of Responsibility</u>
(% in brackets)

	a Managerial	b Academic	c Pastoral	Total Staff
Shottsford Mixed SM	2 (50)	10 (59)	5 (50)	35 (51)
Melchester GS	2 (40)	5 (29)	3 (30)	18 (25)
Egdon Heath Boys' SM	1 (10)	2 (12)	2 (20)	<u>17 (24)</u> 70

(other appoint-
ments 13 total 83)

a. Members of the Senior Management Team
b. Heads of Department or Teachers in Charge
c. Heads and Deputy Heads of Year

At first glance the most striking point to be drawn
from this crude table is the success of Shottsford
candidates in capturing posts of responsibility in
the new school. Clearly this situation contradicts
the frequently quoted adage about amalgamations of
this sort that 'the grammar school staff get the
academic posts and the secondary modern staff the
pastoral posts'. Shottsford staff obtained 10

Heads of Department posts including English, Languages, Physical Education and R.E. There is an interesting point of contrast here with Riseborough's (1981) account of the establishing of Phoenix Comprehensive. However, I shall hope to show that this case does not represent an absolute contradiction of Riseborough's analysis. He found that the Secondary Modern staff involved in the reorganisation which created 'Phoenix Comprehensive School' suffered 'vertical' and 'horizontal' demotion (Becker 1952). They were viewed by the newly appointed Head as 'bad' teachers 'vis-à-vis his organisational goal of a "'pressured' academic environment"' (p.360).

Certainly this scenario hardly applies to the Shottsford Mixed teachers. In the Casterbridge case, it is the Egdon Boys' teachers who lost out in the competition for posts, they are in this sense the 'victims' of the amalgamation. It is the Egdon teachers who are under-represented in all three areas of responsibility shown in the table. The clearest basis for understanding these differences in outcome between the schools lies in the markedly different ethoses, goals, practices and pupil composition of the two secondary modern schools. It is normally the case that the cultures and traditions of grammar schools and secondary modern schools are contrasted in terms of two straight-forward ideal-types based on differences in status, areas of teaching competence, and relationships with pupils (e.g. Hargreaves 1980). But the secondary modern tradition is itself internally differentiated and a number of commentators have suggested that two ideal-typical forms can be isolated. Hargreaves identifies one type which apes the curriculum and the goals of the grammar school and another which responds to 'progressive slogans that teaching must be based on pupils' interests, on relevance to life, and on "learning how to learn"' (1980, p.139). In point of fact this dichotomy is not particularly helpful in capturing the differences between Egdon Boys' and Shottsford Mixed, it tends to blur important points of distinction and probably concentrates too much on the curriculum as a basis of contrast between schools. Reynolds and Sullivan (1981) suggest what is, perhaps, a more powerful and certainly a more apposite dichotomy. Their first ideal-type reflects very much the accepted stereotype of the secondary modern as a child-minding institution, as described for example by

Partridge (1968), such schools are considered to have adopted 'coercive collectivist strategies and generated a somewhat rebellious unqualified delinquent output' (p.132). Their second, in contrast, is portrayed as 'emphasizing the "expressive" goals of relationships using incorporative control strategies . . . collectivistic in orientation and having a conventional view of the knowledge to be inculcated.' They go on to ask:

> What sort of changes were introduced in these schools? Many modified their streaming system (moving to banding or to complete unstreaming) hoping to develop more positive attitudes to learning amongst those in lower streams. Many moved towards a 'truce' on issues like length of hair, uniform, chewing gum and smoking, thus permitting greater autonomy. Many began to incorporate parents by means of parents' evenings, the encouraging of parental visits and the like. Many tolerated a more relaxed atmosphere and flattened status hierarchies between age groups, ability groups and between staff and pupils. They entered more pupils for external exams (up to 50% were entered for CSE or 'O' level in some schools) and many introduced 'progressive' teaching methods such as group work and pupil involvement in lessons of various kinds. Although the number of secondary modern schools attempting all those innovations would have been small, the great majority of secondary moderns would have been attempting some of them.
>
> In essence, the schools were attempting to fulfil their allotted role of attaining goals concerned with social control/instrumental development of talent/expressive development of qualities of humanity and citizenship by attempting to tie their pupils into an acceptance of adult society and adult standards by means of developing relationships with teachers who represent the adult society.
>
> Crucially, the schools were collectivistic in orientation, since pupils were treated as members of classes and given a school experience common to all in the group and since the pupil's place as member of the wider collectivity was frequently stressed, with a substantial emphasis upon the need to

> "get on with" others in that collectivity.
> (pp. 124-5)

Elements of such a regime are certainly evident in the accounts offered by the staff of Shottsford Mixed themselves, even among those who had had previous experience in comprehensive schools. Gabriel Oak, who was second in the English Department and a year tutor at Shottsford, described his application for a post at the school as:

> a shot in the dark, I never wanted to teach in a secondary modern again but the school had special 'touches', and (the Head) was a magic person . . . the ethos was his, materialistic if you like, but I liked the direction he steered in. Shottsford was a fine school.

Miss Henchard had also taught for one year in a comprehensive before moving to Shottsford, and described it as:

> quite a forward looking secondary modern school. We had a sixth form. We did 'A' level. After a couple of years they gave me a whole lot of 'A' level to do and we got kids who had failed their 11+ and were getting a grade A in English.

It could well be argued then that the appointment of Shottsford staff to posts of significant influence in the comprehensive school would provide a starting point for the development of an innovative approach to comprehensive education. Certainly the English and the Languages departments could be said to have made a contribution in this direction. The Head of English was a staunch advocate of mixed-ability groups right through to the fifth year. And the Languages Department continuing from the Shottsford Mixed days provided a Mode III CSE course which enabled the Department to maintain a 70% rate of pupil participation in language courses in the fourth and fifth years. However this was the only Mode III CSE on offer in the new school.

The Headmaster of Casterbridge said of Shottsford Road that:

> although it wasn't a comprehensive school it had elements of the comprehensive school

philosophy behind it. And that in fact was the single biggest school of the three that we amalgamated and provided therefore a larger proportion of the new staff than any of the other schools. That has helped enormously, in that there were a body of staff that were used to working with that kind of philosophy although they perhaps didn't experience the full breadth of ability that a comprehensive school provides, nevertheless they were in a secondary modern school with quite a wide breadth. And had I not had the Shottsford background and the nucleus of Shottsford staff, it would have been much more difficult to get that philosophy accepted. I don't think there's any doubt about that at all.

Here already there are indications of the sorts of differences in school philosophies and teacher perspectives that were to be in competition in the new school. The Headmaster's account of Egdon Boys' differs profoundly from that of Shottsford Mixed.

I think the Egdon philosophy was a very pragmatic one. It basically saw its role as doing - I'm not sure it had any overall philosophy behind it - I think it saw itself fulfilling a sort of social role, in difficult circumstances in an acknowledged difficult area. I think it played it from year to year in a very pragmatic way. And the emphasis was very much on discipline, almost on repression, rather I think - and this is only a pretty subjective viewpoint of someone who was outside the system - than having clear educational aims. So it saw itself fulfilling a social role in that particular neighbourhood. Which might have had some educational spin-offs, but those educational spin-offs were not the most important part of their work. So discipline became more important than the curriculum. And I think that came about because it went through a period when it had a lot of problems; staff movement and difficult pupils. I think it was almost forced upon them just to survive - to have repressive discipline.

As the Headmaster declares this is his subjective viewpoint on Egdon but it is a viewpoint that was reflected in the 'reputation' of the school in the community and backed up by the comments of many of the Shottsford and grammar school staff and some of the Egdon teachers. The importance of the statement lies in the fact that it represents the 'official' and commonly held view of Egdon, irrespective of its veracity. It was on this basis that the Egdon teachers were interviewed for posts in the new school and on this basis that the Egdon teachers were perceived and evaluated by their new colleagues.

Naturally enough the Egdon Boys' teachers did not share this version of their school and its ethos, although they were aware of its existence and its effects. Describing the amalgamation Mr. Dillon, who served for 23 years at Egdon, remarked

> We were unknown quantities. Because of what the Egdon School was, which was sitting in the oldest part of the Melchester Council estate our kids got a name for being tough and uncontrollable and of course the teachers were also classed under that heading.

Much of the value system and preference orderings of the Egdon teachers are captured in the following comments by Mr. Dillon. In both cases, as is often the case in forms of definition and explanation, major points are made through contrast. First:

> There was a period of time when we had a Headmaster who, if you look at it on paper was very successful with O-levels, A-levels, CSEs, GCEs you name it, but in my opinion he was using the school and using the kids. He was trying to make a lot of silk purses out of pigs ears. All right for a while he did. But like water it always finds its own level and you find that some of those kids who were pushed into one or two subjects and studying them to get a GCE or CSE found themselves floundering when they got out of school.

Here there is sense of the anti-academic orientation of the school and the strong belief in the fixed and low level of ability among the children, the school was essentially fulfilling social rather than academic goals. Second:

> Let's face it we used as many modern ideas as we could but we had to be down to earth. The

kids were down to earth. You had to start with them and gradually work up to your level. You couldn't start off with any airy-fairy level as you might do in a grammar school and expect the kids to follow you. You had to go down there, you had to lead and you had to take them with you, to gain their respect. Now if you got that you were all right. But if you didn't they'd run you out of the school in no time flat and they did to a number of teachers.

Here the 'good' teacher is defined. Someone who can survive and work with the most difficult pupils, who learns the trade, the craft of teaching, in the 'school of hard knocks'. Who is 'down to earth' rather than 'airy-fairy'.

The third party in the amalgamation, the boys' grammar school, fits very well the archetypical public school model of grammar schooling. The East Block in the new school, the ex-grammar school building, retained many features of the iconography of its previous use; portraits of previous Heads, a mural of the staff in academic gowns, display cases full of dusty cups and trophies; and the roll of honour in the wood pannelled hall, showing, in gold lettering, the Oxbridge scholarships obtained by past pupils. The ex-Deputy Head of the grammar (now deputy in the comprehensive) explained

Its a great shame, you see, because the year before we went comprehensive we had 7 Oxford and Cambridge awards and places and no more now. One of those boys got a 1st Class Honours degree at Oxford in Law, just been published . . . it's a shame.

It was by these criteria that the grammar school measured its success and it was to these ends that the staff looked for their personal rewards and professional satisfaction. And to achieve these ends . . .

. . . everybody did Latin in the first year but the L-stream, as it was called, the Latin stream, continued to do Latin up to the 4th form, they took it in the 4th form. They had to be streamed otherwise they couldn't do Latin and Physics, Chemistry and Biology, if they wanted to be doctors and so on. But the rest weren't.

The <u>individual teachers codes</u> then (the attitudes and norms and active principles of interpretation and action), that are the basis for choice and action made by any individual (Arfwedson et al (1979)), and the <u>school codes</u> (the dominating tendencies) of each of the three schools differ in significant and conspicuous ways. These differences produced not only a basis for tension and potential disagreement between the teachers from the three schools but also they provided the substance for conflict over the definition of the school code of the new school. The competing coalitions which emerged in the micropolitics of the new school were essentially founded upon the existing social relationships among the teachers. And the preference orderings (i.e. individual goals) (Cyert and March 1963) with which the teachers worked tended to strongly reflect the <u>dominating tendencies</u> within their previous school. New appointments also tended to align themselves with one or other of the existing coalition groups.

The mainlines of conflict within Casterbridge were represented by, on the one hand the grammar school tradition, carried by the ex-grammar staff, and on the other, an assertive comprehensive philosophy maintained by the ex-Shottsford Mixed staff. As far as the Egdon Boys' teachers are concerned, as the appointments shown in Table 1 indicate, they are significantly under presented in positions of formal status and influence at Casterbridge and indeed this together with their low informal status, tended to make them the poor relations in the new school. They carried with them as personal and professional baggage the unfortunate reputation of their previous school. And found themselves landed with 'a stigmatized, spoilt, professional identity' (Riseborough, 1981). They were often antagonistic towards their more 'successful' colleagues and felt themselves to have been ill-treated by the system of making appointments to the new school. They told stories of 'rigging' and 'fixing' going on outside of the interviews. They were 'skidders' (Wilensky and Edwards, 1959), they could not see any future possibility of movement up the career ladder and no way out of their career impasse. They perceived their careers to be at an end. And such realizations had profound implications for 'perception of self and role performance' (Riseborough, 1981, p.363). The attitudes of the new staff at Phoenix towards the 'old' secondary modern teachers, as recorded by Riseborough, are replicated exactly at Casterbridge in the Shottsford Mixed teachers' views of their Egdon Boys' colleagues.

> They were caricatured by the new staff and the Head as irrational diehards, educational backwoodsmen because of their calls for returns to traditional standards of change; their belief that small is beautiful; their selective schools; and the end of all 'trendiness' in educational ideas. (p.365)

The Head of History at Casterbridge, a new appointment and active advocate of comprehensive education and educational innovation, described the Egdon teachers as follows:

> I think the Egdon teachers would have the classic secondary modern thing of 'it hurts the poor little sub-normals to push them' and 'They are happy knowing where their place in life is' you know, 'All you do is stir them up and give them ideas beyond themselves'. And there's also this sort of craftsmanlike approach, 'if you give me a well-streamed group, I'll push them through' and 'I used to get fantastic results from streamed groups' you know, 'this mixed-ability, well'.

This is exactly the sort of caricaturing that Riseborough describes.

Ironically, but perhaps also predictably, the Egdon Boys' teachers tended on many of the controversial issues at Casterbridge to side with the grammar school teachers. Both groups were opposed to changes like the introduction of mixed-ability, (more of which later) and were in favour of measures like the retention of caning. In addition, the Egdon teachers tended to see the Shottsford Mixed staff as soft, weak and unrealistic in their views about children. The successful reputation of Shottsford was regarded as exaggerated, just a facade beneath which things had gone badly wrong. Comments made by Mr. Dillon about the previous Head of Shottsford and one of the senior pastoral teachers from Shottsford, who was appointed to a similar post in the comprehensive school, illustrate these views. Talking about the Head he said scornfully:

> So much was swept under the carpet and ignored as though it did not exist because it didn't agree with his ethos. That there were no bad kids, that discipline wasn't necessary, that he had no problems. And that a gentle talking-to the kids and 'go and have a walk around the playground' and 'have a cup of coffee and we'll discuss it' and it will turn out all right in the end - it didn't.

Here perhaps is some reciprocal caricaturing. And describing the position of the pastoral teacher:

> He's not making the grade. He's got too many non-practical ideas, too much theory. Although you've got to have a background of theory it becomes a different matter when you've got to put it into practice. And the kids know he's weak and that goes for the lot of them. You will find that the teachers who are respected most are the teachers who are hardest because there is the security.

Here again is the contrast between weak teachers and those with too much theory, as against the hard and practical disciplinarian, who is both able to achieve control in the classroom and gain the respect of pupils.

The Headmaster clearly felt himself to be hedged in by the presence of the grammar school and Egdon Boys' teachers in Casterbridge. Their views and 'preference orderings' inhibited the sorts of developments that he saw as necessary if Casterbridge were to develop and become a 'real' comprehensive. He identified the 'attitude' of teachers as the 'predominant' factor working against comprehensive education in the school. He tended to be scathing about the 'role performance' of both the grammar school and the Egdon teachers.

> There are some teachers who do not like teaching in a comprehensive school, who do not like having to teach children of lesser abilities. Although there are others who also do not like it, not because they have children of a higher ability than they were previously used to, but because its a much more demanding school to teach in . . . It therefore couldn't be the school we would like it to be until all those teachers have left . . . It is a very demanding type of education and ideally a

school that should be staffed by people totally committed to the comprehensive idea. We haven't got that because of reorganisation. I doubt whether any school will ever totally have that.

The grammar school teachers in particular were clear in their lack of sympathy for comprehensive education. Mr. Bishop explained:

Well almost without exception, except for two or three who thought it might be their only means of promotion, I should think they were, except for them, 100% against it.

And they also had their own sense of injustices done in the reappointment procedure, Mr. Bishop again, described

. . . people getting upset because they didn't get the job they thought they were going to get. Even on the academic side of the grammar school they found that they weren't getting the academic jobs. Nobody from the grammar school got Head of English or Languages, despite the fact that the grammar school Head of Languages was on a scale 4, was an Oxbridge man and spoke two languages and so on . . . there was also some feeling because suddenly out of the blue Gabriel Oak got a job that nobody knew was going.

Mr. Durbeyfield, ex-grammar school and Head of Resources at Casterbridge expressed the typical opinion.

I'll be frank I didn't think that comprehensive schools were a good idea. I now don't think that comprehensive schools were a good idea, even though they've given me a job which I personally enjoy and find fulfilling. And I'd only get that in a big school.

LINES OF BATTLE AND BASES OF POWER

To refer again to Table 2.1, it is important to note, despite Mr. Bishop's comments, the proportional over-representation of the grammar school teachers in posts of responsibility. While grammar school encumbents failed to gain some of the high-status subject headships - like English and Languages - two of the three deputy headships were captured by grammar school teachers - Mr. Bishop, who was put in charge of the West Block, and Mr. Gordon who was given responsibility for curriculum development and timetabling. Mr. Bishop had previously been Deputy Head in the grammar school having arrived there as an assistant teacher in 1951. He had become, over the years, the 'keeper of tradition' for the grammar school. He kept and maintained an enormous scrapbook of photographs, press-cuttings and memorabilia from the grammar school and had been editor of the school magazine. Mr. Gordon had taught in the grammar school for a number of years and was in addition an old boy of the school. These men together with the Head, the other deputy (from Egdon Heath, in charge of Pastoral Care), the two senior teachers (both ex-Shottsford) and the 6th form tutor (ex-grammar school), constituted the senior management team in the new comprehensive. This group, as is normally the case, was responsible for making school policy. Mr. Oak, a senior teacher, described the senior management team

> as a reacting body rather than an initiating body. It merely responds to what has gone wrong. Alan Jones (that ex-Egdon Heath deputy) and I are very disappointed about that. That's symptomatic of what happens at all the meetings. Nothing new is happening, nothing is being initiated, what has been has come from Alan and I. It's a difference in experience and background. He has been in different schools. He was a deputy in a comprehensive school, he is aware of recent developments in education. Clive Bishop has been at the same school for 28 years. Dan Gordon almost as long. They are happier with a school with tradition not in transition. Its understandable in terms of their background.

The command of key positions of authority in the comprehensive school provided the ex-grammar teachers with direct access to formal policy-making. But as 'carriers of tradition' and on the basis of long-established relationships these particular men were also able to wield considerable influence among the staff through informal channels. Hoyle (1982, p.90) makes the point that

> Influence differs from authority in having a number of sources in the organization, in being embedded in the actual relationships between groups rather than located in any abstract legal source, and it is not 'fixed' but is variable and operates through bargaining, manipulation, exchange and so forth.

The sixth-form and the East Block staffroom were both, in different senses, bases of power and influence for the ex-grammar teachers. The ex-Shottsford Mixed teachers were in the majority in the West Block staffroom, in their old school, and it is symptomatic of the marginal position of the ex-Egdon Boys' teachers that they, after their site was closed, had no natural territory of their own in the new school. Bailey (1982a) notes a similar situation in another amalgamated school where differences between buildings were cultivated by staff, it was 'as though the teachers were perpetuating the perspectival/cultural differences between the schools' (p.120).

For many of the Casterbridge staff, even up to four years after the amalgamation, the differences in values and perspectives between the ex-grammar and ex-Shottsford teachers continued to be the basis for tensions and conflicts in the school, and the driving force behind the institutional micro-politics. One of the ex-grammar staff even talked about the 'malice' and 'hostility' of some of the Shottsford teachers.

> There were certain members of staff - high up members of staff over at what was then the Shottsford School who looked forward to - with malice to . . . I could never understand them - to the amalgamation, because they said 'You'll learn what life is really like, by God we'll grind you down to size, and so on'. There was real hostility. I couldn't understand it. But there was and there still is in little areas; but it's not in departments, it's just individuals putting some people down.

While typically the Shottsford Mixed teachers spoke of the 'pervasive influence', the 'strategies' and the 'opposition to change' of the ex-grammar staff (see below). In particular the grammar school staff were seen as wanting to re-establish streaming and setting to replace the mixed-ability grouping which had been introduced in a few departments, to restrict entry into the sixth form to A-level candidates, and to prevent any subject integration. The following comments were made by ex-Shottsford teachers.

> There was a major row about the sixth form because the person who had been appointed Head of Sixth Form was a disaffected ex-grammar school bloke who started off very negative, saying, 'We're not having the riff-raff in the sixth form'. And in the first year there was a sort of major campaign by one or two people to get established the idea that the open sixth form - the one year sixth form - was valid and those were customers that should be treated with equal status to the other customers. And that worked.
>
> See, the whole strategy of the ex-grammar school teachers is quite simply a ratchet and it's very blatant - I mean, the History bloke, coming back once a term about selection in the fourth year. Now he's going to give me a paper in September about he could select them at the beginning of the third year. And, of course, he'd really want to select them after the first term of the second year. And they've done the same thing.

> But it's just - it's part of this process whereby the grammar - I think, on the whole, the grammar school has had a very pervasive influence, you know, it's used all sorts of subtle strategies to keep things going, keep things comfortable.

One teacher who had taught in both schools prior to amalgamation, spoke of

> a far greater camaraderie between colleagues in the Shottsford school and what I would have called a much more positive caring attitude to the pupils, which I liked very much.

Using Burns' (1955) terminology the ex-grammar teachers may be seen as constituting a <u>cabal</u> attempting to 'promote the occupational success' of its members and 'to restructure situations and values in the interests of its members' (p.480). And adapting Lacey's (1977) typology of strategies

the ex-grammar staff may be seen as engaged in
strategic maintenance, the calculated defence of
the values and practices of the grammar school
against the threats of innovation posed by the
Shottsford Mixed teachers. Lacey argues that a
crucial factor in understanding the effectiveness
of social strategies is 'the ability of the
performer' (p.73). This was a significant feature
of the strategical work done by the ex-grammar
teachers. They were able to refer back to the
'successful' performance of the grammar school as
'good grounds' for opposing change.

> What was sad, I suppose, for a lot of people
> was, in the last few years of the grammar
> school - the boys' grammar school - the A-
> level results had got better and better and
> more and more people went to university and to
> Oxford and Cambridge - I think this is partly
> a reflection of what I've just said, isn't it?
> In the past, we really had a tremendous
> academic record which I feel, perhaps, we've
> thrown away when we've sill got the material
> here; but through lack of effort and time,
> there aren't the teachers to shove the kids
> now - they're too busy doing other things.
> So, from that point of view, obviously it was
> a come-down.

In meetings and discussions the grammar school
staff would often appear deliberately not to
understand or see the relevance or usefulness of
innovations being proposed by the Headmaster or by
the ex-Shottsford teachers. Overt opposition was
rare, as we shall see below, apathy or lack of
interest were more common responses. As a result
discussions would get nowhere, action would not be
taken, decisions would be referred to other
meetings (see Gabriel Oak's comment on the S.M.T.
above).

The Headmaster was clearly very aware of the
opposition of the grammar school staff to change
and to comprehensive education generally, but he
described this opposition as 'mainly passive'. The
tension and antagonisms which underlay the
discussions in meetings often had to be read as a
sub-text (Marland, 1982) which was only accessible
through asides and allusions. In 1981, the school
held a closure day to discuss 'problems of pupil
motivation'. The staff were divided into small
discussion groups, of approximately ten members,

and a rapporteur in each group produced a report for later circulation. The report from one group, written by an ex-grammar teacher, concluded that

> although personal antagonisms seem to be less than formerly there is still a wide philosophical division within the staff between the 'positive progressive' group and the 'reactionary realist' group.

There were moments however when these divisions came out into the open, as the Head explained:

> Occasionally, like a bubble, certainly in the first two years, it sort of burst through. Sometimes at unexpected times . . . I can remember in the second year, when an academic board meeting was devoted to discussing provision for our more gifted children. And we had already then set up the system we have, of attaching our more gifted children to our senior staff, and I have eight attached to me, to monitor their progress and try to bring some enrichment programmes, where appropriate, to their work. And when we discussed this there suddenly arose a nucleus of the academic board, mainly, those who have been in the grammar school, that this was a totally unnecessary expenditure of energy and time on the part of senior staff, if we'd had rigid streaming, as in the grammar school, and these pupils were all in one stream, and were taught just normally, then all this other thing would come as part of the teaching programme and there would be no need for these other groups. And it was a very emotive meeting. Suddenly out of a situation I wouldn't have expected to give rise to these sorts of things, suddenly the whole anti-comprehensive feeling of these teachers came out very strongly indeed.

The most senior of the ex-grammar school teachers described the same meeting to me and his comments illustrate the problems that can arise when groups with different experiences and interpretative frameworks are brought together in a single institution.

> I think the Head's against any form of streaming. I don't think the Head is pro it. You see we had a meeting of the Pastoral Board, or

one of these wretched Boards we have that
lasts for hours on a Wednesday afternoon, and
he was saying 'what is the best way to encourage the bright child'. But what annoyed me
was, as far as I could see, the best thing you
could do for them, would be to treat them as
you treat the remedial children at the other
end. If you've got your remedial groups in
small groups with a specialist, why can't you
spare a specialist graduate to teach the other
extreme, who's willing to take them 35 at a
time. I can't see this. I can't see why. I
can't see what the objection to it is. And I
got up a thing, a sort of round robin not just
from the grammar school people, people who
were Heads of Department who felt the same
way. The discussion was nonsensical because
the only way to teach them was to teach them
according to their ability. And he got very
upset about this. And said was this the grammar school clique again and was it coming to
the fore and all this, that and the other ...
but I didn't do this out of any kind of spite.
I didn't know what they were talking about.

Here again the teacher suggests that he simply
cannot understand what the advocates of mixed-
ability are trying to say, it does not make sense
to him. The grammar school staff saw mixed-ability
as being one of the unacceptable features of the
'positive progressive' views of the Shottsford
teachers. The feeling was that the grammar school
teachers were wasting their talents in being
expected to teach mixed-ability classes. Their
skills and experiences, it was said, had prepared
them best to teach top stream groups.

There are people who think and still
think, and I agree with them that their
talents are diluted because they're trained to
teach the most able children and that's what
they're best at doing and they find it very
difficult teaching less able children and yet
they spend a proportion of their time doing
that and they report to me - a common grumble
- that it just tires them out so they can't
give their best to the more able children.
And I'm sure it's true. You get very tired of
stroppy kids.
But the person I'm thinking about really
was a very dedicated teacher; a high-flier;

his dream of worldly success was to get everybody to Oxford or Cambridge and so on. And he spends most of his life now, you know, sort of restoring order in mixed-ability classes. And he just gets very, very tired.

In their opposition to mixed-ability the grammar school teachers were defending their own interests and commitments to teaching and speaking as they saw it in the best interests of the more able children. There were even some suggestions that the secondary modern staff lacked the necessary experience and training to teach more able groups, especially sixth-form, competently.

Have you ever thought, only the grammar school teachers have ever taught grammar school children and even not all of them have been released on the sixth form. It was always the Heads of Department or a few lucky others who were allowed loose on the high fliers. And of course last year some people who had been in the secondary modern school, quite highly qualified, had had a go and they made mistakes, they admitted they'd made the most ghastly blunders and I think they're reflected in the results.

THE HEADMASTER

It is normally taken for granted in the English school system that the Headteacher is 'to a large extent, responsible for devising and maintaining his (sic) school as a formal organization, and thus, in a most revealing way, his school becomes the expression of his authority' (King 1968, p.88). Bearing this in mind the role of the Headteacher at Casterbridge becomes a particular interesting question. To what extent can he be regarded as the 'critical reality definer' in the new school? To what extent does it stand as 'the expression of his authority'? Briefly, the Head was an Oxford graduate in languages and obtained a PGCE from Exeter. His first teaching post was at a direct grant school in London, obtained through the Oxford appointments service, which he left after 2.1/2 years 'slightly disillusioned', as he put it, with the 'very rigid structure' of the school. He then obtained a post in a large state maintained grammar school in the south of England. After six years this school was reorganized and became a 12-16 comprehensive, the Head described this as a 'traumatic' and 'unsettling' experience, but in the reappointment process he became Head of Languages. He had already been in charge of German and a year tutor in the grammar school, 'from then on' he explained 'because of reorganization my career developed very quickly'. The new school reorganized its academic structure and the Head became Chairman of the Faculty of Communications. He found the new teaching situation 'stimulating and satisfying to such an extent that I then decided that I would want to continue in comprehensive schools for my career'. He spent two years in the new school before obtaining a deputy headship in a split-site comprehensive school in a county adjacent to Melchester, with responsibility for one of the school sites and curriculum and timetabling. He held this post for three years before, at the age of 38, he obtained the headship of Casterbridge.

In several ways he must have looked like the ideal compromise candidate for the new school. An Oxford man with the direct-grant and grammar school experience which should have pleased and satisfied the grammar school staff, he had also had first hand experience of the traumas of reorganization followed by authentic comprehensive school experience, which should have appealed to the Shottsford Mixed teachers. Indeed he saw himself as strongly committed to the comprehensive ideal.

But in a number of ways neither his leadership style nor his strength of commitment satisfied either the grammar or the Shottsford teachers. For the grammar school staff he was far too unsympathetic to their views, they saw him as a dangerous reformer. For the Shottsford teachers he was too accommodating to the grammar school perspectives and did not pursue strongly enough the reforms which they felt to be basic to achieving a comprehensive system in the school. In other words, he did not provide a strong enough lead. The grammar school teachers felt that he gave too much leeway to the 'comprehensive' teachers and allowed them to make decisions about school policy which should have been his prerogative, they believed in a 'strong' Head. One of the ex-grammar school teachers brought this out when comparing him with the old grammar school Head (who had retired at the time of reorganization).

But, in a way, they are both very pleasant

people. In a way, they were very alike. The old grammar school Head used to say we could always walk in and talk to him and it was really true and was really quite difficult in that - I mean, you might find three or four people in the room at the same time when you talked to him. But he really was open like - but the school was run how he wanted it. Now I get the impression that the school's run by a committee. This is what Mr. Tregaskis wants, I presume, and it is not really run exactly according to what he wants but how the majority want. Or at least the majority on the committee. He takes the attitude that ultimately it is his decision but in fact the decisions that one is discussing or arguing about or complaining about aren't really his but what everybody wants.

This stance is paradoxical in a number of ways, the grammar school staff believe in the virtues of having a 'strong' Head but distrust Mr. Tregaskis' commitment to comprehensive education and oppose his attempts at innovation. They criticise his willingness to allow committee based decision-making but use the committees effectively to stifle or postpone changes that they see as threatening to cherished values or traditional practices.

The Head's grammar school experience seemed to carry little sway with the ex-grammar school teachers at Casterbridge, his commitment to comprehensive education put him into the opposition camp.

Well, yes, of course. I mean, Mr. Tregaskis wants to get rid of all forms of elitism, doesn't he? I mean, he actually says that. If you say, 'We don't want mixed ability at this level because we think that so-and-so stands a chance of getting into university if he's tutored with his ability group', it isn't on. He says, 'Oh, we can't have that kind of elitism'. So obviously his beliefs are different from, say, mine or the previous Head's.

But what were to the grammar school teachers strong, doctrinaire and irrational ideological positions were to the 'comprehensive' teachers weakly presented and unfulfilled commitments.

51

> I would have thought people were concerned
> that the Headmaster is not imposing certain
> things on the school. For myself, for
> example, I think we should have a Mode 3 in
> practically every subject and I think the
> school - it's not the sort of thing which
> happens unless the school has a positive
> policy towards it, as we had in our
> department.

For the 'comprehensive' teachers he was too
conservative, too academic, too much under the
influence of the senior staff from the grammar
school.

> The Headmaster takes an introvert low key
> role, philosophically he swings towards the
> academic, whether he's got to or not I don't
> know but I think he feels he's got to . . .
> There's a little bit of criticism that he's in
> his office, he doesn't look around the
> corridors . . . I don't think he's got a
> strong senior management team to back him up,
> which would make him the effective Head I
> think he wants to be . . . I still don't
> think you need a bully boy Head but I think
> you probably do need a more sort of
> charismatic person about the school. And a
> Head usually fulfills that sort of role. But
> I respect his views and respect his
> philosophy.

Here the Head is caught between the competing
demands and preference orderings of his diverse
staff. In a situation of career stagnation in
teaching there was little opportunity for the Head
to 'build a team' in the new school which would
reflect his views. There were few new appointments
to be made and indeed falling rolls meant that
younger staff on scales one and two were being
redeployed out of the school. The implications of
this were soon recognized by those teachers who
were anxious to promote changes. One of the very
few outsiders appointed to a Head of Department
post was acutely aware of the stultifying effects
on the school of career stagnation.

> If you've been in the school all that time,
> what the hell do people mean by coming up to
> you and saying, 'Look, we've got to think

about whether this school works or not'. And the attitude of the people is, 'Of course it bloody well works', you know, 'I've been here for twenty-five years and there's nothing wrong with it'. It's that entrenchment; that's one of the sort of side-effects of the falling roll situation, I think. Whereas if you had young people coming in from college and so on, saying 'This is ridiculous; why are you doing this?' it'd be easier for me to say, 'Yes, I agree with you'.

Increasingly, the Head was left to rely on the older, more traditional staff, especially from Egdon Boys' and the grammar school, to run the school. There was no 'new blood' with new ideas coming into the school. Rather the established staff, especially those in senior posts, were 'growing old' in their jobs. The school was becoming increasingly top heavy. As the Head saw it:

I believe we are trying to develop a comprehensive school in possibly the most difficult circumstances that man could actually devise. And its ironic that the first talks about reorganization in Melchester, I understand, took place about some time like 1965, and it was put off several times. We've now reorganized at a time of falling rolls. Both of which make the development of courses extraordinarily difficult to achieve . . . We can see needs, as the school develops, for different types of courses to suit different types of pupil. We sometimes can't provide them because we are losing staff and not appointing them.

There is little evidence here of the Head as 'critical reality definer', either in 'pursuing desired organizational goals' or in constructing and sustaining 'through interaction the professional identities of teaching staff', as was the case in Riseborough's Phoenix case-study. The Headmaster was neither able to control the definition and ethos of the school nor exercise control over the teachers by acting as arbiter of their careers. Indeed, as far as teachers' careers at Casterbridge are concerned the process of reorganization itself and the concurrent drastic decline in promotion opportunities nationally meant that the Head's power as 'teacher career gatekeeper' was severely curtailed. And whenever points did become available for internal promotions the jostling for preferment which ensued tended to revive and reinforce the latent tensions and antipathies within the staff. Furthermore, in contrast to the Phoenix situation the status, perspectives and skills of the 'old' staff, at least as far as the grammar school teachers are concerned, were not devalued by the creation of the comprehensive school. They could not be 'marginalized' and labelled as 'bad' teachers as had happened to the 'old' secondary modern staff at Phoenix and the Egdon Boys' teachers at Casterbridge. Indeed, in the light of the community's expectations for the new school and the inter-school competition for pupils and publication of examination results required by the 1981 Education Act, the skills and experiences of the grammar school teachers were increasingly important to Casterbridge. Events outside the school tended to reinforce the status and influence of the ex-grammar school staff especially within their sixth-form power-base. Their arguments against mixed-ability grouping and in favour of using 'experienced' teachers to teach the most able pupils could be put forward as being in the best interests of the school in the context of an increasingly 'wild' environment. However, survival in the organization must still be seen as a political act. The pursuit or maintenance of interests and priorities is an interactive, political process, 'politics in organizations involve the tactical use of power to retain or obtain control of real or symbolic resources' (Bacharach and Lawler, 1980, p.1). This is what the grammar school teachers were engaged in.

During the fourth year after reorganization Mr. Tregaskis began to look for and apply for headships in his home county and quickly obtained a post in a small, well-established comprehensive school not far from where he was born.

DISCUSSION

At Casterbridge the struggle to control the definition of the school can be explored in individual and group terms. Certainly, any analysis of the school must recognise the significance of the differences in ideology and ethos, and experiences and commitment, between the three institutions and three groups of teachers involved in the amalgamation. Within the clash of ideologies crucial vested interests are at a stake. Cherished values, self-esteem and career futures are all under threat. For some the amalgamation would open up new career possibilities and an opportunity to assert their 'preferred view' of education. For otheres reorganization would mean an end to personal development and the betrayal of their professional investment in teaching.

These elements of conflict within the newly created institution are played out in and through the micro-political matrix. The matrix is constituted by, on the one hand, a set of ideological, personal and interpersonal factors - teacher and school codes, individual values and beliefs, perceptions of others' biographies, official reputations and informal status. These intersect, on the other hand, with a set of organizational and situational factors - formal organizational control and informal influence, territorial occupation, the tactical use of power (e.g. in committees and staff meetings), community support and patterns of recruitment and promotion. And the ideological and the organizational factors are to a large extent inter-dependent and mutually conditioning. Thus, individuals who have formal positions of authority but carry a damaged reputation or a suspect biography may find themselves effectively powerless in public arenas of decision-making. Conversely, high status practitioners without formal position may find themselves able to achieve innovations in the face of dogmatic opposition. Promotions or appointments which 'officially' rely on merit and expertise may in fact be made in the light of the 'political' allegiances and educational values of the candidates. Traditional rights of territory can be used to defend and camouflage principles of interpretation and action at odds with publically acknowledged school policy. Effective control and definition of the institution emerges from the interplay between formal authority and informal influence, between positional power and personal status. That is not to say that the balance of power is fixed once and for all. The outcome of particular issues or decisions cannot be predicted with absolute certainty. The political process is dynamic, struggles are on-going. The outcomes, in terms of teaching and organization in the school, are often messy and confusing (Bailey, 1982b, p.102).

As we have seen, the different groups within the school employ different strategies, although they all in various ways attempt to legitimate their arguments by reference to the success of previous practice. The grammar school teachers point to sixth form achievements and Oxbridge places, the Egdon Boys' staff to their firm discipline, and the Shottsford Mixed teachers o their high levels of participation in examination courses and 'humane' relationships with pupils. These claims are countered by disparagement and by gossip about classroom problems. Criticisms about being 'out of date', 'out of touch' are parried with censure of 'trendiness' and of 'airy-fairy theories'. For the most part the grammar school teachers seek to retain or return to more traditional forms of teaching and organization. They use their formal positions of authority to stifle attempts at change by delaying discussions or by failing to take proposals seriously. Attempts at innovation fall by the wayside through a combination of disinterest and the use of barbed scorn. Strategic maintenance relies to a great extent on <u>non-policy making</u>, the avoidance of decisions. Even when decisions are made, when the Headmaster uses his formal authority to push through changes, gaps between <u>formal</u> and <u>effective</u> policy open up. Policies are not implemented, exceptions are found and exploited, issues which seem to have been firmly resolved are reopened for further discussion and questioning. Crucially, at times both the advocates of change and the defenders of tradition are able to make claims about the legitimacy of their position by pointing to trends in public policy or parental opinion outside the school. Such claims are doubly effective when they are related to the 'survival' of the school in an increasingly turbulent socio-economic environment. Such strategies must however be used with care, individuals who 'cry wolf' too often are liable to be labelled as scaremongers, their political influence will suffer. The political process is most apparent in the contest over <u>critical decisions</u> (like mixed-ability, caning, an open sixth form, etc.) which formally shape the definition of the school, and over <u>critical appointments</u> (like Heads of Department and Head of Year), who have formal authority in significant areas of practice. But as a sub-text of meaning it can also make itself felt in the day-to-day social relationships between teachers. Patterns of friendship, social interaction, interpersonal influence and support and sponsorship strongly reflect the patterns of micro-political allegiance among the staff.

My argument here is that educational change (or lack of change) as represented in forms of school organization and the learning experiences of pupils is fundamentally related to institutional micropolitics. The micro-political matrix of the institution needs to be recognised as a powerful mediator when changes are proposed internally or are required by external agencies. The sociological analysis of educational change in recent years has for the most part, been focussed either on the all-embracing effects and implications of structural movement (be it cultural or economic in origin), or on the responses, adaptations and strategies of individual actors. Indeed, the past ten years have been dominated, in the sociology of education, by the continually regurgitated motif of micro vs. macro, structure vs. action, freewill vs. determinism. In important ways this has led to both an underemphasis of and misrepresentation of the other major areas of analysis in sociological study - the group and the organization - what we might call the meso level.

In the rush to disown and disengage from the chains of functionalism at the end of the 1960s British sociology of education also seems to have given up an interest in the study of the school as a social organization. As I indicated earlier there has been an enduring interest in the relationship between technical aspects of school organization (particularly pupil grouping) and educational inequalities, and there has been a recent revival of concern with 'school effectiveness' (Reynolds, Gray, Rutter et al), but issues like school leadership, and school administration and organizational innovation and development have been left almost exclusively in the hands of those who work under the heading of administration and management (represented by BEMAS) or to be carried on by researchers and writers whose work is now unfashionable in mainstream sociology of education (like William Tyler and Eric Hoyle). Clearly, there is still much to be wary of in this alternative tradition. American organizational research with its normative, prescriptive and empiricist orientations is still a major point of reference for many writers in this country. But there are other theoretical interests that are making themselves felt in the United States and in Britain in organizational research that should have a more sympathetic reception in and share many areas of common concern with British sociology of education (the work of social psychologists like Bacharach and Lawler (1980), political scientists like Baldridge (1971), writers employing a Marxist perspective like Salaman (1979), Braverman (1974) and Clegg (1977 and 1979), conflict theorists like Collins (1975) and March and Olsen (1976) and anthropologists like Bailey (1977) and Boissevain (1974)).

If I can misquote a now famous dictum, the school is both the site and the subject of conflict and struggle. In the institutional politics of the school inhere both limits upon and the possibilities for educational change, they are an arena of dispute where conflicting ideologies and interests engage and compete. While the outcomes of these disputes are in no way divorced from the organizational environment and its political and economic structures neither are they inevitably or completely determined by them. It is probably true to say that at any time certain ideological tendencies are dominant in the majority, but not all, of our schools. But the existence of these dominant tendencies must not be allowed to blind us to the continuing existence of and efforts of assertive groups and their ideologies.

In explaining the differences between schools and the process of educational change it is important to recognize the role played by institutional conflict and the ways in which internecine guerilla warfare in the corridors and staffroom and staff-meetings of schools is related to influence and control over school policy.

NOTES

1. Having said that I would also argue that it should be possible to use the analysis of conflict to specify the conditions within which consensus is possible.

2. The case study reported here is based upon occasional fieldwork over a four-term period. I observed school committees at work, attended staff and departmental meetings and speech day, school plays and other events, I spent time sitting and chatting in the staffrooms and observed a small number of classes. In

addition I tape recorded twenty-nine
interviews with twenty-four different members
of staff (that is twenty-eight per cent of the
whole staff including all the key figures
involved in the amalgamation).

REFERENCES

Arfwedson, G et al (1979) Skolan och Lärana : om
skola närsamhälle och lärares arbetsvilkor.
Rapport 6. Forskningsgruppen for läro-
plansteon och kulteveproduktion. Högskolan
för lärutbildning 1 Stockholm. Institutionen
för pedagogik.
Bacharach, S.B. and Lawler, E.J. (1980) Power and
Politics in Organizations, Jossey-Bass, San
Francisco.
Bailey, A.J. (1982a) The Pattern and Process of
Change in Secondary Schools: A Case Study.
Unpub. Ph.D. thesis, University of Sussex.
Bailey, A.J. (1982b) 'The Question of Legitimation:
A Response to Eric Hoyle', Educational
Management and Administration, Vol. 10, No. 2,
pp. 99-106.
Bailey, F.G. (1977) Morality and Expedience: the
folklore of academic politics, Basil Blackwell
Oxford.
Baldridge, V.J. (1971) Power and Conflict in the
University, John Wiley, New York.
Ball, S.J. and Lacey, C. (1980) 'Subject
Disciplines as the opportunity for group
action: A measured critique of subject sub-
cultures' in Wood, P. (ed.) Teacher Strategies
Croom Helm.
Ball,S.J. (1981) Beachside Comprehensive, Cambridge
University Press, Cambridge.
Ball, S.J. (1984) 'Becoming a Comprehensive School?
Facing up to falling rolls', in Ball, S.J.
(ed.) Comprehensive Schooling: A Reader,
Falmer Press, Lewes.
Becker, H. (1952) 'The Career of the Chicago Public
Schoolteacher' in Hammersley, M. and Woods, P.
(eds.) (1976) The Process of Schooling,
Routledge and Kegan Paul, London.
Becker, H. and Strauss, A. (1956) 'Careers,
personality and adult socialization' American
Journal of Sociology, Vol. 62, pp. 253-63.
Boissevain, J. (1974) Friends of Friends, Basil
Blackwell, Oxford.
Braverman, H. (1974) Labour and Monopoly Capital,
Monthly Review Press, New York.

School Politics, Teachers' Careers and Change

Bucher, R. and Strauss, A. (1976) 'Professions in Process' in Hammersley, M. and Woods, P. (eds.) The Process of Schoolint, Routledge and Kegan Paul, London.

Burns, T. (1955) 'The reference of conduct in small groups', Human Relations, Vol. 8, pp. 467-86.

Clegg, S. (1977) 'Power, Organization Theory and Marx: a critique' in Clegg, S. and Dunkerley, D. (eds.) Critical Issues in Organizations, Routledge and Kegan Paul, London.

Clegg, S. (1979) The Theory of Power and Organization, Routledge and Kegan Paul, London.

Collins, R. (1975) Conflict Sociology: Toward an Explanatory Science, Academic Press, New York.

Cyert, R.M. and March, J.G. (1963) A Behavioural Theory of the Firm, Prentice-Hall, Englewood Cliffs, New Jersey.

Goff, T. (1980) Marx and Mead, Routledge and Kegan Paul, London.

Hammersley, M. (1981) 'Ideology in the Staffroom? A Critique of False Consciousness' in Barton, L. and Walker, S. (eds.) Schools, Teachers and Teaching, Falmer Press, Lewes.

Hargreaves, D.H. (1980) 'The Occupational Culture of Teachers' in Woods, P. (ed.) Teacher Strategies, Croom Helm, London.

Hoyle, E. (1982) 'Micropolitics of educational organisations' Educational Management and Administration, Vol. 10, No. 2, pp. 87-98.

Hughes, E.C. (1958) Men and their Work, Free Press, New York.

Hunter, C. (1981) 'Politicians Rule O.K.? Implications for Teacher Careers and School Management' in Barton, L. and Walker, S. (eds.) Schools, Teachers and Teaching, Falmer Press, Lewes.

King, R. (1968) 'The Head Teacher and His Authority' in Allen, B. (ed.) Headship in the 1970s, Basil Blackwell, Oxford.

Lacey, C. (1977) The Socialization of Teachers, Methuen, London.

March, J.G. and Olsen, J. (1976) Ambiguity and Choice in Organizations, Universitets forlaget, Bergen.

Marland, M. (1982) 'The Politics of Improvement in Schools', Educational Management and Administration, Vol. 10, No. 2, pp. 119-34.

Musgrove, F. (1971) Patterns of Power and Authority in English Education, London, Methuen.

Nias, J. (1984) 'Professional Socialization and the Definition of Self in Primary School Teaching' Paper presented at the International Sociology of Education Conference, Westhill College, Birmingham, January 3rd-5th.

Partridge, J. (1968) Life in a Secondary Modern School, Penguin, Harmondsworth.

Reynolds, D. and Sullivan, M. (1981) 'The Comprehensive Experience' in Barton, L. and Walker, S. (eds.) Schools, Teachers and Teaching, Falmer Press, Lewes.

Riseborough, G. (1981) 'Teacher, Careers and Comprehensive Schooling: An Empirical Study' Sociology, Vol. 15, No. 3, pp. 352-80.

Salaman, G. (1979) Work Organizations: resistance and control, Longman, London.

Woods, P.E. (1979) The Divided School, Routledge and Kegan Paul, London.

Wilensky, H.L. and Edwards, H. (1959) 'The Skidders: Ideological Adjustments of Downwardly Mobile Workers', American Sociological Review, Vol. 24, pp. 215-31.

THE LOCAL STATE AND TEACHERS: THE CASE OF LIVERPOOL

Henry Miller

> Schools slowly die. They become difficult to
> staff efficiently. They prove less attractive
> to teachers and parents. Key subjects
> disappear. Less able and highly gifted pupils
> suffer. Range of examination subjects
> shrinks. Standards of performance and
> behaviour decline. Demoralisation of staff,
> pupils and parents sets in. The school
> becomes a source of social and educational
> disadvantage to those associated with it.
>> Proposals for County Secondary Re-
>> organization 1984-5, p.2. A consultative
>> document. Liverpool Education Committee.

This is a quotation from a document produced
in 1983 by Liverpool's newly elected Labour
majority administration which has been engaged in a
major confrontation with the Conservative central
government. It refers to the reasons why it had
become desperately necessary to introduce a wide
ranging re-organisation of secondary schools in
Liverpool. A consideration of those proposals and
the Local Education Authority's relation to
teachers' local lay union officials provides an
opportunity to explore some aspects of the work of
the local state in relation to the national state
and the economy.

Sir Ronald Gould, General Secretary of the
NUT, wrote (<u>The School-master</u> of 10 September,
1954):

> I have heard it said that the existence in
> this country of 146 strong vigorous LEAs
> safeguards democracy and lessens the risks of
> dictatorship. No doubt this is true but an
> even greater safeguard is the existence of a

> quarter of a million teachers who are free to
> decide what should be taught and how it should
> be taught.

and Asher Tropp, in The Schoolteachers, a classic
work, wrote:

> Through the activity of professional
> associations it is possible to reconcile the
> desire of the individual to fulfill his
> professional conscience with the needs of the
> state. (p.270)

These two quotations from the 1950s raise the
questions of the relationship of the state to
teachers and their organisations. Thirty years on
it is apposite to consider what changes have taken
place in the state and in teachers' response to it
and how to explain these developments. Sir Ronald
Gould's quote seems to suggest Local Education
Authorities as something separate from the central
state and rests on a liberal pluralist theory and a
political experience formed by opposition to Hitler
and Stalin. Tropp's account suggests a Whig or
even Hegelian political philosophy which identifies
the beneficial action of the state and the
possibility of realising individual teachers
aspirations through appropriate organisations.

Another view has been developed by Marxists
(e.g. Castells, 1978; Cockburn, 1977) which seeks
to explain the action of the state in terms of its
relation to economic production and consumption,
but which also includes an examination of the
political and ideological. The focus of this
chapter will be on the local state. The Local
Education Authority (LEA) constitutes in terms of
activity, provision and finance one of the major
parts of the local government unit, thus it can be
seen as constituting an important part of the local
state and its activity.

The relations of the LEA to the DES and
national politics on the one hand, and local
teacher union leaders on the other, finds varying
degrees of control, co-operation, and contestation.
With reference to the politics, policies and
practices of one local authority, Liverpool, I hope
to show, on the one hand, that there is a
specificity related to the local state of class
struggle and political power as well as
administrative procedures but also, that the weight

of the central state, itself mediating economic pressures, is ever present.

LIVERPOOL

Any local state operates within its own time and space, but in Liverpool in 1984, demographic economic and financial conditions, culture and politics cannot be understood without some knowledge of the historical forces that have produced them. The broad lines of changes in demography, economy, polity and educational problems of falling rolls or comprehensive reorganisation have national contours but in any particular city they take a specific shape. The balance of class forces, trade union and political power have been shaped by employment and occupational structures, past and culture and tradition so it makes sense briefly to sketch in some salient features of Liverpool's economic social, political history (at least in the 20th Century) before turning to the relation of education teachers to the local state in 1984. Even at a personal level the attitudes and actions of many of the teachers' leaders were influenced by local family traditions and by affiliation to the Liverpool city life, its problems and possibilities.

Lebas (1981) puts this perspective:

The historical and political role of cities is significant in that it constitutes for those who live in cities a sense of place from which to organise and to resist. (p. xxviii).

and argues for the utility of the discussion by Gramsci (1971), 'The Historical Role of Cities'.

Each major city has its own specific economic structure and politics. There is a question as to whether Liverpool is a deviant case or an extreme case; it certainly has its own peculiar characteristics. Briggs (1963) remarks, writing of Victorian times:

Liverpool also was markedly idiosyncratic: religion shaped political affiliation, and the presence of large numbers of Irishmen in the city gave a special twist both to Conservative and later to Labour politics. (p.391)

Conservatives were able to use anti-

catholicism and the Orange order to maintain
support in working class districts. The Irish
Nationalist party was the second largest party in
the 1920s and the gradual transmutation and
transference of support via the Catholic Party and
Centre party to constitute a significant part of
the Labour party by the 1950s, meant that the
religious issue remained not only potent between
parties but within the Labour party it was, and
still is, of some significance.

The rise to power of the Braddocks, Tom and
Bessie, in the Liverpool Labour party was against
Catholic influence, but their brand of politics in
the 1950s was not decisively different. There was
no encouragement to develop a democratic base.
Merseyside Socialist Research Group (1980, p.79),
suggest they established a form of boss politics
with the support of Catholic notables and right-
wing trade union officials. When Labour eventually
came to power in 1955, its housing policy of
building high-rise blocks was not popular and left
room for the development of Liberal community
politics. Since the late 1970s the left in the
Liverpool Labour (including supporters of Militant)
have steadily gained ground, (Crick, 1984). Local
constituency parties have selected left Labour MPs
to replace SDP defectors and the District party,
under left control itself, exercises decisive influence over the Labour group on the city council.
The relationship of trade unions to politics
and even more specifically the relationship of
teachers' unions to local political establishments
is certainly influenced by religious affiliation
but it is also decisively influenced by the
structure of the local economy and changes in
occupational patterns. A brief history may help an
understanding of the current situation in
Liverpool.
Liverpool's maritime fortunes, founded on the
slave trade, continued to prosper in the 19th Century; up to and beyond the 1st World War the port
and associated transport, financial, commercial and
ancillary trades rather than manufacturing was the
basis of the local economy. The incomes, working
and living conditions of workers in these industries were low and precarious. The system of hi-
ring on the docks and irregularity of employment
led to the establishment of a system of casual work
which might have had some benefits in terms of
individual independence but which also made workers

difficult to organise and volatile in terms of trade union and political allegiance. Workers in the docks and transport did not initially play an important part in local Labour party organisation and even at times disaffiliated from the Trades Council.

Before the Toxteth riots of 1981, Liverpool had a tradition of riots and militant action. In 1911 a series of strikes in the docks and transport industry was followed by riots and two strikers were shot dead by troops. Two gunboats were anchored in the Mersey. The settlement was a victory for workers union-recognition and better conditions were won. Dockers' and seamen unions constituted the heart of working class organisation right through to the 1950s and 1960s. There were considerable tensions between local spontaneous militancy and the attempts by national union organisation, epitomised by the figures of Bevin and Havelock Wilson to impose discipline and control.

In the 1926 general strike, Liverpool was again the scene of militant actions and riots and this time of the Battleship Ramilles appeared in the Mersey. By the mid-1920s a pattern of mass unemployment had emerged related to the decline of traffic through the docks as the traditional heavy industries of the north (coal, shipbuilding, steel and cotton) were not able to compete on the world market. The tension between local militancy and central control in the Transport and General Union and Seamans' Union remained. It was not until the 1960s that rank and file movements made substantial gains in democratising these unions and by then employment in the docks and shipping had drastically declined. There were 18,000 dock workers in 1948, now there are less than 5,000; fewer than the number of teachers in Liverpool.

In the 1950s and 1960s, Liverpool did share, if only to a limited extent, in the prosperity of the long boom. A combination of government grants, regional policy and cheap labour did attract manufacturing plants to Merseyside - notably the Ford Leyland and Vauxhall motor companies to Halewood, Speke, and Ellesmere Port. These and other plants were owned by multinational corporations. When profitability was squeezed through the establishment of parity in wages with more affluent parts of Britain or through changes in trade conditions - work was transferred to areas with more favourable conditions for capital.

A similar process has been documented for Birmingham, Gaffiken (1984). Beynon (1973) has described the development of a democratic militancy amongst the workers at Fords and while, because of the general decline in the docks and manufacturing unions in this sector now play a less important role in local politics than public sector unions, the traditions of militancy handed on through the culture of family pub and union branch are an important feature of Liverpool life.

The importance of public sector unions became more visible with the establishment of the Joint Shop Stewards Committee in 1978. This grew out of co-operation between unions in the Direct Labour Department of the Council to defend jobs and to mutually support each other. The Committee now has affiliated nearly all the TUC unions representing over 30,000 workers employed by Liverpool Council. Thus affiliated, are manual workers unions like the General and Municipal Workers, National Union of Public Employees, Transport and General Workers Union and the Confederation of Engineering Workers but also significant are the National Association of Local Government Officers, with over 9,000 members and the National Union of Teachers, with over 2,000 members, and NATFHE, with 900 members. Not affiliated are the National Association of Schoolmasters/Union of Women Teachers, nor AMMA, the Head Teachers Associations or the Professional Association of Teachers.

The organisation of teachers' unions itself reflects changes in Liverpool's social, political and religious cultures. The large Catholic sector and associated tradition of single sex schools is part of the basis for the large NAS/UWT organisation. Liverpool is probably the only major city in England where this union is larger or as large, depending on whose claims are believed, as the NUT. The present office holders in the NUT are predominantly Labour party members (with an influential Communist as general secretary) which replaced what they present as a less militant Catholic dominated caucus in 1979.

The current concerns of teachers leaders might be characterised as being dominated by the issues of reorganisation and redundancy. These two issues are related not only to the immediate political and financial crisis but also to the legacy of the previous decades falls in employment, population, income, school rolls and political credibility in Liverpool.

1974-84 ADMINISTRATION AND EDUCATION

1974 can be taken as a crucial year in marking the development of a number of trends which determine the present situation. While at national level the Labour Party took power after the second major miners' strike and the three day week, the government soon capitulated to the demands of the IMF to cut public expenditure. At the ideological level the previously dominant view that educational investment was an efficient way to promote equality, meritocracy and the growth of the economy was being increasingly eroded. By October 1976, Callaghan, at Ruskin College, was questioning whether value for money was being obtained from education and Conservative populism, epitomised by Rhodes Boyson and the Black Papers, was gaining ground (CCCS, 1978).

At local level in 1974, Labour lost control of the City Council and there began a period, which lasted until May 1983, in which no single party had an overall majority on the City Council. Liberals were able, through effective community politics, to capitalise on the deficiencies of the housing policies of the right-wing Labour administration.

1974 was also the year of local authority reorganisation. In the case of Liverpool this did not involve amalgamation of previously separate authorities but it did involve internal reorganisation like that recorded by Cockburn (1978), Wallace et al. (1983) and Fergusson and Brown (1982), involving a move towards corporate management, typically a chief executive officer working with elected members on overarching co-ordinating committees. In this system the Policy and Finance committee can oversee policy and expenditure and establish priorities and monitor expenditure over the whole range of council services.

While the local education authority has a definite legal status with statutory duties imposed on it by central government, it is, at the same time, very much a part of local government. Its budget, which is usually over 40% of current expenditure, is only rivalled by housing. Much of this expenditure is to meet statutory requirement or debt changes so that there is very little room for manoeuvre when there is pressure for cuts. Pressure for cuts has been developing steadily since 1974. The shifts in the ideological, political and

economic climate reached a climax in the monetarist
rhetoric and public expenditure cuts of the 1980s.

In terms of the local public economy there has
been increasingly tight central government control
through the Rate Support Grant. In 1976/1977 the
RSG was calculated by a formula which did not
include a growth element and allocation was made
within specific cash limits. Since 1979, the
Conservative government has attempted more directly
to influence council rents and rates. In 1984 rate
capping legislation has been passed and penalties
have become the commonplace of local government
political vocabulary and action.

In the case of Liverpool the pressure on
education expenditure has been exacerbated by
Liberal/Conservative administrations which have
pushed council rents up but attempted to keep rates
low. Interest payments on the massive municipal
housing developments of the 1950s and 60s
constitute a considerable debt commitment even when
some of the housing has had to be knocked down as
uninhabitable. The incoming 1983 Labour majorities
program was to maintain services and jobs, cut
council rents by £2, without a rate increase, and,
by threatening an illegal budget and fiscal and
social chaos, to force the Conservative central
government to restore cuts and remove penalties.

While the economic and political constraints
on local authority education expenditure are not
peculiar to Liverpool the economic and demographic
decline and its effect on rate base and disruption
of school provision has indeed been extreme. The
decline of docks, and more recently of
manufacturing industry, and concommittant increase
in unemployment are dramatic as the Merseyside
Socialist Research Group (1980) has shown and show
little sign of abating. The loss of population has
been comparably extreme.

POPULATION AND SCHOOLS

The average birthrate for the United Kingdom
as a whole has fallen from 17.1 per 1,000 from
1966-1970 to 12.1 in 1976. In Liverpool it was
17.3 per 1,000 from 1966-1970 and 12.0 in 1976. If
we take total population figures and actual school
enrolments the changes can be seen to be even more
considerable. The census of 1931 showed a
population in Liverpool of 856,072, by 1981 that
had declined to 510,306, a decline of over 40%
(Brown and Fergusson, 1982). Live births in 1962

were 16,479, by 1977 that had declined by 62% to 6,166. This dramatic fall is partly explained by many people moving out of Liverpool, not only was the birth rate falling but there was a considerable net movement out of the city by a disproportionate amount of women of childbearing age (Liverpool City Council, 1977).

The movement from and within the city was uneven, population movement being heavily affected by slum clearance and the building of new housing estates on the edge of the city. Clearly something of the effect of these movements and decline of school population must have been apparent before the mid-1970s. Prior to that point however, the general favourable attitude to educational expenditure and the feeling that a reducation in school class-size was a good thing, reduced the urgency to reorganise and reduce education in terms of total provision of the educational system.

Reorganisation was taking place but it was in terms of establishing a comprehensive system within the county sector. The Roman Catholic sector did not go fully comprehensive until 1983. There was some little attempt to rationalise primary school provision before 1974 but paradoxically after 1974 this movement slowed down despite a special committee being set up to deal with this question!

The reasons for the failure of the city council after 1974 to come to terms with the need to reorganise and reduce primary and secondary school provision are complex, but Brown and Fergusson (1982, a,b) provide a useful discussion. Even summarised the factors indicate the complexity of the interaction of economic, political and administrative constraints. There was certainly pressure to reduce educational expenditure. Teachers' salaries constitute over 60% of current education expenditure, there was a reluctance on the part of any of the political parties at that time to face the teachers' unions in a battle over compulsory redundancies, which meant that encouragement to retire early, redeployment and internal recruitment were used, but this proved inadequate to deal with problems over proper curricula provision. This situation pointed to a policy of school closure and amalgamation. However, in terms of Liverpool politics this was extremely difficult.

Local schools often focus local loyalties. An extremely dramatic case of this has been the struggle over Croxteth Comprehensive school which, after being threatened with closure, was occupied by parents and staffed by volunteer teachers. Subsequently the school has been reinstated to become part of the Liverpool Labour party's plan for secondary reorganisation and the establishment of 16 community comprehensive schools (Corspeken and Miller, 1984, 1984 a,b). This is perhaps an extreme case of mobilisation by a community but the recognition by local politicians of parents' opposition to the closure of their local school has meant that they have been reluctant to push through plans involving closure or amalgamation in their ward. The political context of annual elections in each ward, where one third of the city councillors are returned and the state of the parties with neither Labour, Liberal nor Conservatives having majorities on their own between 1974 and 1983, meant that there was endless room for manoeuvre and delay in the interests of local political advantage.

In Liverpool in 1984 those working in education and including those leading teachers' organisation faced a situation of crisis traceable back in the end to the dynamics of international capitalism and its mediation through central and local state. These crises have been crystallised in the need for secondary and primary reorganisation to deal with the pressure to provide adequate curriculum to an unevenly declining school population within an ever-tightening budget. The determination to avoid compulsory redundancies, the difficulties of redeployment and the politics and hesitations induced by many years of a hung council has meant that realistic overall plans for reorganisation in the county secondary sector came only when a majority Labour council was returned in May 1983. This has meant that the educational reorganisation proposals were entwined in the general political confrontation between Liverpool's left-wing Labour council, determined to maintain services and employment and reluctant to raise rates, and a Conservative central government bent on controlling what in their eyes are extravagant local authorities and extremely reluctant to accede to Liverpool's demands.

UNION OFFICIALS AND THE COUNCIL

As in most other cities the main teachers' unions are the NUT and NAS/UWT. As we have already noted, Liverpool is unusual in that the NAS is much stronger here than elsewhere, Liverpool being one

of the founding branches of the association and the
NAS/UWT has maintained its strength particularly in
the Catholic sector, where NAS/UWT claim it
organises 85% of the secondary teachers.

Both unions now have a fairly young group of
officers in their 30s and 40s in control. In the
case of the NAS/UWT as one officer put it

> We found ourselves two years ago with a series
> of unfortunate tragic deaths amongst officers
> who had been around for twenty odd years in
> the Liverpool association. Well-known at the
> council offices, they had exceptionally good
> relationships with the officers. The
> association went through a hiatus of uncertain
> leadership until the existing leadership came
> together.

The development of the present NUT leadership
is a stormier story. Present officers claim that
the NUT and NAS/UWT were both effectively run by
the Catholic Teachers Association. In the mid-70s
there was some opposition in the NUT, from the
'rank and file' group, in which motions on abortion
would be countered by busloads of nuns turning up
to meetings. By 1976, the present general
secretary, a member of the Communist party with
Trade Union experience in the Engineering industry,
had arrived on the NUT scene in Liverpool and a
broad left grouping was able eventually to wrest
control from the right by campaigning on issues
like redeployment.

Up to this period the local associations had
been dominated by head teachers who had good
personal relationships with councillors and
officers but, in the view of the present general
secretary, 'the union did not really negotiate - it
talked to influential people and as a consequence
not much was done to improve the lot of the
membership - so basically the service depended on
the education committee . . . The union had little
or no say.' He reports that 'the executive member
for the area has since become a Liberal councillor
campaigning on education cuts'.

Some two or three hundred members were lost in
the period of left take-over in the late 1970s.
Since then teaching relief has been negotiated for
union officers and a proper filing system has been
established and the NUT is now installed in a
permanent office near the NALGO and education
offices. The NUT now plays an active role

negotiating over conditions of service, redeployment and reorganisation and has regained membership.

The formal machinery of negotiation and consultation is the same as for the Liberal administration before May 1983 but now, under the Labour administration, it works in rather different ways.

There are a number of levels of decision making. Firstly, there is the committee where teachers' associations are represented which consults and negotiates, usually with the Director of Education. Secondly, there is the education committee on which there are teachers' representatives elected from all the teachers in a particular part of the system, e.g. Secondary, Infant, Special, FE and HE who have a vote along with 3 representatives from the churches. In the period of the hung council the teachers' representatives votes could be decisive. There are various sub-committees of the education committee, schools, further education etc. Quite crucial in the system of corporate management is the process by which any matter requiring expenditure goes to the Policy and Finance committee, initially, in fact, to the Performance Review Financial Control sub-committee of the Policy Finance committee. Labour, before May 1983, refused to serve on this sub-committee because they saw that this would involve them in legitimating cuts in jobs and services. Measures approved by Policy and Finance go to the full Council. At any of these stages, of course, decisions can be reversed through effective lobbying and that has occurred particularly when there was no one party with an overall majority.

It is interesting that Labour has maintained this committee structure, indeed strengthened it with a Policy Review group on the Performance Review sub-committee, dealing with items which the committee does not wish to approve immediately. This is corporate management but with effective political control over the policy options and spending rather than corporate management developed from any strategy of chief officers or chief executives. Labour has used the structure to maintain control over the prioritisation of different items of spending. It is in this structure that the union leaders have to negotiate and attempt to influence policy.

There is some agreement among teachers union officials in the assessment of the changes since

May 1983 and on what constitute current problems nd
issues. An NAS official puts it this way:

> Under the Liberal administration, because
> there was no possibility of the Liberal group
> being able to implement a specific set of
> policies at any level but particularly at the
> secondary level - affairs were very much in
> the hands of the professional officers of the
> authority, the Director - Assistant Director -
> we usually found that at meetings of the Joint
> Teachers Association and the authority that it
> was the Director who came along - who more
> often than not then transmitted our views to
> the politicians suitably amended or altered
> and there would be a response. Clearly the
> Director very often had to talk to the three
> leaders of the education groups. But while we
> made progress substantially over a number of
> issues where there was broad areas of
> agreement mainly related to conditions of
> service, redeployment, premature retirement
> compensation supply staff that, nevertheless,
> did not solve the major problem in Liverpool
> which was very much relating to county
> secondary reorganisation and we had a number
> of fruitless meetings over that which
> culminated in a number of piecemeal
> reorganisations.

The NUT and NAFTHE officers' view places more
emphasis on the importance of negotiations with
political leaders prior to May 1983, who, because
of the sensitive balance of Liverpool politics in
this period, were reluctant to leave too much to
the officers. There was also a period when the
Director of Education was suspended. However, when
Labour came to power in 1983, both the fact of an
overall majority and the importance of the Joint
Shop Stewards committee meant a change in the
relationship between councillors, officials and the
teacher unions.

A NAS official saw the situation like this

> Because the Labour administration now has an
> absolute majority on the city council, the
> negotiation tends to be directly with the
> chairman of the education committee but in
> Liverpool that is somewhat complicated
> because, I think, its generally accepted that

a major input to the Labour administration is through the Joint Shop Stewards committees. Now we did have an invitation to join that and we refused because we saw the possibility of clash of interests and that clash has now occurred between the NUT and the GMW over the issue of caretakers sharing a staffroom with teachers.
(NAS Officer)

NUT officials agree on the shift of emphasis to direct negotiation with the chairman of the education committee rather than with the director. The general secretary of the NUT, who is also assistant secretary of the Joint Shop Stewards committee stresses also how in meeting on a liaison committee with the leaders of the Labour Group and the District party important issues are negotiated which could be then binding on the chairman of the education committee. This emphasis is rather different from that of an official of NAFTHE or indeed of the Secretary of the SSSC itself, a NALGO official, who, while recognising the role of the committee, seems to see it as part of a more diffuse set of power relations with rather more limited, defensive, trade union powers rather than an active policy forming body or even negotiating body.

The joint stewards doesn't really negotiate over anything - that's one area of problem we've had with the Labour group. They want to use us as a central negotiating body, well we won't do that - that's not our role . . . it's basically to fight redundancies and if people require help then they come to us and we take it up - we're there over the big issues if you like - and for us to get involved in things imposing agreements on some unions which didn't like them would be just a nightmare.
Secretary of JSSC

The NUT was taking on an increasing union identity partly through being involved with JSSC. Also, the NUT officers have been able to negotiate directly with Labour politicians partly because of their general pro-Labour stance. But while most of the officers are Labour party members, many of the members are not Labour supporters and would not have supported an illegal budget with no rate-rise. Also, the NUT has to continue its role as a union negotiating for its members with an employer

75

notwithstanding the sympathy of individual Labour party officers for the Labour council's problems. Over both secondary reorganisation and over the designation procedure for staffing, it has been able to get much of what it wanted. This is in contrast to the NAS/UWT which, while still probably the larger association in the secondary sector has, it seems, been marginalised.

SECONDARY SCHOOL REORGANISATION

Something of the background to the problem of secondary re-organisation has already been outlined in terms of demographic changes, falling roles, and the difficulty of organising a system whereby a reasonable range of curriculum could be taught. There was much delay and several attempts at piecemeal solutions, such as the attempted closure of several schools including Paddington, which was reprieved after the Riots of Toxteth, and Croxteth, which was occupied by parents. Unexpectedly achieving a majority in May 1983, the incoming Labour group had to work out a plan.

Any plan for secondary reorganisation would necessarily involve some closure and/or amalgamation, given the existing resources and population trends. The two main possibilities were 11-18 Comprehensives or a system of 11-16 schools with tertiary colleges or open-access sixth forms. Labour party NUT and NAS/UWT were all agreed in their opposition to selection and in their approval of co-education. The critical HMI report on the Boys' Institute had undermined some of the support for selection but support for single sex education was to prove considerable amongst parents, of whom 70,000 signed petitions.

There was considerable debate in both the NUT and NAS/UWT and AMMA about the merits of the 11-18 and 11-16 tertiary sixth form college system, many of the officers in both associations favouring the break at 16 as being the only way of securing adequate curriculum coverage in large enough units for advanced work. The NUT general meeting voted for 11-18 schools, with 12 schools with 8 form entry, based on local communities. It seems the favourable view of John Hamilton, an ex-teacher and the leader of the council, towards 11-18 schools was also influential. The NUT proposals were largely accepted except that 16 community schools were proposed, which included Croxteth and Paddington school which was to amalgamate with the

Institute schools. These community schools were to have 6 rather than 8 form entry.

Whatever reservations the teacher union leaders and the directorate may have had about it, it was seen as being a viable, definite plan that could be implemented and immensely preferable to the previous policy of piecemeal closure, stasis and decline.

If we look at the Liverpool Education Committee's consultative document 'Proposals for County Secondary Reorganisation, 1984-5' we find in the language and proposals an emphasis, as in the opening quotation on the urgency of the situation and on the need for a clear, overall, principled reorganisation rather than a rationale relating to the needs of the local or national capitalist economy or indeed a strong explicit commitment to a socialist form of education, compare with Hargreaves (1984) account of the West Riding move to Middle Schools.

The first two sections of the proposals deal with the need for reorganisation. Firstly, in terms of the opportunity for the Labour majority committed to secondary reorganisation. It notes the Secretary of State's request for a plan in June 1982, and that informed opinion including parents, government bodies and teachers' associations and staff all accept the need for reorganisation and are pressing for a planned, overall once for all and coherent scheme which avoids 'mixed economy' and 'market economy' alternatives. Mixed economy in this context means combinations of 11-16 and 11-18 schools such as has been adopted by a Conservative administration in Birmingham which threatens to reintroduce selection; market economy means a system which allows free movement of pupils across the city to the school of their parents choice irrespective of catchment areas. The document at this point points to the September 1983 reorganisation of 43 schools in the Catholic sector into 15 new comprehensives as another factor pressing the urgency of reorganisation.

The second section defines the case for reorganisation in terms of the statistics of falling roles, the effects on schools, the inadequacy of short-term solutions and the dangers of delay. There is reference to the overall contours of the falling rolls numbers, and the document points out that the then current capacity is 182 forms of entry and asserts this needs to be reduced to 96 by September 1979. Further, the

1982-83 average size of sixth form at 68 pupils and only 12 schools guaranteeing a full range of A-level courses is reported.

The concluding paragraph of this section includes the words:

> The secondary system in Liverpool is in danger of sliding into a moribund state. It is already characterised by gross inequality of opportunity, lack of parity between schools and an escalating waste of and imbalance of human and material resources.
>
> Liverpool Education Committee (1983, p.3)

Thus the case is defined primarily in terms of the failure of the council to reorganise to take account of the effect of falling rolls with its consequent deletarious effects on the quality and parity of education.

The principles and objectives laid out as the basis for reorganisation can be summarised as a commitment to fully comprehensive 11-18 schools, co-educational, neighbourhood and community schools; opposition to sexual and racial discrimination and commitment to improving educational opportunity and achievement for girls and to multi-cultural education for all children. Included in the principles and objectives section are statements recognising the need to improve the numbers of pupils staying on in the sixth form, and asserting that a school requires at least six classes in the entering age group to provide an adequate range of subjects for fourth and fifth years. Also there is a paragraph arguing for a planned, rather than a free market use of resources to ensure a stable future for schools.

The crux of the proposals is the balance struck between community and curriculum needs and the rejection of selection, separate education for boys and girls and a tertiary system. The original proposal of 16 11-18 co-ed comprehensive schools with 6th form entry, it is argued, would give adequate numbers for an adequate curriculum in fourth, fifth and sixth forms and would produce sufficient schools to relate to local communities. It is ambiguous what precisely constitutes a neighbourhood or community.

Neighbourhoods and communities can be defined in terms of patterns of housing and communication but also by the effective mobilisation of people to secure services. In Liverpool the campaign to retain Croxteth, based on the Gillmoss housing estate, was prominent and perhaps influential in influencing thinking about community schools. Croxteth became one of the originally proposed schools. The only major change of plan before the proposals were put to the minister was to accommodate the expressed demands for their own school of another nearby well-defined community at Walton, this put the total number of schools up to 17 and in the opinion of at least one teachers' representative weakened the scheme making it more difficult for schools with sixth form entry or less to reach a sixth form size sufficient to provide an adequate range of curriculum.

Although the consultative documents records a wide range of comments and strong objections to its proposals, apart from the provision of the one more community school, the Labour group did not modify its proposals. Both major teacher concerns dissented from the plan. The NUT arguing for 12 schools with 8 form entry 11-18 schools and the NAS/UWT for 11-16 schools with open access sixth form system both, it seems, being concerned at the provision of adequate sized sixth forms. The other major objection has been in terms of arguments for retaining single sex schools. The proposals argue that provision for boys and girls can be better made within co-ed schools and that without them an adequate curricula spread would be difficult. The argument for 16 or 17 11-18 schools rather than 12 larger schools is rejected in terms of the need to retain closeness to neighbourhood and community. The arguments for open access sixth forms or tertiary colleges have been well-developed and it is interesting that the Labour group's adherence to 11-18 schools coincides with Sir Keith Joseph's preferences. Hunter (1983) in reporting the difficulties of Manchester and Croydon LEAs which had opted for 11-16 and 6th form colleges quotes Sir Keith 'only in exceptional circumstances can it be right to reduce good schools from 11-18 to 11-16'.

In the event, when Sir Keith finally gave his verdict on the proposals in June 1984, the pressure for single sex schools did presumably influence him to press for the retention of two such schools in one area but in general it is remarkable how widely the councils' plans have been accepted and how little parental opposition over the closure of particular schools has been translated into votes against the Labour party. In 1984 Labour increased its majority on the council from two to seventeen.

The relationship of gender to class, religion and ethnicity in Liverpool underlies the way in which both the Labour group and teachers' union leaders all advocated the establishment of co-educational community comprehensives rather than the retention of some single sex schools. The plan set out its proposal and rationale as follows. Two of the principles refer to a commitment to co-educational schools and opposition to sex discrimination and commitment to improving educational opportunity and achievement for girls and the general proposals referring to the establishment of comprehensive co-educational schools requires that there is

> Ending of single sex education at secondary school level. The proposals imply the firm belief that a true comprehensive education must be co-educational and that the social and educational needs of girls and boys at their most specialised can best be met and equal opportunity guaranteed in viable, mixed schools of forms of entry, in which a balanced curriculum would counter the disadvantages of sex stereotyping. The survival of small single sex schools of limited viability is not consistent with the establishment of multi-purpose comprehensive schools designed to serve the main neighbourhoods of the city. Given agreement of the voluntary sector it should be possible to meet demands for single sex education deriving from ethnic minority religious needs.
> (Liverpool Education Committee, 1984)

Co-education is here defined as part of what is meant by comprehensive education and, while there is recognition of girls' educational disadvantage, it is assumed that this is best overcome in co-ed. schools with a wide curricula. This is clearly contentious because of the way in which, in co-ed. schools curriculum choice may still lock girls and boys into gender stereotypes. However, in the Liverpool context, perhaps because of the size of the problem of declining roles, the considerable pressure for retention of single sex education was seen by practically all progressive political and teacher union leaders as reactionary rather than representing a viable feminist position. Those arguing for single sex education were seen as attempting to use it as a way of retaining selection by other means, and thus preserving class advantage, or as representing archaic views of the relations of the sexes or even representing covert racist views that their daughters would be molested by black boys. Thus there was a remarkable unanimity amongst these teachers' leaders negotiating and considering the plan proposed by the Labour group, that co-education was an essential, if contentious, principle, if curricula range and community relations criteria were to be met. Questions of gender and schooling in Liverpool were locked into a debate where feminist arguments for separate schooling for girls (Shaw, 1984) could have little weight.

The process of negotiation with the teacher unions over reorganisation shows the effect of wider economic and political considerations on the detail of educational policy and practice. We have already noted how the political stance of the NUT leadership gave them an advantage in influencing the Labour party and education committee over the basic principles of the reorganisation, but this also extended to the discussion of the details of designation. With the establishment of 17 new institutions replacing 25, re-allocation of staff was going to be a considerable problem. Under the Catholic reorganisation staff had been interviewed and put in categories of highly recommended, recommended or not recommended. The NUT leadership, fearing the possibility of commissioners being imposed on Liverpool, was anxious to avoid any documentation that listed staff in a way which could be used to facilitate sackings to reduce costs, so they devised a system of guidance meetings with an adviser and an allocation by a designation committee of councillors which avoided this.

At the same time, it was clear that there would be a number of Heads of Department who could not continue their current role in the organised system. Their salaries would have been protected but the NUT managed to retain the existing points within the system and they are to be allotted to new scale 3 posts dealing with Race-Relations, Special Needs, Equal Opportunities and Community Relations, using Parent Support Units in each school. Thus, some of the existing Heads of Department will find new posts which will give them status as well as money. Whether this institutionalised arrangement will effectively support the political and educational policy initiatives designated by the posts without stranger propogation of policies than has yet eminated from the council, remains to be seen. However, these examples suggest the interplay of local political and trade union negotiation is, as one might expect, influenced by the wider economic, occupational and national political pressures.

CONCLUSIONS

The local Liverpool political scene has been characterised by the combined effects of the influence of the Catholic/Protestant divide and an employment pattern and trade union tradition of what might be termed 'bossism', which had little base in large or democratic local parties. A populist, community campaigning Liberal policy was able to develop in the 1960s and 1970s which attracted substantial working class support. From 1974 to 1983 there was a hung council, which was unable to deal with the problems of falling school rolls and school reorganisation effectively.

This is within a context where the city of Liverpool was suffering from the sectional decline of a substantial section of capitalist industry thus reducing rate income and generating substantial and prolonged unemployment. At the same time, the national state was increasingly intervening to control and limit and reduce local authority expenditure, on the thesis that public expenditure was a drain on the sources of profitability.

In the late 1970s, the Liverpool Labour party, with the support in particular of the public sector unions, was able to regenerate itself so that in 1983 it won a marginal and in 1984 a substantial electoral victory which placed it in a position where it had to attempt to deal with the substantial housing, employment and educational problems of the city. The Labour group, with the support of most of the public sector unions, adopted a policy of confrontation with the Conservative government in terms of its general budget. Its educational plans although, to some extent, controversial in terms of their commitment to co-educational, 11-18, comprehensive, community schools yet presented what appeared at least a reasonable overall plan, so, that with the exception of the provision for two single sex schools, it was acceptable to the Secretary of State. At nearly the same time, a deal was negotiated between the Minister of the Environment on the Liverpool budget which allowed the commitments to no job cuts and maintenance of services to be maintained at the cost of a 17% rate increase. Interestingly, in both instances, the Liverpool Labour Leaders, Hamilton and Hatton, claimed that 90% of their demands had been met and agreement was reached.

In reality the deals are more of a compromise and certainly, in the case of education, Sir Keith Joseph must have been relieved to get an overall plan that looked as though it stood some chance of working.

Following Castells (1978), the city and local state can be seen as an arena where different class forces contend. The difficulties that capitalism on an international scale faces in maintaining profitability are translated in two ways into city politics and the cities political economy. Firstly, international corporations increasingly move their operations to areas where profit can be most easily maintained. Liverpool has certainly suffered from this movement and this has effects both in terms of demographic decline, with attendant problems for the organisation of schooling and on the rate base to provide the finance for schooling, housing and other social services. Secondly, at central state level, whether unwilling under Labour or willing under Conservatives, there has been an increasing attack on the level of public expenditure (particularly local expenditure on public services) which are not seen as contributing to profitability or wealth creation. This has meant increasing intervention, control and reduction of resources available to local authorities to maintain their services. But these services have been generated by popular pressure. They support and are supported by large sections of the population including organised labour, tenants' association and parents concerned about their childrens' education. Thus it became increasingly possible to mobilise support for councils appearing to support these services and local democratic control against what is seen as the dictatorial intervention from central government.

Teachers are one of the groups which might ally with more traditional working class Labour supporters in this context. We have seen that in the case of Liverpool some of the teachers' leaders particularly in the NUT are able to exercise influence on reorganisation plans. The NUT has also affiliated to the Joint Stewards Committee, representing public sector unions, which itself has been a major support for the Labour council in its confrontation with central government. It is true that sympathetic as the leadership of the NUT have been to the Labour council, it was not able to persuade NUT members at a general meeting to back a 24 hour stoppage in support of policies advocated by the council involving no cuts in services, employment or rate rise. On the other hand, as the final quotation illustrates, teachers' prospects of employment, as well as their consciousness, are likely to be affected by their involvement in such organisations of trade unionists.

> The general secretary - very influential bloke - has led the union into a much more - um - into an attitude of the NUT being a trade union rather than a professional body and the fact that we have linked-up with the joint shop stewards - the very fact that we're sat down alongside blue collar workers has come as a shock to very many union members and I'm damn certain that they're not totally happy with it. One is meeting blue collar workers with whom generally one has very little contact and it is a different world - because the teachers, the NUT, didn't support the council on its March 29th day of action. We received a tremendous amount of stick from the GMW and TGW and they said if there are going to be cuts in jobs let the bloody teachers take the cuts in jobs and you can't deny their right to say that. But on the other hand the very fact that we're teamed up with the Joint Shop Stewards committee over the past 3 or 4 years, I think, has undoubtedly saved teachers jobs. Earlier on this year - and this is the Labour council when they inherited the Liberal budget, (in May 1983) they realised they had severe problems . . . and I think it was only I think through the intervention of the Joint Shop Stewards that Derek Hatton (deputy leader of the Liverpool Council) and Labour backed down. So there are 150 teachers in the city today who are there because of our action, and because of the support we got from the Joint Stewards Teachers.
>
> [Secondary school rep on Education Committee, NUT member].

NOTE

This chapter draws on field work done in
Liverpool from January 1983 to June 1984. Until
July 1983, I was teaching one day a week at the
occupied Croxteth Comprehensive School (Carspecken
and Miller, 1983, 1984a,b). This gave me contact
with and perspective on local education policy.
Between February and May 1984 I interviewed ten of
the officers of the NUT, NAS/UWT, AMMA and NAFTHE,
three of the teacher representatives on the
education committee and the secretary of the
Liverpool Shop Stewards' Committee, using semi-
structured tape-recorded interviews lasting from
half an hour to one and a half hours and conducted
variously in school, home or union office. I asked
questions about how people came into teaching, how
they got involved in the union, what their union
work involved and how they saw current problems in
Liverpool. The particular focus was on the
relationship of the interviewees to the officers
and elected members of the council and their
perception of the changes that occurred between the
period of Liberal administration and the accession
of Labour to power in May 1983. I made clear my
interest in the relationship of teacher
professionalism and unionism, my own involvement
with Croxteth and membership of the Labour party.
The account and quotations taken from these
interviews present a view from a particular
perspective; that of local teachers'
representatives or leaders and many councillors,
officials or rank and file teachers probably saw
the situation differently.

REFERENCES

Beynon, T. (1973) Working for Ford. London,
    Penguin.
Briggs, A. (1963) Victorian Cities. London,
    Odhams.
Brown, P.J.B. and Fergusson, S.S. (1982) 'Schools
    and population change in Liverpool' in Gould,
    W. and Hodkiss, A.G. (1982) The Resources of
    Merseyside, Liverpool University Press.
Carspecken, P. and Miller, H.D.R. 'Croxteth
    Comprehensive', in Donal, J. and Wolpe, A.M.
    (ed.) Is There Anyone Here From Education.
    London, Pluto.

Carspecken, P. and Miller, H.D.R. (1984a) 'Croxteth Comprehensive - Curriculum and Social Relationships in an Occupied School'. In Socialism and Education, Vol. 11, No. 1, London SEA.

Carspecken, P. and Miller, H.D.R. (1984b) 'Community Education in Croxteth' in Forum, September 1984, Leicester P.S.W. (Educational).

Castells, M. (1978) City, Class and Power. London, Macmillan.

Centre for Contemporary Cultural Studies (1981) Unpopular Education. London, Croom Helm.

Cockburn, C. (1978) The Local State. London, Pluto.

Crick, M. (1984) Militant. London, Faber and Faber.

Fergusson, S.S. and Brown, J.B. (1982) 'Issues relating to decision making in the planning of inner city primary school provision'. In Buhr, W. and Frederick, P. (eds.), Planning in Stagnating Regions, Baden Baden.

Gaffiken, F. and Nickson, A. (1984) Job Crisis and the Multinationals. Birmingham, Trade Union Resource Centre.

Gould, R. (1954) The Schoolmaster, 10th September 1954, London, NUT.

Hargreaves, A. (1983) 'The Politics of Administrative Convenience', in Ahier, J. and Flude, M. Contemporary Education Policy, London, Croom Helm.

Gramsci, A. (1977) 'The historical role of cities' in Hoare, Q. (ed.) Antonio Gramsci: Selection from political writings 1910-1920. London, Lawrence and Wishart.

Hunter, C. (1983) Education and Local Government in the Light of Central Government Policy, in Ahier, J. and Flude, M. Contemporary Education Policy, London, Croom Helm.

Lebas, E. (1981) Introduction in Harloe, M. and Lebas, E. (eds.) City, Class and Capital. London, Edward Arnold.

Liverpool City Council (1978).

Liverpool Education Committee (1984) Proposals for County Secondary Reorganisation 1984-85. Liverpool, Liverpool City Council.

Merseyside Socialist Research Group (1980) Merseyside in Crisis, Manchester, Manchester Free Press.

Shaw, J. (1985) 'The Interaction Between Sex, Class and Social Change' in this volume.

Tropp, A. (1957) The School Teachers. London: Heinemann.

The Local State and Teachers: The Case of Liverpool

Wallace, G., Ginsberg, M. and Miller, H.D.R. (1983)
    'Teachers Responses to Education Cuts' in
    Ahier, J. and Flude, M. (eds.), Contemporary
    Education Policy, London, Croom Helm.

ACKNOWLEDGEMENTS

    I am grateful to John Bowen and Terry O'Donell
for reading and commenting on the draft; to the
households of Phil Carspecken, Janet Strivens and
to Dave Robertson for help and hospitality in
Liverpool, and to the lay officials of Liverpool's
teacher organisations and teacher representatives.

TEACHER BASHING AND TEACHER BOOSTING:
CRITICAL VIEWS OF TEACHERS BETWEEN 1965 AND 1975

Gertrude H. McPherson

For about a decade, from the mid 1960s to the
mid 1970s, American and Canadian teachers were the
uncomfortable target for volleys of brickbats,
custard pies, rotten eggs, and an occasional limp
rose. Who threw them? Everyone - journalists,
parents, community leaders, academics of all
stripes (including sociologists), educators,
novelists, administrators, and yes, even teachers
themselves. Everyone in that period of crisis was
a critic - of the society, of the education system,
of teachers.
     In our present concern as sociologists of
education to be heard and understood by teachers,
it is appropriate to reflect on some of the
characteristics of that earlier barrage. Can we
learn anything for the present from briefly and
selectively examining the recent past?
     I shall restrict my attention in this paper to
the American scene in that decade, and within it to
reformist (rather than radical) criticism[1]. My
distinction between reformist and radical criticism
closely parallels that made by Diane Ravitch (1977)
and the somewhat different but similar distinction
made by David Hargreaves (1974). Within the
reformist camp I shall contrast two types of
reformist critics[2] whom I call the teacher
bashers and the teacher boosters. I shall contrast
the stances[3] they took on the formal position of
the teacher, contrast the images[4] they held of
existing certified public school teachers, and
analyze the relation between the stances and the
images. The reformists had explicit images of real
teachers and these explicit images were important
to the stance a critic took. More often the
radical critics tended not to express images of
teachers, nor to justify the stance they took in

88

terms of images.

Not all of these reformist critics were hostile to teachers; some were kindly, many were condescending. I believe that this spectrum of more and less negative attitudes is still with us, although muted. Whenever a crisis in education demands a scapegoat, teachers become readily available to fill the position. Academics seem to find it hard to believe that public school teachers are capable of thinking, analyzing, knowing, or acting correctly. The criticism in the sixties was strident, out in the open. We have less strident, but often not much friendlier attitudes.

REFORMIST STANCES

Critics with reformist stances affirmed the fundamental legitimacy of the society and of the school system, but they wanted gradual, more or less complete change in both. They agreed that the system needed rebuilding and repair rather than dismantling. In addition, they accepted that there should be a legitimate formal teacher position, but they differed on how it should be defined and grounded. For some, legitimacy would be increased by providing greater professionalism for teachers; for others, legitimacy required more administrative and/or community control over teachers.

The difference between the two kinds of reformist criticism is clearest in the context of the battles - in writing and in action - that were fought over urban ghetto, particularly Black, education[5]. Stances were developed in relation to two important concerns, seen by some critics as separate, by others as linked: one concern, the power structure of the school - disagreement over who did and who should control the schools, and so the struggle for and against community and Black control; the other concern, disagreement about the reasons for the imputed failure of the schools to give minority group children a 'decent education' (Featherstone, 1976: 7). It was no longer considered proper or correct practice to blame the children, their families, and their neighbourhoods. Rather, the critics sought the sources of trouble and the solutions within the schools. This was as far as agreement among the critics went.

Were teachers part of the evil power elite running the schools? Were teachers responsible for all that went wrong for children in the urban classrooms? How should the teacher's position be changed - more power or less power - to meet either or both of these concerns? Were teachers powerful villains resisting change or powerless victims of the system? The answers to these questions composed two distinct, even contradictory, stances about what the teacher's position should be and why.

Critics with one stance advocated giving more control to administrators and the community over presently-powerful, evil-doing teachers (unable and/or unwilling to do better). Only thus would they become more accountable: force them to do a better job or eliminate them. These critics we shall call the teacher bashers. Critics holding the other stance advocated increasing the autonomy and professional status of presently powerless but good-hearted teachers. If they were freed somewhat from administrative control, they would show how well they could learn to teach. Their ineffectiveness was not irremediable, nor entirely their fault. These we shall call the teacher boosters.

Despite the usually powerful relationship Leonard Fein (1971) postulated between perceptions of effectiveness and perceptions of legitimacy, in this crisis period effectiveness was not the crucial determinant of a critic's stance on the legitimacy of the teaching position. Most critics, in fact, believed that teachers were less than effective, expert or competent[6].

TEACHER BASHERS

Teacher Power

Until this period, the conventional understanding had been that teachers were more like bureaucratic employees than true professionals. They had limited autonomy and authority inside the classroom and almost none outside of it. This view was beginning to be challenged at this time by some highly vocal critics who argued that teachers were becoming dangerously powerful. Also, and evilly, they were making false claims to professional autonomy and using their power to avoid accountability to administrators and to the community. What had brought about these new beliefs?

One element certainly was the increasing teacher militancy and demands for collective bargaining by teacher unions (Lortie, 1975). Even more important, this teacher militancy was developing at the same time as the growing public demand for greater community participation in education, decentralization and community control. The two trends, particularly in New York City, were on a collision course. The UFT and its leader Albert Shanker defined the community control movement as a real threat to the union (Rosenthal, 1969: 154); on the other side, those academics, community participants and liberal intellectuals for whom community control was the new gospel defined the teachers and their union as the evil villain, thwarting the wishes of the community. The UFT was clearly not the only organization attacking various proposals for decentralization and community control in New York. But for many educational critics it was the real villain, because it had 'let them down'. The union they had once wholeheartedly supported was now, they believed, fighting against the powerless, trying to prevent the downtrodden from acquiring even a little power. For these critics, the rights of the powerless took precedence over any of the union's rights - even rights to job security and tenure. The teachers and their union were one, and together they controlled New York education.

Since the teachers were powerful and evil, their claim to professionalism through their union, a claim to autonomy and some control over education, was illegitimate. For some of these critics, professionalism as demanded by teachers signalled lack of accountability:

> A teacher is never held responsible for failure to teach . . . This violence against the mind and spirit of the Black or Puerto Rican child is facilitated by the magic of inviolable professionalism.
> (Stein, 1971: 195)

or Ryan (1971: 35):

> . . . the monopolistic control of education by the teaching profession.

For others, professionalism for some occupations was fine, but as claimed by teachers it was an aberration, a distortion: 'discredited' (Schrag, 1967), 'elite' (Gittel and Hevesi, 1969), or 'pseudo' (Cuban, 1970) professionalism. Teachers were part of the dominating establishment of 'school professionals' (Scribner and Stevens, 1975:

16-17) who misappropriated power and prevented lay control. Nat Hentoff, for example, was horrified at the idea that 'only professional educators are qualified to evaluate professional educators' (Hentoff, 1977: 7). Swept along by his own rhetoric, he asserted that teachers and other educational professionals were better protected from the consequences of the harm they did than doctors. Permeating all of these writings is angry hostility toward teachers, a view of teachers as powerful villains. If they were not villains, they would be working with students and parents against bad schools and pushing for, not against, community control and their own accountability.

The solution? Make teachers directly accountable to the parents, or directly accountable to the principal who would be directly accountable to the parents. Then, through negative sanctions (such as paying teachers by the number of students they attracted - Scribner and Stevens, 1975: 39) and through ignoring teacher rights in some circumstances (e.g. it might be necessary 'to temporarily disturb job security of some adults' to ensure children's rights, Ibid., 44), education would then noticeably improve.

Despite the devastating attacks these critics made on teacher competence, they must have attributed some competence to teachers, or competence to some teachers. Otherwise, how would making them directly accountable and punishing them make them better teachers? As we shall see, what was important was not competence per se but good will. If teachers could not be trusted and had no good will, it was necessary to control them more and reduce not increase their power. Such images of teachers, rarely supported by empirical data, certainly influenced these critics' solutions to the serious educational problems of the day.

Ill Will

Those reformist critics who attacked teacher power also generally 'blamed' the teachers for the damage done to minority group and poor children in urban ghetto schools. (Teachers in other settings were also frequently 'blamed'. But the thrust was strongest and clearest in the urban ghetto context.) If these teachers were powerful and failed, they must have chosen to fail - been unwilling to change (to become effective), or have been incapable of being different. They were villains, not victims. Some reformist critics not particularly disturbed about teacher power joined the chorus of blame about what went on inside the classroom[7]. While it was no longer acceptable to blame the victim - the child or his family, it was now quite fashionable to blame the teacher, a form of what Alvin Gouldner called blaming the caretaker (1970: 122). Blame usually implies an imputation of responsibility for what happens. To blame the teacher then usually implied a belief that teachers were free to do good work and if they did not, they chose not to and were responsible. Sometimes, however, teachers were blamed because they were certain kinds of people - blamed for their social class background, their low native intelligence, their age, their sex, their race. That a critic would agree that teachers could not help doing what they did and still blame them suggests both a generalized hostility and also an attribution of responsibility to them for possessing these ascribed characteristics, as if they had evilly chosen to be lower-middle class. Since we are dealing here with feelings and not with logic, we should not be surprised at the contradictions such a stance could produce. The teacher who behaved well (usually a man!) despite his background was seen as remarkable, unusual, a hero - the strong and brave individual who against all odds triumphed over bad ascribed characteristics. On the other hand, the teacher who predictably did not escape the influence of her background was still crossly blamed for not being a heroine.

The decision a critic made as to how to control the teachers he blamed and did not trust related in part to the basis on which he blamed them. If he believed that teachers were 'unwilling' to be good, he would recommend greater sanctions that would make them be good to avoid punishment. If unregenerate, they would have to be eliminated. If he believed that teachers were 'unable' to be good, more often he would recommend changing the nature of the job, introducing programmed learning or teacher-proof curricula, or reducing teachers to skill trainers[8]. Or he would recommend the selection of different kinds of people to be teachers. Some critics went so far as to set up their own schools or sent their children to 'free' schools where the parents had some control over the selection and conduct of the teachers.

Since these reformist teacher bashers believed in preserving the framework of public education, they also believed teachers were a necessary evil.

Teachers were not competent, and, worse than that, they lacked fundamental good will. Therefore, one could not expect voluntary change from them and they should not be granted greater professional status and autonomy.

The Social Class Taint

In addition to attributing illegitimate power and ill will to teachers, many teacher bashers believed that the social backgrounds of teachers determined their bad behaviour; they were tainted by their ascribed social characteristics. In probing this stance, we must remember that, at this time, American critical writing - whether produced by sociologists, other academics, or nonacademics - was permeated with the 'normative' paradigm and little influenced by the 'interpretive' paradigm becoming important to sociologists of education in Great Britain. (American sociologists were, therefore, more prone to overdeterminism than to the problem that afflicted some of the British sociologists working in the interpretive paradigm - failure to recognize the important social constraints and limitations on change.) There was a marked tendency among radical as well as reformist American critics to view human actors as puppets pushed around by social structures or determined by social background to behave and think in particular ways[9].

For some of the teacher bashers, these ascribed characteristics were seen as bad in themselves. It was sufficient to label teachers as women, veteran, white, stupid, or lower-middle class if one wished to damn them.

We shall confine our attention to the critics' treatment of the teachers' social class backgrounds. Other ascribed characteristics of teachers - age, sex, intelligence or race - were, of course, the focus in many of these writings and were handled in a similar way by these critics. Social class has long been a valuable, central explanatory variable for sociologists of education. It is not surprising that all kinds of critics were sensitive to social class and attributed much of what they saw as problematic to it. Some of the critics in this period, however, failed to define the terms they used, did not provide evidence for their assertions, and drew conclusions about the importance of the teacher's social class position that were not carefully qualified. Generalizations about the influence of social class on teachers' attitudes and expectations and the impact of these on the behaviour and achievement of students were simplistic and sweeping. For example, it was frequently stated that because of their class backgrounds, teachers had negative expectations for lower class and Black children which resulted directly in low student self-images and student failure. This was the popular translation of Rosenthal and Jacobson, Pygmalion in the Classroom (1968). Middle class or lower-middle class teachers inevitably imposed their middle class expectations, inevitably did not understand the behaviour of lower class children and inevitably then failed them. It was obvious!

The social class attribution was also used by some to explain why teachers claimed professionalism and professional power (wrongly, of course). These claims which protected teachers illegitimately from those they should be working with derived from the small status advantages teachers had acquired over their clientele by becoming teachers. From their, at best, lower-middle class backgrounds, they could escape into a branch of the civil service by draping themselves in the professional myth (Cuban, 1970: 38-39). Or, as Gittell and Hevesi put it, teachers supported the status quo because of their life patterns and backgrounds, backgrounds which put great value on professional status (1969: 6).

The opposition by teachers to lay or community control was also the direct result of their class and race.

> Most teachers are of low social and econaomic origins, barely 'escaped', as some perceive it, from the ghetto. They have ambivalent, often strongly hostile, feelings toward the ghetto children they teach . . .
> (Lauter and Howe, in Gittell and Hevesi, 1969: 225)

The once-progressive teachers' union that had been aligned with the working class and civil rights movement had become nothing but a middle class group that was anti-Black. The teachers' strike, these critics claimed, was a racist strike (Sol Stern, in Berube and Gittell, 1969: 179) whatever the union said about job security, tenure, professionalism. For Jason Epstein, the battle in New York was a 'classic revolutionary situation' (in Gittell and Hevesi, 1969: 290), with an excluded class trying to improve its position against an 'established, if largely ineffective, professional group' that was trying to maintain the prerogatives it had won through bitter struggle. This professional group stood in the way of the 'legitimate ambitions of the emerging class boiling up just beneath it' (Ibid.: 319). True, teachers were underpaid and unemployable in other capacities, and they had invested years in their jobs (Ibid.: 315), but they had no choice. Their 'discredited professionalism' would have to give way to this 'apparently irresistible surge of democratic fundamentalism' (Ibid.: 321-322).

The class and status advantages of teachers over the children they were oppressing were for these critics minor - 'two penny' status advantages, 'crumbs of status'. Why did they cling forlornly to these crumbs? Patrick Harnett, sympathetic to the teachers, argued that this kind of question illustrated the inability of liberals and intellectuals - the upper-middle classmen - to understand or to support the lower-middle class ethos of teachers. In fact, the upper-middle classmen were willing to tolerate

> unquestionable violations of professional and human rights of one group of people in the professed interest of promoting the human rights of another group
> (Harnett, in Berube and Gittell, 1969: 206)

To Harnett, teachers were a lower-middle class group of people with working class parents and it was ridiculous for the intellectual upper-middle class to consider them either 'dedicated missionaries' or 'ingrained racists' (Ibid.: 210). Teachers were protecting union rights, rights denigrated by those upper-middle class establishment types with their 'built-in contempt for teachers' who could always return to their 'Connecticut Shangri-la' (Ibid.: 211).

Not only did class backgrounds explain the teachers' attitudes toward professionalism and toward the aspirations of poor and Black children and their parents, class backgrounds explained teachers' unacceptable behaviours, their lack of intellectual curiosity, their 'provincial parochial outlook', and their generally lower-middle class ethos of piety, conservatism, narrow-minded morality, and intolerance[10]. The critics' lack of trust, respect or willingness to grant teachers some professional autonomy and power derived, in part at least, from such a negative appraisal of the influence of their social class background on them.

Earlier I suggested more than this - not just that the critics believed social class had a negative influence, but that it was a deterministic influence. This is hard to demonstrate with a few quotations. (As Silberman noted, it is primarily a matter of nuance and tone). However, I feel justified in asserting that many of the teacher bashers believed the class label itself was denigrating and that the class position tainted and stained the teacher irremediably. She could not change. The most forthrightly negative class-linked picture of teachers was presented in 1963 by Edgar Z. Friedenberg in Coming of Age in America. His opinions of teachers were cited approvingly in this period by many of the teacher bashers who in no way shared his particular educational ideal.

Friedenberg made no bones about the irremediable nature of this class stain. Having located high school teaching as the

> first (and often last) step up from the working class for moderately intelligent members of recently assimilated ethnic groups' (Friedenberg, 1963: 180)

he described these teachers in less than flattering terms: 'gossipy and malicious', 'minds of really crushing banality' (Ibid.: 180-181), 'genuine hostility to these children [lower status pupils] and their cognitive style, often expressed as contempt, solidly based upon fear' (Ibid.: 194). And, believing that internal change was not possible, the only way out of this dreadful situation for Friedenberg would be to hire 'what we used to call a better class of people . . .' (Ibid.: 250). Since 'the wrong kind of people' went into teaching, programmed instruction could be used to reduce the number of teachers. With fewer teachers, 'from a better class', the status, dignity, and competence of teachers would rise. No longer would teaching act as a

> vehicle for the gentle ascent of common men, or as an anteroom in which poor but respectable girls can occupy themselves while awaiting the possibility of marriage; what has been essentially a lower-middle class

vocational preserve would become more nearly
an upper-middle class profession.
(Ibid.: 260)

In sum, teacher bashers believed that teachers
were powerful, full of ill will, and tainted, even
determined, by their lower-middle class
backgrounds. While few of these beliefs were
grounded on cited evidence, they were strongly held
and they deeply influenced the position these
critics thought teachers should occupy.

TEACHER BOOSTERS

Teachers as Powerless
    The contrasting reformist stance defined
teachers as more powerless than powerful. But if
teachers were not the powerful villains, who were?
Two different answers were given: in one, the
teachers' union (particularly the UFT in New York)
was the villain, seen as an entity distinct from
the thousands of 'potentially good' teachers; in
the other, the bloated bureaucracies of the school
system and their agents were the villains. Some
critics (like Marilyn Gittell) condemned both the
union and the bureaucracy.
    Critics who condemned the union while
exempting the teachers tried to persuade the
teachers to join the community control movement and
to become part of the push for the 'new
professions'. New professionalism and some form of
community control were considered compatible and
developing them together would signal a return to
an old but forgotten American tradition. Often,
the spokespeople for this point of view were the
same liberal intellectuals who in an earlier time
spoke so eloquently for universalism and protection
of the professional from parochial, particularistic
community pressures. These critics now joined two
seemingly antithetical goals, one for community
control over education and the other for
professional control over education. The
'tradition' supposedly being returned to was that
laymen would set goals and policies, while
professional educators would implement these
policies and give advice on the goals. Education
was a public business, one never intended to be a
professional monopoly. As Superintendent Donovan
put it in the Bundy Report, professional educators
must not be left accountable to 'nobody but
themselves' (Fein, 1971: 271).

The degree of community control desired by these critics, many governmental spokesmen and some educators was limited, less than that advocated by some radical critics and teacher bashers. Also, the new professional movement advocated limiting professional autonomy more than the traditional supporters of the professions would have accepted: no longer monopoly of expertise in the hands of a small group; credentialing open to the many worthy aspirants now not qualified; professionals more responsive to their clientele through client involvement in decision making[11]. By thus limiting the power of both professionals and the community they were made to seem compatible allies.

An advocate of the new professions believed that expertise was needed, that an appropriate body of knowledge existed in a particular field and that training was available to provide future professionals with this expertise. A critic taking this stance about teaching then might be expected to believe that teaching and teachers were necessary and that expertise was available or could be acquired. However, waffling, disagreement, and uncertainty surrounded this issue. Some believed that, although teachers presently had very little expertise, they could in time acquire it. Others were less sanguine, believing that the technical and theoretical body of knowledge necessary was nowhere near complete (Dreeban, 1970). Advocates of the new professionalism were not sure that teaching qualified to become a new profession. If they did include teachers as new professionals, they asked that control over budget, personnel, pupil policy and curriculum should go to the community, away from the power-hungry teachers' union (Gittell and Hevesi, 1969: 366).

Such a stance did not indicate wholehearted faith in the good will or trustworthiness of present teachers. 'Education is much too important to be left up to educators' (Braun, 1972: 17, in his diatribe against the AFT). But since skill and professional expertise were necessary, these critics were ready to accept the teachers' right to display them as long as the community had some control over them. (Strong spokespeople for such a position were, for example, Marilyn Gittell, 1969 and Mario Fantini, 1971.) This was a more hopeful and less angry stance than that of the teacher bashers but, since these critics believed that the professional group should not have control over professional standards, entry, decision making or the definition of competence, some would argue that whatever was 'professionalism' in the status had been cut out.

As noted above, some critics (like Gittell) attacked both the union and the 'remote, static bureaucratic structure' which was not responsive to the needs of local communities (Gittell and Hevesi, 1969: 3-4), the bureaucracy that alienated parents and the community in the name of 'professionalism'. Other critics focused all their attention on the evils of over-institutionalization and the bureaucratic 'fortresses' (Cuban, 1969: 256) of education.

While one major strand of radical criticism also attacked over-institutionalization, i.e., recommending the elimination of schools and formally-certified teachers (Illich, 1970), the reformist stance was less extreme both in its definition of the problem and in its proposed solution. Not elimination of organizations or formal teachers, but reformation, reduction in size and humanization of institutions was sought[12].

Some of the reformists were far more disturbed by the evil the bureaucracy did in protecting professionals from clients (Rogers, in Skolnick, 1970) than by the teachers' lack of freedom to become more professional themselves. Others, however, were also concerned about teachers' autonomy and rights to professionalism. For example, Featherstone spoke eloquently of the need to move away from the 'pathological professionalism' of the large educational bureaucracy to smaller, more pluralistic institutions built on a human scale. But he also argued for the need to help teachers - decent and well-meaning people - to become true professionals, loyal to students rather than to superiors or the system. As he said, the teachers did not create the problems. They were trapped by the institutions.

> Baiting teachers . . . denying that they are
> people too, is becoming common, a senseless as
> well as a morally ugly practice.
> (Featherstone, 1971: 154)

Featherstone's writings in this period are landmarks of sanity and cogency. Throughout his work he deplores the 'faddishness of our educational concerns', the 'quicksands of nostalgia', the 'amnesia' afflicting us in our handling of educational dilemmas, and the 'conceptual swamps' we fall into in our sloganizing about participation, quest for community, accountability and youth. 'Peter Pan ought to have travelled on an American passport . . .' (1976: 108).

A few of the critics who wanted the teachers to become more responsive to their clientele believed that this could not be achieved simply through lay or community control. A wish for some control over professional performance did not imply for all (Featherstone, 1971, 1976; Mayer, 1969; Cuban, 1969, 1970) that education should be completely turned over to the control of parents and the community. In a clearly reasoned discussion of 'participation' and 'community control', Featherstone argued that we must not accept any simple but nostalgically appealing answers to complicated questions. Noting that neither institutions nor professionals could be wished away, he said we must work for coalitions of parents and professionals, for quasi-professional bodies to work to counter school bureaucracies (1976: 181-2) rather than naively assume that all that was necessary for good education was to turn the schools over to the communities. Similarly, Larry Cuban:

> . . . the desire to control schools comes from mixed motives and the power to hang the sword of dismissal over a teacher's neck will not extract a competent performance.
> (1970: 231)

However, in this crisis of legitimacy, few, even of the teacher boosters, took such a stance. Many others, like Leonard Fein, believed that the schools had become so illegitimate in the ghetto that concentration on improving teacher effectiveness, teacher performance and responsiveness would not be sufficient to re-establish legitimacy. These critics advocated community control of education, not because they believed it would necessarily make education in the ghetto better, but because the present power structure had been too undermined to continue. And education could not be any worse than it was.

Good Will

As noted above, the teacher boosters wanting teachers to be new professionals were not always convinced that teachers had the necessary expertise

Teacher Bashing and Teacher Boosting:

or body of knowledge to qualify. As Fantini said:

> . . . teachers do not really know how children
> learn, what knowledge is most valuable, how
> best to teach, how best to organize a school,
> how to evaluate learning . . .
>   (Fantini, 1974: 68)

Teacher boosters were as likely as teacher bashers
to believe that teachers were prejudiced and racist
as well as incompetent. Their portraits of
teachers were quite as bleak (e.g. Arthur Pearl,
1972). They differed from teacher bashers in the
attribution of responsibility for the problems and
the solutions offered. Teacher bashers, as we have
seen, defined teachers as villains full of ill
will needing to be controlled, punished, even
eliminated. Teacher boosters, on the other hand,
labelled the union and/or the bureaucracy and its
representatives as the villains and advocated
freeing the teachers - giving them a chance to show
what they were capable of doing. Because these
critics imputed basic good will to the teachers,
they trusted them enough to recommend giving them
some autonomy and some professional status, along
with better training and lots of support. The
educational results, they suggested, might be a
pleasant surprise.

They had hope rather than conviction. Teacher
boosters hoped that teachers could become 'good' or
'true' or 'real' professionals and grounded their
hope on a quite different appraisal of the position
of teachers in the school bureaucracies than the
appraisal made by teacher bashers. Teachers were
bureaucratic employees, possessing some limited
autonomy within their classrooms, with almost no
decision-making power in the school or over their
own occupation - entry, recruitment, standards,
peer evaluation. Dan Lortie's (1975) analysis of
teachers tends to support this appraisal.

A seemingly simplistic version of this
approach was put forward by Charles Silberman. As
he put it, he had been brought around from his
'Hobbesian or conspiratorial view of teachers as
the villains' to believe that teachers were '. . .
as much sinned against as sinning' (in Passow,
1971: 83). If one reversed the self-fulfilling
prophecy with children, one also should with
teachers. If we thought well of teachers, they
would blossom in response to our new faith in them
(Silberman, 1970: 272). Put this way, it sounds

almost as naive as the common suggestion (once Rosenthal and Jacobson's work became the new gospel) that all that was needed to improve students' performance was for teachers to think better of them. To be fair to Silberman, in addition to thinking better of teachers, he recommended specific ways to help them improve and to increase teacher autonomy.

> If placed in an atmosphere of freedom and trust, if treated like professionals and as people of worth, teachers behave like the caring, concerned people they would like to be.
> (Ibid.: 142)

Frequently, critics supported this argument by citing the superior quality of teaching in British primary schools, noting the high degree of professional autonomy teachers had in their classrooms and in school decision making. Critics would then argue that there was no reason to believe that British teachers in general were more extraordinary than American teachers. (Some of the critics did seem to fear that maybe British teachers really were more extraordinary!) If American teachers were less effective, it was a result of the barriers in the American public school system to competent and effective teaching.

Teacher boosters rejected the snobbery of those who blamed and condemned teachers. Michael Katz:

> Education has not suffered from any freedom granted teachers to run schools as they see fit; it has suffered from the suffocating atmosphere in which teachers have to work
>
> . . . teachers do not run the schools
> (1971: 348);

Eleanor Leacock:

> . . . the responsibility for poor education cannot be laid at the door of the individual teacher any more than poverty is the responsibility of the individual family
> (1969: 21);

teachers were 'experienced, hardworking and capable', trying to do their best within the limits of their training and situations; '. . . it is only a most unusual person who can surmount the limits of the educational system' (<u>Ibid</u>.: 22). And with this stance the critics asked for some autonomy for teachers: Arthur Pearl:

> Teachers must have the right to go their own way. They must have independence in decision-making. It is only when decisions can no longer be defended logically within the context of educational goals that teachers or administrators can be restricted
> (1972: 149).

Even Peter Schrag, whose general approach to Boston teachers was rather sour, wrote

> . . . when teachers are given a little trust, are treated like professionals, and are given the freedom to function, they will respond
> (Schrag, 1967: 110)

Not all teacher boosters recommended that teachers become new professionals. Even those who did, although they emphasized the need to increase professional competence and effectiveness in part by increasing professional autonomy, did <u>not</u> advocate turning teachers into 'full-fledged professionals' in the traditional meaning of the phrase. Almost no writers in that period did(13). The teacher boosters believed that it was neither feasible, nor more importantly, <u>right</u> to turn education completely over to the teachers. However difficult it might be to balance the rights of parents, students and communities with the rights of teachers, however difficult it might be to provide teachers with professional autonomy while they continued to teach in constraining bureaucratic schools, these efforts had to be made. Teachers treated as professionals could work effectively within the modified institutional framework of our imperfect society. And they could be counted on to do this in the future - to translate into reality their potential expertise and effectiveness, because they had basic good will.

The Ability to Change

These critics challenged the teacher bashers' treatment of social class backgrounds on two grounds. First, they objected to the snobbery and class bias. Second, they insisted that teachers could change and could learn.

Charles Silberman spoke most strongly to the first point. He criticized the stance of Friedenberg and his followers for its 'aristocratic insouciance'. Approvingly quoting David Riesman:

> . . . the spirit of so many self-made American intellectuals who feel they must demonstrate their superiority to the lower-middle class world of lace curtain taste out of which they have come and identify on the taste ladder of the aristocracy . . .
> (1970: 8-9),

he cleverly if nastily turned the tables on Friedenberg! Silberman noted a trend in recent years toward a 'nasty and somewhat spiteful form of bigotry' and 'snobbery of the upper-middle class toward the white collar, lower-middle class world of teachers, social workers, civil servants, and policemen' (Ibid.: 141-142). To him, what was involved was a virtual denial of humanity.

Silberman, like Harnett, deplored the tendency noted by Lee Rainwater (in Wasserman, 1974: 200-202) for intellectuals (others too, but intellectuals with less excuse) to attack the 'dirty workers', those like social workers and policemen who do the society's dirty work for low status and reward. Some of the teacher boosters were deeply disturbed by the hostility such critics expressed toward the lower-middle class teachers, the caretakers, while at the same time they were glorifying the underdog and the open and spontaneous working class values and attitudes.

With reference to the second point, the ability of teachers to change, the teacher boosters had faith that basically well-meaning teachers could change when the power structure was revamped to free them a little. These critics did not see lower-middle classness as a permanent irremovable taint. Few of these critics believed that teachers came anywhere near possessing a sound body of theoretical pedagogical knowledge or had strong command of the skills necessary for good teaching or had the right values and attitudes. And even teacher boosters often associated these deficiencies with social class backgrounds. But they also sincerely believed that better training and interning would make a difference in the performance of teachers from lower-middle class backgrounds with moderate intelligence and average

105

school grades. Teachers could, with help, transcend their limitations. These critics, believers in the teachers' ability to change and grow, as well as in their basic good will, wanted different selection procedures for teachers - procedures better attuned to what teachers had to be and do. Miriam Wasserman, for example, showed how the New York credentialing requirements selected for the most rigid, timid, cautious and rule-minded candidates (1970: 44). But, once selected, teachers did not have to be 'extraordinary' people in order to do well. They could be ordinary people quite capable of learning to do a good job.

Implications and Conclusions

I have presented two neat, well-formed stances complete with appropriate images. Far too neat and well-formed! And to some degree, false! Critics spill out of the categories. There is no perfect one-to-one relationship between the image of teachers held by a particular critic and the stance that critic took on the teacher's position. Not all critics put power, ill will and determinism in one package, or powerlessness, good will and freedom into the other. But, no matter how muddy reality always is, no matter how jerrybuilt the structure, I believe I am justified in claiming that there are reasonably consistent assumptions underlying the variations played on the surface. These assumptions guided the way critics thought about teachers, what they hoped for or despaired of, and they influenced different critics to draw opposing conclusions from the same visible reality.

Our attitudes towards teachers and the ways in which we academics conceptualize them make a difference in how well we are able to communicate and work with them. Among reformist critics, the teacher boosters were more generous than the teacher bashers. But even they were more condescending and patronizing than positive. They too found teachers a somewhat inferior species.

I fear that our attitudes have not significantly changed. We are as prone as any nonacademic to cherish our untested assumptions, to let our feelings colour our choices, to attribute a kind of brute determinism to the actions of others that we would deny to our own.

One attempt we can make is to apply our own theories reflexively. We should then be able to comprehend why teachers are often sceptical about us, why they take what we say with more than a few grains of salt, why they protect themselves from our condescension and hostility. When we and they can talk to one another directly, even if negatively, we may be able to bring some of our hard-won knowledge and insight into communication with theirs. And we can then both learn.

NOTES

1. The research on which this paper is based is part of a larger project in process analysing radical as well as reformist critical stances on teachers.

2. The term 'critic' encompasses all those who wrote on education for the general public - negatively or positively, analytically or dramatically. In this period, everyone who published had an agenda. Objective description and analysis easily blurred into subjective polemic. Critics cared too much to be detached.

3. My attempt is to delineate stances, using the writings of particular individuals for illustration. In actuality, individual critics overlapped stances, or slipped in and out of them. In this paper, we cannot analyse the work of individual critics in all their unique richness.

4. By images I do not mean completely false or distorted pictures of reality. Images are more or less true, more or less based on fact, more or less distorted. They grow from diverse sources, often without one's conscious awareness of the process. Images may be broadly generalized to all teachers, or more narrowly specified to high school rather than elementary, urban rather than rural, ghetto rather than middle class teachers. Also, images may be constructed and dramatized to support an argument from another source. I shall not probe the truth or falsity of the images. I shall probe whether they were related to a critic's stance on the teacher's proper position.

5. New York was the focus of much of the writing and struggle. Comparable conflicts occurred in other U.S. cities, although not always posing teachers against parents. Similar struggles occurred over Native education in Canada.

6. Philip Jackson (1971: 62) is a rare exception. He found the schools better than a century ago with 'more humane and better educated teachers'.

7. Blaming the teachers was also a sport engaged in by non-reformist critics. Some of the most popular critical works of this period were morality plays, recounting the devastating but gripping personal experiences of a brave, dedicated teacher (the author) fighting a hopeless battle in the school against the evil being perpetuated by the other insensitive, bigoted, incompetent and cruel teachers. Such an intense experience sent Jonathan Kozol to free schools (1967, 1972), Herbert Kohl to open classrooms (1967, 1976), and John Holt to deschooling (1964, 1976).

8. See Carl Bereiter (in Levine and Havighurst, 1971) for this kind of approach.

9. Some radical critics like Miriam Wasserman deplored this tendency as did some reformist critics like Diane Ravitch.

10. See Silberman (1970: 141) for a discussion of this kind of class bias against the 'white collar, lower-middle class world of teachers.'

11. See, as an example of this approach, Gross and Osterman (1972).

12. For an example of this approach, see Seymour Rosen in Gartner et al. (1973: 100).

13. One exception was Donald Myers (1973).

REFERENCES

Berube, M. and Gittell, M. (eds.) (1969) Confrontation at Ocean Hill-Brownsville: The New York School Strike of 1968. New York: Frederick A. Praeger.

Braun, R.J. (1972) Teachers and Power: The Story of the American Federation of Teachers. New York: Simon and Schuster.

Cuban, L. (1969) To Make a Difference: Teaching in the Inner City. New York: The Free Press.

Cuban, L. (1970) 'Teacher and Community', Harvard Educational Review 39, no. 2: 256-272.

Dreeben, R. (1970) The Nature of Teaching: Schools and the Work of Teachers. Glenview, Illinois: Scott, Foresman and Company.

Fantini, M. (1974) What's Best for the Children? Resolving the Power Struggle Between Parents and Teachers. Garden City, New York: Anchor Press.

Featherstone, J.(1971) Schools Where Children Learn
    New York: Liveright.
Featherstone, J. (1976) What Schools Can Do New
    York: Liveright.
Fein,L.J.(1971) The Ecology of the Public Schools:
    An Inquiry into Community Control. New York:
    Pegasus (Bobbs-Merrill Co., Inc. Pub.).
Friedenberg, E.Z. (1963) Coming of Age in America:
    Growth and Acquiescence. New York: Random
    House.
Gartner, A., Green, C. and Riessman, F. (eds.)
    (1973) After Deschooling: What? New York:
    Harper and Row Publishers.
Gittell, M. and Hevesi, A.G. (eds.) (1969) The
    Politics of Urban Education. New York:
    Frederick A. Praeger, Publisher.
Gouldner, A. (1970) 'The Sociologist as Partisan:
    Sociology and the Welfare State', in Jack
    Douglas (ed.), The Relevance of Sociology.
    New York: Appleton-Century-Crofts.
Gross, R. and Osterman, P. (eds.) (1972) The New
    Professionals. New York: Simon and Schuster.
Hargreaves, D. (1974) 'Deschoolers and New
    Romantics', in Michael Flude and John Ahier,
    Educability, Schools and Ideology. London:
    Croom Helm.
Hentoff, N. (1977) Does Anybody Give a Damn? New
    York: Alfred A. Knopf.
Holt, J. (1964) How Children Fail. New York:
    Pitman Publishing Company.
Holt, J. (1976) Instead of Education. New York:
    E.P. Dutton and Co., Inc.
Illich, I. (1970) Deschooling Society. New York:
    Harper and Row, Publisher.
Jackson, P. (1971) 'A View from Within', in Daniel
    Levine and Robert Havighurst (eds.), Farewell
    to Schools? Worthington, Ohio: Charles A.
    Jones Publishing Co.
Katz, M. (1971) 'The Present Moment in School
    Reform', Harvard Educational Review 41, no. 3:
    342-359.
Kohl, H. (1967) On Teaching. New York: Shocken
    Books.
Kohl, H. (1976) 36 Children. New York: Signet
    Books, The American Library, Inc.
Kozol, J. (1967) Free Schools. Boston: Houghton
    Mifflin Company.
Kozol, J. (1972) Death at an Early Age: The
    Destruction of the Hearts and Minds of Negro
    Children in the Boston Public Schools. Boston:
    Houghton Mifflin Company.

Leacock, E.B. (1969) _Teaching and Learning in City Schools: A Comparative Study_. New York: Basic Books, Inc.

Levine, D.U. and Havighurst, R. (eds.) (1971) _Farewell to Schools?_ Worthington, Ohio: Charles A. Jones Publishing Company.

Lortie, D. (1975) _Schoolteacher: A Sociological Study_. Chicago: University of Chicago Press.

Mayer, M. (1969) _The Teachers' Strike, New York, 1968_. New York: Harper & Row Publishers.

Myers, D.A. (1973) _Teacher Power - Professionalization and Collective Bargaining_. Lexington, Mass.: D.C. Heath and Co.

Passow, A.H. (ed.) (1971) _Reactions to Silberman's 'Crisis in the Classroom'_. Belmont, Ca.: Wadsworth Publishing Co.

Pearl, A. (1972) _The Atrocity of Education_. New York: E.P. Dutton, Inc.

Ravitch, D. (1977) _The Revisionists Revisited: A Critique of the Radical Attack on the Schools_ New York: Basic Books, Inc., Publishers.

Rogers, D. (1968) _110 Livingstone Street: Politics and Bureaucracy in the New York City Schools_. New York: Random House.

Rosenthal, A. (1969) _Pedagogues and Power: Teacher Groups in School Politics_. Syracuse: Syracuse University Press.

Rosenthal, R. and Jacobson, L. (1968) _Pygmalion in the Classroom_. New York: Holt, Rinehart and Winston, Inc.

Ryan, W. (1971) _Blaming the Victim_. New York: Pantheon Books (Random House).

Schrag, P. (1967) _Village School Downtown: Politics and Education - A Boston Report_. Boston: Beacon Press.

Scribner, H.B. and Stevens, L. (1975) _Make Your Schools Work_. Now York: Simon and Schuster.

Silberman, C. (1970) _Crisis in the Classroom_. New York: Random House.

Skolnick, J. (1970) _Crisis in American Institutions_ Boston: Little, Brown and Company.

Stein, A. (1971) 'Strategies for Failure', _Harvard Educational Review_ 41, no. 2: 158-204.

Wasserman, M. (1970) _The School Fix, NYC, USA_. New York: Outerbridge and Dienstfrey.

Wasserman, M. (1974) _Demystifying School_. New York: Praeger Publishers.

JUDGING TEACHERS: THE SOCIAL AND POLITICAL
                   CONTEXTS OF TEACHER EVALUATION

Gerald Grace

The beginnings of a systematic sociology of assessment and evaluation has brought into sharp focus a recognition that these activities are not simply to do with technical measurements but have ideological and political dimensions. Assessments and evaluations in education have, as Bernstein and others have pointed out, implications for the distribution of power and the principles of social control and as such are of fundamental sociological interest. The fact that assessment and evaluation activities have a dual character, partly technical and partly ideological, provides scope for differences of emphasis in the literature. On the one hand a liberal reformist strategy in education has emphasised the objective and technical aspects of these procedures and has looked towards an increasing refinement of them as the crucial means for the realization of the meritocratic principle. On the other hand, from various conflict perspectives such procedures have been regarded as primarily devices for the legitimation of the cultural and social status quo. Here the emphasis has been upon the ways in which assessment and evaluation procedures in education although apparently open and meritocratic can be viewed as effectively reproducing the social relations, the personality dispositions and the distribution of cultural capital necessary for the maintenance of existing social arrangements. The need to locate assessment and evaluation principles and procedures in relation to wider structural, economic and political frameworks; the need to recognise the conflicts and contradictions of their dual character and the need to clarify the historically changing nature of these principles and procedures has been recognised by writers such as Young

(1971), Bernstein (1977), Bowles and Gintis (1976), Hextall and Sarup (1977) and Broadfoot (1979, 1981). While such contributions have significantly extended the range of questions to be raised, the emphasis of much theoretical writing and of much empirical inquiry has been upon the assessment and evaluation of pupils by teachers and examiners or upon the assessment of educational institutions by external agencies. These are clearly important areas of concern but preoccupation with them has tended to overshadow another area of concern, that of the assessment and evaluation of teachers by headteachers and inspectors, or, as begins to be the case in some local authorities, by management consultant specialists.[1] I want to argue that contemporary educational, social, economic and political conditions are making the assessment and evaluation of teachers and of teacher competence a crucial issue for all those interested in the fate of state provided education. At one level of analysis, many significant educational changes such as the move to comprehensive school organisation, to mixed ability grouping and to integrated forms of pedagogy and curricula have implications for the assessment of teacher competence. At another level of analysis, the tightening network of accountability, monitoring and control in education has important repercussions in this area. Expenditure cuts in education, falling school rolls, the redeployment or making redundant of teachers necessarily bring into sharp focus the principles and procedures for assessing and evaluating teacher competence. Politically it is clear that a growing emphasis in ministerial and official statements upon the existence of 'incompetent teachers in our schools'[2] has not emerged at this particular historical juncture merely by chance. Such an emphasis serves a number of very useful ideological functions. In the first place it diverts attention away from the effects which educational expenditure cuts per se are having upon educational standards and achievements by concentrating upon purported teacher deficiencies. In the second place, it legitimates policies for closer control and monitoring by implying that excessive teacher autonomy exists and in the third place it provides a useful 'quality control' argument to be used in strategies involving the reduction of teacher numbers and of their training institutions and in decisions involving teacher redeployment and redundancy.

Judging Teachers: The Social and Political Contexts

I want to suggest that our critical understanding of these contemporary developments will be enhanced if we locate our analysis of teacher evaluation historically. One of the most promising developments in contemporary sociology of education has been the re-discovery of the heuristic power of historically located inquiry. Such inquiry, the virtues of which were well known to the founding fathers of sociology and which were proclaimed in a later period by writers such as C. Wright Mills,[3] has many advantages. It guards against (as I have written elsewhere) an unfortunate tendency towards a disembodied structuralism on the one hand or an unrelated world of consciousness on the other.[4] More positively it has the advantage of sensitizing us to the principles and procedures which have been dominant in the past so that we are alert to the mode of their reproduction, reconstitution or change. It has the advantage also of concretely exemplifying and making visible the relations between educational structures and processes and wider structures of power, economy and control in particular periods of social change. Such exemplification and such making visible can provide us with suggestive hypotheses and useful models in our attempts to clarify the present form of those relations.[5]

It is for these reasons that my approach to the study of teacher evaluation related to changing social and political contexts in this country proceeds historically. In the space available however it is only possible to elucidate main trends, characterise general principles and procedures and suggest tentative relations. Detailed confirmation or refutation of these must wait upon the outcomes of further socio-historical and empirical inquiry. Because of the structural variety of the teaching profession and its change over time, it is not possible to trace all the strands of such an analysis. The intention is therefore to concentrate upon those principles and procedures and contextual forces which relate to teachers in working class schools in particular. Such teachers, known in the nineteenth century as 'the teachers of the people', are those whose workplace has been in Britain historically the urban elementary school and subsequently the secondary modern and the contemporary inner city school.

HISTORICAL LOCATION (1): EVALUATING THE 'TEACHERS OF THE PEOPLE'

British state schooling was marked from its origins by a concern about teacher quality and competence and this concern was most explicit in the case of the teachers of urban working class pupils. As Johnson (1970, p.119) has argued, fears about the maintenance of social control in the cities gave a particular urgency to the role of schooling in processes of class-cultural transformation: 'supervised by its trusty teacher, surrounded by its playground wall, the school was to raise a new race of working class people – respectful, cheerful, hard-working, loyal, pacific and religious'. The question of what constituted a 'trusty teacher' was therefore of some significance. A scrutiny of the historical literature suggests that three dominant emphases were used in nineteenth century evaluations of teachers in the popular system of schooling. These were principles of ideological reliability; principles of competent social control and principles of efficient pedagogic work production. Such principles may be traced in the writings of influential agents of the state such as James Kay-Shuttleworth (the first Secretary to the Committee of Council on Education); in the reports of the school inspectorate and in evidence presented to Commissions of Inquiry into the state of popular schooling. While these principles coexisted throughout the nineteenth century and beyond, it is possible to discern the ways in which particular principles of evaluation came into particular prominence as social, educational, economic and political conditions changed.

The first and arguably the most important of the principles of evaluation was that of ideological reliability expressed initially in notions of the religious and moral character of the teacher and in notions of his or her respectability. It is clear that in the opinion of the Victorian providers of elementary schooling, 'goodness' was much to be preferred to 'cleverness' for the teachers of the people. Whereas a religious and moral character might be taken as an indicator of respectability and reliability, cleverness per se was unpredictable in its consequences. Thus Kay-Shuttleworth (1862, p.401) stressed the need for the elementary teacher to be 'the gentle and pious guide of the children of the

poor' and not 'a hireling into whose mind had sunk
the doubts of the sceptic and in whose heart was
the worm of social discontent'. The language of
teacher evaluation and of teacher selection
especially during the crucial founding period of
English popular schooling is replete with such
observations. So for instance we find the British
and Foreign School Society writing to the Committee
of Council on Education in 1843 on the difficulties
of obtaining suitable students for training:

> To obtain youth of considerable talent, or
> shrewd and clever mechanics whose ability
> would reflect credit in any public examination
> is not difficult if moral and religious
> character can be regarded as a secondary
> consideration but to secure persons who are
> decided as to their religious views, persons
> who have given some evidence of their desire
> at least to cultivate a degree of seriousness,
> humility, patience and meekness it is
> frequently necessary to be content with a less
> amount of talent.
> (In Tropp, 1957, p.17)

The good student and the good teacher was
preeminently at this time one whose character and
general ideological stance was acceptable to the
authorities and one who could be relied upon to act
as an agent of social control and social cohesion
especially in the schools of the great cities. The
training colleges had crucial functions in
monitoring and shaping such acceptability during
the teacher's occupational formation. This was
accomplished by careful ideological screening upon
entrance; a regime of constant busyness during
training; a high degree of surveillance of
students at all times and a closely controlled
curriculum. Such a regime, the regime of the
'total institution'. distanced the students from
economic and political controversies and indeed
from intellectual and ideological enthusiasms of
any sort - even from religious enthusiasms. Thus
an inspector of training colleges could reassure
the Newcastle Commission in 1861 that,

> there is very little opportunity for the
> students in training colleges to indulge in
> irregularities or to consort with improper
> companions . . . no set of young men of the
> same age are kept under such close restraint

and could add 'there is very little active feeling with regard to political or ecclesiastical questions among the students' (Newcastle Commission, 1861, Vol. 4, p.404). If the young teacher survived the regime of the college and even if his or her route into teaching by-passed the college, the school inspectors and the school managers provided yet another mechanism for ideological screening once the teacher had arrived in the school. The teacher of the working class in other words continued to be subject to a high degree of social surveillance even in the work situation, and this situation was to last until well into the twentieth century.

If principles of ideological reliability were the first requirement in the evaluation of the teacher of the poor, the second was to be found in principles of social control expressed in notions of management, discipline and good order. The success of teachers in working class schools was seen to be related to 'the role of maintaining exact order and ready and active attention as the first necessity and after that as much kindness to the children as is compatible with a habit of entire obedience', (Newcastle Commission, Vol. 2, 1861, pp.258-9). The conditions of the teacher's work situation at this time generated a technical imperative of dominance and control from which it was virtually impossible for even the most idealistic of teachers to deviate. As one of them wrote, 'so large were the classes and so unruly the boys, one could not educate, one could only subjugate'[6]. Teachers who could not manage in this sense, who could not dominate in the first instance and then subsequently establish principles of obedience, hierarchy and respect through the schooling process could hardly be expected to survive in the classroom. Teachers judged to be competent were those who did establish good order in the classroom and those who did survive with resilience the conditions of the school as workplace.

This provides us with an example of the ways in which the technical and the ideological elements in teacher evaluation at this time were compounded together. With large classes, cramped space and an arid curriculum, the strategy of a survivor-teacher had to involve dominance, hierarchy and respect. In the situation as constituted these became the necessary qualities for teacher survival.[7] At

the same time however wider socio-political
concerns about the rate and direction of social
change and about the weakening of principles of
hierarchy and of respect gave to such classroom
practice a wider structural significance. The
competent teacher not only engaged in the
production of good classroom and institutional
order but was also crucially engaged in the
production of the conditions for socio-political
order. Thus teacher evaluations at this period
were themselves a product of both constructed
technical imperatives of the workplace and of
ideological and political concerns generated by
industrialization and urbanization.

Now the danger with the sort of socio-
historical analysis which I have engaged in so far,
is that it can lead to an over-determined linear
view of the education system and of the position of
teachers within it. It is relatively easy to
demonstrate that the providing classes had certain
intentions for the schooling enterprise. It is
relatively easy to demonstrate the existence of
certain principles of teacher evaluation related to
wider structural concerns. The more complex part
of the analysis is to try to examine the mechanisms
and mediations of these intentions and of these
principles; the conflicts and contradictions which
existed in the practice of elementary schooling;
the unintended consequences and lacunae and the
resistances, overt and covert. For while social
control and class-cultural transformation may have
been the dominant intention of the providing
classes and while the elementary teacher as the
crucial agent of this process was to be carefully
evaluated, this is not to say that these intentions
and these evaluations constituted a total hegemony.
There were spaces, there were contradictions and
there were resistances. It is important that as
the sociology of education rediscovers the value of
historically located study it should not only
reconstruct hegemonic intention but should also
recover the more complex nature of educational
practice.

Something of this complexity can be discerned
in the struggles within British elementary
schooling in the second half of the nineteenth
century. The educational reaction of the 1860s in
Britain was provoked among other things by the
complexities and contradictions of practice. This
reaction, exemplified in the imposition of the
Revised Code and of payment by results and

exemplified in the undermining of the status, security and economic position of elementary school teachers and their tutors, was fuelled by middle class fears that the apparatus of popular schooling which they had brought into existence had got out of control. Despite existing mechanisms of surveillance and screening, the system had perversely developed its own dynamic which had resulted in forms of curriculum development, forms of teacher initiative and forms of cultivation of intelligence which had never been intended for working class schooling. The costs of the enterprise had risen dramatically and new subjects had been introduced into the curriculum. Elementary school teachers had become more confident and assertive. As standards within the provided system rose the dreadful prospect that working class education might soon surpass in quality that provided by many middle class private schools suggested, as one writer put it, that there would be 'an inversion of the orders of society'.[8] In short, the system in practice had turned out to be altogether too good for the working class.

It was the teachers themselves who were largely held responsible for this state of affairs. They were being, it was claimed, over-educated in their training colleges and this over-education had led to over-ambitious aims within the elementary schools. They had become interested in the novel and the unusual and were neglecting the basics of instruction. Collectively, it was said, they had become an over-paid and over-confident vested interest within education whose potential for independent action seemed to be growing. Thus Robert Lowe warned the House of Commons in 1861 that 'a state of things will arise that the control of the educational system will pass out of the hands of the Privy Council and of the House of Commons into the hands of "the persons working that educational system" . . .' (in Tropp, p.87). The educational and political reaction of the 1860s was intended, among other things, to cut back the pretensions of elementary schooling and of elementary schoolteachers. It was thought necessary to tighten the apparatus of control around the schools, the teachers and the training colleges. The most favoured means of doing this was by a vigorous application of market economy principles to elementary schooling. The mechanism would be the Code and the agents of assessment would be the inspectorate. The Code would define the product required; the inspector would assess the extent to which it had been achieved; the teacher would be paid and evaluated in relation to his or her measured efficiency in production. Teacher competence would be apparently a matter of mechanical efficiency - of meeting the requirements of the Code. The training colleges would be expected to prepare for that mechanical efficiency. The dominant principle was now to be that of efficient pedagogic work production with an emphasis upon 'basics'.

The second half of the nineteenth century saw therefore a determined attempt to reassert control, to restructure elementary schooling and to reappraise teacher status and teacher competence. The mechanism of the Code was powerful and the inspectors as agents of assessment were active and yet even in these conditions it is possible to discern countervailing principles and agencies. The situation was contested. Although the intention of certain groups was to establish a principle of efficient work production as a decisive element in teacher evaluation, this was overtly resisted by the teachers and, it can be argued, covertly resisted by a sector of the inspectorate. The teachers collectively began their long struggle to have themselves evaluated as professionals and not as pedagogic technicians. They condemned the restrictions placed upon elementary schooling and the narrow and mechanical criteria now applied to the assessment and evaluation of teacher competence. The following denunciation, taken from a speech at the Nottingham conference of the National Union of Elementary Schoolteachers in 1879 is typical of the reaction of the more spirited teachers -

> What is the first question asked by the manager visiting a school or engaging a teacher? What percentage did you pass last year? Upon what is the salary, nay the reputation of a teacher made to depend? Upon his ability to turn out so many yards of reading, writing and arithmetic from his human machines at 3 shillings per yard.
> (In Gautry, 1937, p.119)

In resisting the application of the ethic of industry, of measured production and of close surveillance, the teachers began collectively to forge the ethic of professionalism as a weapon in the ideological struggle. As I suggested in Teachers, Ideology and Control (1978) and as Ozga and Lawn have suggested in Teachers, Professionalism and Class (1981) constructs of professionalism became a first line of defence against pedagogic and cultural imposition. In the name of professionalism, elementary schoolteachers called for evaluations which took into account intelligent and humane teaching as well as mechanical teaching. They called for improved status and working conditions; for greater autonomy and 'freedom from obnoxious interference'. At the same time they urged that the agency of assessment itself, the inspectorate, should be open to talented elementary schoolteachers and should not remain a closed elite recruited largely from graduates of Oxford and Cambridge. In short, the attempt by the state to cut back on educational expenditure and to exercise tighter control over teachers and curriculum had the effect of provoking the teachers into more vigorous forms of association and into a more assertive form of occupational ideology.

While the teachers engaged in overt resistance to an imposed code of mechanical measurement and quantification in schooling, a code applied both to the pupils and to themselves, a sector of the inspectorate provided some strategic support.(9) It is here that we have yet another example of the way in which socio-historical study in the sociology of education can help us to resist the element of over-determination in theories of social and cultural reproduction.(10) It would fit the premises of such theories to find that the school inspectorate was an homogenous and unified agency of surveillance and of code transmission and implementation. In fact, as definers of pedagogic excellence, influential members of the inspectorate notably Matthew Arnold and in a later period, Edmond Holmes made clear their criticisms of the code and of the narrow and mechanical criteria for the assessment of teacher competence which it enshrined. Arnold in particular sought to establish against the model of the elementary schoolteacher as competent technician a model which stressed the teacher's appreciation of culture. For Arnold and others in this literary-romantic tradition teacher assessment and evaluation could not be reduced to a mechanical process. Whatever else they were, elementary schoolteachers were 'missionaries and preachers of culture', agents for the dissemination of refining and ennobling sensitivities and values among the working class achieved through the study of great literature and poetry.[11] Such work was essential not only for the civilising of that class but also for the realisation of a new principle of social solidarity and harmony against the threat of growing class conflict. As Martin Wiener (1982) has shown in English Culture and the Decline of the Industrial Spirit 1850-1980 a contempt for the values of industrial capitalism permeated the universities and the public schools of later Victorian Britain. Given that the majority of the inspectorate were Oxford and Cambridge and public school men it is hardly surprising that elements of this contempt or at least cultural distancing were mediated even into elementary education. These countervailing influences and agencies meant that even at the high point of code domination and also in a later period of growing pressures for more industrial and technical emphasis in the curriculum, elementary education was not in direct correspondence with the requirements of the state or of the economy. While it is important therefore to recognise a crucial degree of non-correspondence between these structures and while it is important to recognise the contested nature of the criteria for teacher assessment and evaluation, it cannot be denied that in the second half of the 19th Century elementary school teachers were under tighter control, closer surveillance and more specific assessment criteria than at any other period. This surveillance incorporated not only the apparently technical production criteria of the codes but also a renewed interest in the ideological commitments of the teacher. The rise of socialism in the late nineteenth and early twentieth centuries brought sharply back into focus the principle of ideological reliability in the assessment of elementary school teachers. Thus we find a writer in 1908 warning the British nation that,

> the socialist leaders already perceive what a splendid field the elementary schools afford for their peculiar propaganda. What better career can they offer to their sons and daughters than to enter the teaching profession and in a discreet way play the socialist missionary?
> (in Tropp, p.148)

HISTORICAL LOCATION (2):   EVALUATING TEACHER
                           PROFESSIONALS

The paradox of locating the teacher's position
in working class schooling in the twentieth century
(or at least after 1926) is the paradox of apparent
freedom. In the discourse of the teachers
themselves and in much of the literature which
focusses upon such teachers can be found a strong
celebration of autonomy;[12] of the absence of
close control and surveillance and even of the
absence of very specific criteria for assessing
teacher competence. This sense of freedom has led
commentators as different as Frank Musgrove (1969)
on the one hand and Rhodes Boyson (1975) on the
other to assert subsequently that teacher autonomy
has become excessive and ought to be cut back. Now
unless such teachers and writers are the victims of
a false consciousness about teacher autonomy (and
this seems unlikely) a considerable transformation
of the teacher's situation in working class
schooling seems to have occurred this century, even
if its extent may have been exaggerated. If this
is the case, it raises some very important
questions for socio-historical study in the
sociology of education. How, for instance, is this
transformation to be explained? How has it come
about that the teachers of the working class, once
so closely controlled as the strategic agents of
social and cultural formation, should, in the
context of modern capitalist Britain, appear to
enjoy so much freedom, or at least sense of
freedom?

John White (1975) has suggested, convincingly
in my view, that the change from a relatively high
degree of control and monitoring of such teachers
to a relatively high degree of autonomy was the
result of a political decision at a time of
perceived ideological crisis. In 1926 the Board of
Education in an unprecedented manner swept away the
remnants of code prescription in elementary
education by eliminating all mention of the
subjects (except for practical instruction) which
were expected to be taught in elementary schools.
At the same time, a new concept of the inspector's
role and of the process of school inspection began
to be propagated by the Board of Education. The
inquisitional aspect vis-à-vis the teacher was no
longer thought appropriate and inspectors were now
advised by the Board that their role was to be one
of 'disseminating in convenient fashion, results

and suggestions derived from continuous recorded observations' (Edmonds, 1962, pp.174-75). In effect the modern principle of curriculum autonomy and teacher autonomy was being established at this time.[13] But why? It seems clear from the historical evidence that although a complex of factors contributed to this change, including the sustained campaigns of organised teachers as a pressure group and a rising interest among educationalists in a more open and progressive pedagogy, the decisive factor was political. As both John White (1975) and Martin Lawn (1983) have pointed out, the 1920s marked a high point of Conservative fears about the growth of socialism in Britain and particularly about the political role of education as an instrument of socialism. This fear was constituted at two levels. At one level, that of the teachers in the popular system, there was concern about increased militancy and frustration and the beginnings of alliances between certain sectors of the teaching force and organisations within the labour movement. At another level, that of administration, there was concern that the existence of centralised directions or codes related to an agency of implementation such as the inspectorate provided a mechanism which might be seized by an elected Labour government and turned to socialist ends. All this pointed to the need to win the teachers away from dangerous alliances with the working class by trying to remove their sense of occupational grievance, by taking more seriously their claim to be professionals and crucially by establishing a principle of school and teacher autonomy in respect of curriculum which could act as a countervailing force to any future socialist direction in educational policy. White (1975, p.28) has expressed the Conservative position at the time as follows:-

> If Parliament still controlled the content of education, the Socialists would change the Regulations . . . they would be able to introduce curricula more in line with Socialist ideas. To forestall this it was no longer in the interests of the anti-Socialists, including Conservatives, to keep curriculum policy in the hands of the state . . . If they could devise a workable system of non-statutory controls, the Conservatives had everything to gain and nothing to lose

from taking curricula out of the politicians' hands.

It was in these circumstances that the principle of school and teacher autonomy was effectively born. The political produced the ideology of the non-political - the non-political school, the non-political curriculum and the non-political teacher. This latter construct, the non-political teacher, now became a central strand within the legitimated ideology of teacher professionalism. Such professionalism was now about relative autonomy; it was about particular expertise; it was about white collar status and security and it was about the teacher being at a distance from the political and the economic and the agency of the state. Such a version of professionalism suited the aspirations of many teachers in the popular system and it suited those who saw in such professionalism an effective non-statutory control over the teaching force. What Lawn (1981) has called the 'licensed autonomy' of the teacher could now effectively serve as a buffer against attempted state imposition without much danger that the teachers would exploit such autonomy in any threatening way. The effect of these changes was to alter the modality of control in state schooling from an essentially visible, prescriptive and centralized system to an essentially invisible and diffuse mode. Professionalism had a crucial part to play in this more invisible and diffuse mode of control. The ethic of legitimated professionalism(14) provided the context within which teachers in the popular system were evaluated from the 1930s to the 1970s. This period was marked by a significant change in the agencies, mechanisms and mode of assessment. The legacy of code prescription in popular schooling had gone. The school inspectorate was increasingly presented as an advisory body or as one of them wrote expressing the new ideology - 'H.M. Inspectors regard themselves in the main as advisers and consider such inspections as they hold incidental to their advisory work' (Blackie, 1970, p.89). The inspector was no longer represented as primarily the critical assessor and evaluator of individual teachers. As the culture of legitimated professionalism developed in this period encouraged both by the state and by the teachers' associations, most teachers found themselves distanced from a formal apparatus of control and surveillance. They were less and less accustomed to being observed in the classroom. They were less and less the objects of formal criteria for assessment and evaluation. All of this seemed to be the realisation of that professional autonomy for which they had struggled since the nineteenth century.

An important addition to this rising sense of professional freedom and autonomy among teachers in working class state schooling came as a result of economic change. The economic expansionism and affluence of the 1950s and 1960s, while it created some problems for teachers at the level of income differentials, appeared to strengthen their relative autonomy within schooling. The market situation in terms of teacher supply was in favour of the teachers. As the shortage of teachers became more acute, especially in inner-city areas, the balance of power within many state schools shifted away from the headteachers and towards staff associations. The shortage of teachers especially in urban working class schools, and the associated phenomenon of rapid teacher turnover and teacher mobility assisted in the development of innovative spaces in such schools for those who wanted to attempt curriculum or pedagogic change. With resources available for educational change; with progressive developments in pedagogy and in social relations within schooling and with a new sociology of education celebrating what Whitty (1977) has called 'radical possibilitarianism', the sense of freedom among teachers in state schooling probably reached a high point in the early 1970s. The Houghton Report of 1974 with its considerable salary increases awarded on the 'expectation of professional standards of performance' seemed to consolidate the notion that the teachers 'had never had it so good'. Viewed historically the relative gain in teacher autonomy at this time can hardly be denied. Teachers within state schooling were no longer judged and evaluated by the close, formal and visible mechanisms of the past. This is not to say however that they were no longer being judged and evaluated but rather that the process and the mode had become much more diffuse and indirect. The process of teacher assessment and evaluation was now mediated through notions of legitimated professionalism and the operation of the process was decentralized to individual schools. In effect, the changes of 1926 and the changes in the role of the inspectorate had devolved the process of teacher evaluation upon the headteachers. Headteachers had become the agents of a process now made much more difficult by the existence of the ethic of legitimated professionalism and, in the 1960s and early 1970s, by the existence of a strong sense of freedom and of bargaining power among the teachers. In the face of teachers confident in a sense of professionalism and confident in their market situation, headteachers were in an awkward position as agents of assessment and evaluation. It is true that both HMIs and the local inspectorate could act from time to time as the formal agents of these processes but the new ideology of advisory work tended to play down these functions. The term by term evaluation of teachers was seen to be the business of the headteacher because, among other reasons, it was the headteacher who had to write the references and testimonials which were in high production as a consequence of the fluid teacher labour market. The problem for headteachers was how to carry out this aspect of their role given the absence of any central policies or guidelines on staff evaluation and given the legacy of hostility among teachers in state schooling to any form of surveillance that might be reminiscent of nineteenth century 'obnoxious interference'. In small primary and secondary schools this might be less of a problem but in large urban comprehensive schools the problems were considerable.

Because the whole system of teacher assessment and evaluation had become so de-centralised it is difficult to give general characterisations of the principles and procedures being employed at this time. In my own researches during this period, in the specific context of inner-city schooling in London, I found that headteachers used a range of principles which reflected their own constructs of the needs of the schools and their own constructs of professionalism. In the main, they esteemed acceptable personalities, good organisers, efficient managers and social relations facilitators, and 'good professionals' defined in terms of a distancing of the teacher from the political and the controversial. The correlates of legitimated professionalism for the most part seemed to be dependability, commitment to the school, executive efficiency and good relations with the pupils in the pastoral care role. The procedures used by the headteachers to assess these qualities were of a very general and diffuse kind, almost a form of professional intuition rather than of systematic appraisal.[15]

Bernstein (1977) has suggested that the 1960s saw a shift in pedagogic codes from the visible and the strongly framed to the invisible and the weakly framed. A similar shift can be discerned in the mechanisms and mode of teacher assessment and evaluation. In both cases the transformations resulted from a matrix of educational, economic and political considerations and in both cases there were intended and unintended consequences. As far as the teachers are concerned it could be argued that, for the State, the intended consequence was the creation of a de-centralised network of control mediated by the ethic of legitimated professionalism. It could however also be argued that the unintended consequence was that certain fractions of the teaching group had opportunities to exploit the relatively autonomous spaces now made available. These fractions of the occupational group, if they rejected the ethic of legitimated professionalism could become subversive agents within the schooling enterprise. In other words, the de-centralised network of control depended to an important extent upon an internalised professional ethic established by, among other things, teacher training institutions. Without this internalised professional ethic the system was vulnerable. As it became apparent by the mid-1970s that the ethic of legitimated professionalism was being rejected by significant groups of teachers particularly in urban schools, and as the economic and political context changed from expansionism and optimism to retrenchment and reaction, the conditions were being constructed for a reappraisal of teachers in state schooling – their work situation, their autonomy and their supply and training.

TEACHER EVALUATION: SOME CONTEMPORARY ISSUES

We are now in a period where the social and political context of state provided schooling in Britain is reminiscent in a number of ways of the climate of reaction in the 1860s. Such comparisons must not be overstated but the parallel features (quite apart from a general celebration of 'Victorian values') are striking. There is a cutback of educational expenditure for state provided schooling. There is a growing emphasis upon tighter accountability; a required core

127

curriculum and a concentration upon basics. The role and strength of the inspectorate is being re-appraised and changes can be expected in the ideology and practice of inspection at all levels. Both teacher training and the work of teachers in schools are to be subject to more surveillance and to the application of more specific criteria for the assessment and evaluation of competence. Perhaps most significant of all these are suggestions that teacher deficiencies and the deficiencies of teacher education are at the heart of the 'education problem' today. Constructs of teacher competence are again high on the agenda as are principles and procedures for determining such competence.

As in the 1860s the reasons for this particular reaction and attempted shift in the modality of control are various. There is the usual interrelation of educational, social, economic and political elements. I would argue that the economic context provides the opportunity for the intervention; the political context provides the reason for the intervention and that the target for the intervention is once again the teachers and the teacher trainers. For many, influential in the state, the limits of the ethic of legitimated teacher professionalism have now been reached. Such professionalism has made possible in educational practice in working class schools too much space for the development of a threatening critical intelligence[16] and a threatening critical practice among urban working class youth. A new form of relation between the state and the teachers and the teacher training system now has to be forged. That relation is in the process of emerging at this time. Given a reassertion of stronger control by the state, the important question becomes, what will be the pattern and the form of the resistances to it? The actions that teachers are prepared to take collectively will be as crucial now as they were in the later part of the nineteenth century.

ACKNOWLEDGEMENTS

I am grateful to Dr. Harold Silver for helpful comments on an earlier draft of this paper.
I also learned much from discussion with participants at the Westhill Conference, January 1984 where this paper was first presented.

NOTES

1. A Performance Management System (PMS) undertaken by Hay - MSL Management Consultants is at present in operation with 'volunteer' teachers in the Cambridgeshire Local Education Authority. The PMS claims to be 'not simply another form of performance appraisal, self-evaluation or corporate planning' but an approach which involves 'regular face to face meetings between job holders and their immediate seniors not just to review past performance but to concentrate on future action'. ('A Note on the Hay Performance Management System', p.1).
For a brief discussion of Systematic Performance Appraisal applied to education see D. Martin, 'Systematic Performance Appraisal for Schools' in Secondary Education 10, (2), June 1980, pp. 18-19.

2. See for instance, The Times Educational Supplement, 29th January 1982, pp.21-24.

3. See Wright Mills' (1970) discussion of the 'Uses of History', pp.159-182.

4. See Grace (1978) p.215.

5. For a discussion of some of the advantages but also some of the epistemological difficulties of socio-historical inquiry, see Gareth Stedman-Jones (1976).

6. See Phillip Ballard, Things I Cannot Forget, University of London Press, 1937, p.62.

7. This is not to say that humane relations and innovative teaching were absent from elementary school classrooms. See for instance Edmond Holmes' acknowledgement of 'a noble band of pioneers' of such teaching and see also the work of Edward O'Neill (both cited in Grace, 1978, pp.26-27 and pp.44-46). However it does seem likely that such humanity and such innovation could only appear after certain principles of hierarchy and of respect had been established in early meetings between the class and the teacher - the 'initiation by ordeal' period.

8. J.C. Wigram, Secretary of the National Society (quoted in Tropp, 1957, p.59).

9. Edmonds (1962) notes that 'the opposition case to payment by results was nowhere better stated than by some of Her Majesty's Inspectors themselves' (p.28). He goes on to argue that 'instead of being a constructive

adviser, the inspector had become the harsh dispenser of an all too meagre government grant whose size he determined. Such a burden of responsibility was both unfair to the inspectors and unwanted by most of them' (p.81). It is clear that the opposition of a sector of the Inspectorate was based not only upon educational principle but upon objection to the changed nature of school inspection which had itself become more mechanical and routine.

10. Such theories should, as E.P. Thompson (1978) argues, submit themselves to 'the historical discipline, to historians' own discourse of the proof . . . (which) involves the empirical interrogation of the evidence, the dialogue of hypothesis and 'fact'.' (pp.286-287).

11. See Margaret Mathieson (1975) pp.37-47.

12. There are a number of ways in which the notion of autonomy can be employed in relation to education and the teacher's position:-
    (a) Structural autonomy: which refers to the degree of space and independence possessed by the educational structure vis-à-vis other structures of the state and the economy, i.e. the relative autonomy of education.
    (b) Occupational autonomy: which refers to the degree of self-determination possessed by teaching as an occupation in respect of professional entry, professional formation and professional self-government.
    (c) Workplace autonomy: which refers to the degree of self-determination possessed by teachers in the workplace in relation to curriculum, pedagogy, modes of assessment and evaluation of pupils and crucially the mode of their own assessment and evaluation.
    While it is clear that these three levels are interrelated the discussion in the remainder of the paper refers particularly to workplace autonomy.

13. It can be argued that important elements of curriculum and teacher autonomy were present in elementary schooling before 1926. This is not denied. The argument here however, following that of John White (1975), is that the political conditions of the mid-1920s resulted in a universalizing and a generalising of

14. these elements and that the motive force was political rather than primarily educational.

14. The ethic of legitimated professionalism involves licensed autonomy for the teacher in curriculum choice and pedagogic practice based upon an implicit understanding that the economic and the political should be distanced from the educational. For a criticism of the limitations of this ethic, see White (1979).

15. See Grace (1978) and Grace (1984a).

16. See Musgrave (1980) for a discussion of state response to 'dangerous knowledge'.

REFERENCES

Bernstein, B. (1977) Class, Codes and Control, Vol. 3 (second edution) London, RKP.

Blackie, J. (1970) Inspecting and the Inspectorate, London, RKP.

Bowles, S. and Gintis, H. (1976) Schooling in Capitalist America, London, RKP.

Boyson, R. (1975) The Crisis in Education, London, Woburn Press.

Broadfoot, P. (1979) Assessment, Schools and Society, London, Methuen.

Broadfoot, P. (1981) 'Towards a Sociology of Assessment' in Barton, L. and Walker, S. (eds.) Schools, Teachers and Teaching, Lewes, Falmer Press.

Broadfoot, P. (ed.) (1984) Selection, Certification and Control: Social Issues in Educational Assessment, London, Falmer Press.

DES, (1983) The Work of HM Inspectorate in England and Wales: a policy statement, London, DES Publications.

Edmonds, E. (1962) The School Inspector, London, RKP.

Gautry, T. (1937) Lux Mihi Laus: School Board Memories, London, Link House.

Giroux, H. (1981) Ideology, Culture and the Process of Schooling, London, Falmer Press.

Grace, G. (1978) Teachers, Ideology and Control: a Study in Urban Education, London, RKP.

Grace, G. (1984a) 'Headteachers' Judgements of Teacher Competence: Principles and Procedures in Ten Inner-City Schools' in Broadfoot, P. (ed.) Selection, Certification and Control, Lewes, Falmer Press.

Grace, G. (ed.) (1984b) Education and the City: theory, history and contemporary practice, London, RKP.

Hextall, I. and Sarup M. (1977) 'School knowledge: evaluation and alienation' in Young, M. and Whitty, G. (eds.), Society, State and Schooling, Lewes, Falmer Press.

Holmes, E. (1911) What is and What Might Be, London, Constable.

Johnson, R. (1970) 'Educational policy and social control in early Victorian England' in Past and Present, Vol. 49.

Johnson, T. (1972) Professions and Power, London, Macmillan.

Kay-Shuttleworth, J. (1862) Four Periods of Public Education, London, Lowland Green.

Lawn, M. and Ozga, J. (1981) 'The Educational Worker? A Re-assessment of Teachers' in Barton, L. and Walker, S. (eds.) op.cit.

Lawn, M. (1983) 'Teachers and the Labour Movement 1910-1935' unpublished Ph.D. thesis (CNAA).

Mathieson, M. (1975) The Preachers of Culture: a study of English and its teachers, London, Allen & Unwin.

Musgrave, P. (1980) 'The limits of curricular experience' in Barton, L. and Walker, S. (eds.) Schooling, Ideology and the Curriculum, Lewes, Falmer Press.

Musgrove, F. and Taylor, P.H. (1969) Society and the Teacher's Role, London, RKP.

Newcastle Commission, Report to the Popular Education Commission 1861,Vol.2 & 4, London HMSO.

Open University (1981) The Politics of Schools and Teaching, E353, Block 6. Milton Keynes, Open University Press.

Ozga, J. and Lawn, M. (1981) Teachers, Professionalism and Class, London, Falmer Press.

Rich, R. (1933) The Training of Teachers in England and Wales during the Nineteenth Century. Cambridge, Cambridge University Press.

Stedman-Jones, G. (1976) 'From Historical Sociology to Theoretical History' in British Journal of Sociology, Vol. 27, No. 3.

Thompson, E.P. (1978) The Poverty of Theory, London, Merlin Press.

Tropp, A. (1957) The Schoolteachers, London, Heinemann.

Weiner, M. (1982) English Culture and the Decline of the Industrial Spirit 1850-1980, Cambridge, Cambridge University Press.

White, J. (1975) 'The end of the compulsory curriculum' in The Curriculum: The Doris Lee Lectures 1975 University of London, Institute of Education.

White, J. (1979) 'The Primary Teacher as Servant of the State' in _Education 3-13_, Autumn, pp.18-23.
Wright Mills, C. (1970) _The Sociological Imagination_, Harmondsworth, Penguin Books.
Young, M.F.D. (ed.) 1971, _Knowledge and Control: new directions for the Sociology of Education_, London, Collier-Macmillan.

PART II

SCHOOLS AND SOCIAL CHANGE

THE INTERACTION BETWEEN SEX, CLASS AND SOCIAL CHANGE: COEDUCATION AND THE MOVE FROM FORMAL TO INFORMAL DISCRIMINATION

Jenny Shaw

One of the more recent educational surprises has been the questioning of coeducation and the re-examination of single sex schooling. For girls especially, single sex schools have gone from being the Cinderellas of education, poorly equipped and unloved, to occupying a position of some political importance. Dressed in the garb of positive discrimination they offer clear, if uncomfortable, directions for change. Meanwhile coeducation, once the darling of progressives, is now seen to have certain disadvantages.

Taking these disadvantages as its starting point this paper argues that they result from a growth in informal discrimination. This has been encouraged, or rather permitted by two linked changes. First, certain organisational changes in schools following comprehensivisation, and second, a convergence of class and sexual divisions over the last twenty years. Together these have determined the direction of social and educational change and the paper concludes that these changes represent a shift from system to social integration in the field of education. Social and system integration are theoretical categories first suggested by David Lockwood[1]. They have, by now, become part of the everyday vocabulary of sociological theory, although illustrations are harder to find. It is one of the merits of discussing coeducation yet again that the paradoxical and unintended consequences of its introduction may serve as an illustration of these categories and of a hypothesis derived from them. Thus the purpose of the paper is to identify at two distinct levels the causes of a particular educational problem. It does not offer new research into coeducation although it aims to offer some new insights.[2]

In brief, it argues that what is most interesting about coeducation is that it has been a relative failure. This failure stems from the spread of informal means of class and sexual division which colonised the mixed comprehensive schools. Both the schools and the means of discrimination replaced the earlier system of grammar and secondary schools based on formal differentiation and discrimination. These shifts, important for understanding the changing nature of class and sexual division, are related to the more general problem of access or resource allocation and its solution. Problems which, in fact, underlie all the major historical changes in educational provision from private schools onwards.

The interaction of class and sexual divisions is fundamental to the nature and direction of educational change. It may impede, accelerate or re-direct it. As such it has serious political consequences for any effort to remedy either or both class and sexual inequality. Just as in practical terms the costs of coeducation stem from some of the attempted remedies for class inequality in the form of mixed comprehensive schools so a return to single sex schools as a remedy for gender inequality probably has unavoidable consequences for class inequality, a likely result being to encourage the reintroduction of class selection to British education.

THE FAILURE OF COEDUCATION

Of course coeducation has not been a total failure. The fact that most people claim to prefer mixed schools to single sex ones shows that, but it is equally clear that coeducation has not had the effect it should have of fundamentally altering the educational opportunities of boys and girls in Britain.

As is now well known the majority of British schools went coeducational largely for reasons of administrative convenience following comprehensive reorganisation in the years between 1965 and 1981. In the beginning there was little interest in the specific issue of single sex schools, or indeed, very much interest in girls' educational performance per se. For the minority who were concerned the factor that seemed important was the undeniably poorer existing provision in girls' schools, particularly of science equipment and well qualified science teachers.(3)

At the time there was no organised or noticeable women's movement to defend or promote either single sex or coeducational schools. Equal pay within the profession having been achieved in 1961, the previously forceful and feminist National Union of Women Teachers had disbanded.(4) If anything the ending of formal sex segregation was welcomed on the grounds of it providing equal access. Thus as a primarily economic solution to the costs of comprehensive reorganisation in most local authorities coeducation went through on the nod.(5)

In principle then, when coeducation was introduced and the human and material facilities became equally available to pupils of both sexes there should then have followed some marked changes. Patterns of curriculum choice should have become less sex stereotyped and the gap in educational performance between girls and boys should have swiftly decreased. This did not happen. Indeed not much happened at all. Over a longish period of time there has been a gradual narrowing of the gap in educational performance between boys and girls, but not in the subjects most affected by sex stereotyping or by an imbalance in provision, i.e. mainly the natural sciences. In fact in some respects the situation worsened and despite objectively better provision in the mixed schools the patterns of choice according to gender narrowed and the sex stereotyping of the curriculum increased.(6) What might have been a fundamental redistribution of educational opportunity and outcome turned out to be a change of form, not function.

As is so often the case, social relations intervened to obstruct organisational change. For the trouble with coeducational schools is that they are, as their proponents have always claimed, more realistic than single sex schools. They are more like the rest of the 'heterosexual' social world and they reproduce many of the conditions that lead to the distinctly different and largely unequal life styles of men and women. With hindsight, we can see that the removal of formal educational barriers between the sexes led to an increase in the scope for informal discrimination and differentiation operating primarily at the interpersonal level. · The 'naturalism' of the coeducational school was its main problem for it led, as naturalism in working class education generally does too, to the consolidation of deprivation and subordination rather than to its mitigation.[7] Reproducing the 'both sexes' aspect of life in general within schools led to the reproduction of the sexual division of labour with all its negative consequences and some very specific educational results.

We may be cynical, and maybe these results should have been predicted, but they were not. When interest in sexual inequality surfaced in the early seventies (one of the first four demands of the women's movement was for equal education) it was with genuine surprise that coeducational schools were found to be less than wholly progressive.[8] Coeducation had surely not had the effect it should have of substantially altering the educational opportunities of boys and girls.

The immediate presence of boys and girls in the same classroom dramatically affected both teachers' behaviour towards pupils and the performance of those pupils. Evidence began to grow that mixed schools gave teachers the opportunity, not available in single sex schools, to give more time and attention to boys.[9] They could, and did, structure lessons in ways that suited boys, choosing examples which built on boys' interests, e.g. in old radios, car mechanics, etc., thus admitting boys whilst informally excluding girls.[10] A stress on possible dangers and the need for safety at the start of a science lesson may seem perfectly sensible but it can literally frighten off the girls whilst exciting the boys.[11] Both sexes apparently respond to teachers of their own sex more favourably, thus, as seniority and specialisation cull the women teachers, girls are deprived not only of role models but also of the social situations in which they do best.[12] The social relations between pupils are just as damaging as those between staff and pupils and girls risk becoming collectively constructed as a negative reference group for boys, thereby boosting the boys' egos and performance whilst depressing their own.

In short, what happens in a coeducational setting is that there is direct competition for educational resources between the sexes. How this is resolved clearly depends on a number of factors, not least of which is the economic and political context in which it occurs.

By any standard comprehensive reorganisation created a prolonged period of crisis for the education system: the more so because it was explicitly intended to reform and even abolish its class basis. Much sociological commentary on the progress and consequences of comprehensive education has centred on the capacity of schools to resist change and perpetuate class divisions in educational outcomes. In retrospect not least of these adjustments has been the heightening of gender as a basis for social and academic division.

To understand why gender divisions have, in part, displaced or taken over from class divisions in determining apparently academic choices and structuring educational selection one needs to remember that in the background there is always the question of resources. All subjects are not equally available and all subjects are not equally cheap. We already know that in per capita terms the middle class child is invested in more by the state and receives qualitatively and quantitatively more educational resources than the working class child.[13] We know that this inequality is directly related to factors such as differences in rates of staying on in education[14] and regional inequalities[15]. Furthermore we know that a similar pattern of distribution occurs between girls and boys, on the subjects that they choose.[16].

ACCESS, RESOURCE ALLOCATION AND SEXUAL DIVISIONS

Equality of access to education is a liberal demand enjoying virtually universal consent. And in some measure most of the educational changes of this century have been built on it. However equality of access to educational resources in no way implies equality of distribution. When informal methods of distribution replace formal ones it is frequently tradition rather than progressive social justice that dictates who gets what.

In the British case the problem of a shift towards informal allocation of resources was initially eased by expansion,[17] though it was later to be exacerbated by contraction. The rationale of comprehensive education was that all pupils should be given the chance to develop their full potential, and not be limited by judgements made of their capabilities at the early age of eleven. The caveat to these noble aims was always that equality was interpreted to mean equality of opportunity rather than equality of provision and selection within the new system was simply altered, not abolished. Seen from an organisational or systemic viewpoint the problem is how to be true to the aims of comprehensive education whilst never having sufficient resources to meet all rightful claims of individuals to reach their full potential.

Comprehensive reorganisation was, potentially, explosive. In fact it coincided with a period of unprecedented economic growth and was able to command an increasing share of national resources. Although it did not it could have led to quite unrealisable demands from hitherto underprivileged groups, i.e. working class children, ethnic minorities and girls. Enough good jobs and places in higher education were never, even at that time, going to be available. Yet discontent with educational provision has never taken the direct and explicitly political form of the consumers demanding more. That is not to say that there have not been political manifestations resulting from raising expectations and then failing to meet them but they have, in the main, taken a private, self-critical and defeatist form. One of the earliest, and best known, studies to show the crucial role of sexual divisions in deflecting discontent and educational disappointment into personal channels was Willis' study of young working class boys in Birmingham.[18] He showed how they energetically threw themselves into being young men in a highly macho way, very much as a response and an alternative to facing academic defeat, or success.

The significance of this generally personalised response to failure or, more properly, to the reality of limited educational resources, can be seen in wider theoretical terms. Indeed it is arguably a defining characteristic of 'access' relations in general, of which educational settings are a good example. The increased polarisation between the sexes in the mixed comprehensives are, in one sense, an individual and practical solution to the situation of competition. In another sense it may be viewed as a further example of the individuating, disorganising and isolating strategies that are characteristic of the capitalist state towards subordinate classes in general.

Another, less abstract, way of viewing the same set of issues concerns the introduction of computers and computing studies to schools at present. In principle gender is not a precondition for access to the new technology, or to the new subjects, but in practice it comes pretty near to that. The interest shown in computers by boys has far outstripped that of girls and, given the eclectic nature of the British curriculum, the social consequences which have followed both reinforce existing divisions and give them a fresh impetus along new occupational and educational lines.[19] Even the best off schools cannot afford a computer for every child, thus all schools have to deal with the problem of distributing a new and scarce resource. The effective, though again unintended, distribution has been massively in favour of boys. This creates the problem of how, under formally equal access conditions, and in a very short time, boys as a group of 'collective actors' have established their privileged relation to the new resources.

A small literature on access, mainly concerning political science and developing countries[20], offers a lead into some of these issues and shows the danger of leaving educational reform simply at the point of 'access'. Starting with the attempt to conceptualise non market or administrative systems of allocation in general an argument is presented in terms of the political purposes of such systems. Schaffer and Huang claim that whilst different systems of access produce different politics, in the end the point of all distributive systems designed by public authorities, whether they are strictly administrative or not, is to secure 'integration and mobilisation: loyalty rather than apathy and support rather than revolution'.[21] Such systems may appear to 'include the excluded' but the service offered is frequently inappropriate and the access unreal. Lamb goes further. He observes first, that isolation is the intended effect of all access relations and second, that the form of relations (queues for example) that characterise the access situation are not reserved exclusively for the dominated classes; they appear egalitarian and the dominant classes share in them too, though usually more successfully.[22] These writers conclude, nevertheless, that the experience of access relations, i.e. being given a formal chance, is profoundly significant and structures the politics of access by giving rise to particular ideologies and a vocabulary for voicing complaints and reinforcing loyalties.

If we return to Britain and its education system the general response to criticisms of

coeducation and the mode of access that it
represents is interesting. At the time of its
inception coeducation was not a controversial issue
and it was not seriously contested. (Largely
because it was not seen to relate directly to class
and class inequalities.) Never mind that in
principle it was a more thoroughly redistributive
measure than any other to date, being wholly non-
selective, it passed into the British education
system with hardly anyone being aware of it. No
formal policy was established, although one can
argue that single sex schools were defended in
principle within the private sector through the
exemptions granted to schools by the Sex
Discrimination Act of 1975, allowing them to remain
as single sex institutions.

Again, in principle, a dismantling of
coeducational schools would jeopardise no group's
political credibility and no hard fought for
victory would be lost if some single sex schools
were to be reintroduced. This was unlikely to
happen on a large scale for there is widespread
support for coeducation running across party lines.
Moreover there is probably an even greater
resistance to a return to single sex schools than
there is for a return to grammar schools. Loyalty
or incorporation to a system that is not in fact
egalitarian has clearly been achieved.

To summarise, comprehensive reorganisation was
based on the twin ideals of maximising individual
development and abolishing the class basis of
selection in education. Coeducation trailed along
behind it under a cloak of good intentions to
improve the facilities available for girls. What
in fact happened was that the social patterns
promoted by coeducation served to resolve in part
the stress, strain and competition for educational
resources. These had previously run, and been
resolved, in an uncomplicated and explicit way
along class lines. Occupational destinies were
clearly signposted and a reasonably stable and
predictable labour market provided the framework
and the rationale for the grammar/secondary modern
school system. Comprehensive education, with its
individualistic ideology and healthy appetite for
resources, upset that; later and successive rounds
of cuts and deepening unemployment upset it still
further increasing both the strain and the
competition.

Put starkly, coeducation entered the British
secondary education system the moment before it,

and the economy, entered a period of contraction. It had the effect of permitting gender to be deployed to defuse tensions inevitably created by an inegalitarian and compulsory education system. Since denying children access to subjects on the basis of their gender is now illegal these stabilising outcomes have operated almost wholly at an interpersonal and informal level. This is not new, the sexual division of labour has often been pressed into the service of other ends. It is regularly exploited by other interests, all because gender is currently a weak basis for organised action, resistance and social solidarity.

This, then, is one of the grounds for arguing for a return to single sex schools. It may be surprising but it is possible that formal segregation in separate schools is a form of positive discrimination, and not only for girls.[23] Although, to my knowledge, it has not been tested, single sex setting in arts and languages might show an improvement in interest and performance for boys similar to that shown by girls in science subjects.[24] If this were true then the case would be even stronger for a return to single sex schools, for both sexes would benefit by being enabled to resist stereotyping. Yet for both good and bad reasons a return to single sex schools is generally treated as extreme, if not unthinkable.

The bad reason is that any attempt to improve the position of girls in schools is opposed by large numbers, even within the teaching profession.[25] And because returning to single sex schools would be a form of affirmative action primarily, if not solely, on the behalf of girls then it too will be resisted. Because boys are thought to benefit socially from coeducation and not to suffer academically the opposition to single sex schools must be seen as an example of what Parkin has called a 'strategy of exclusion', practised in this instance on the behalf of boys against girls.[26]

The good reason is that there is a serious and dangerous possibility that it would aggravate class inequality. It is, after all, no coincidence that both the issues of single sex education and the revival of grammar schools have surfaced, or at least been publicly promoted, at more or less the same time. Both are reactions to the cuts and to varied attacks on the education system. Both are seen as essentially conservative although one could argue that in this respect they are not the same. Selective education preserves a class domination through control of educational resources and means; single sex education does not secure either male or female advantage, minimally it offers a way of keeping track of resources and ensuring that they are equitably distributed. It represents, if you like, a quota system rather than a free market. However, what is also likely is that if single sex schools were reintroduced and were well subscribed to this could help create the conditions for quasi or disguised selection in much the same way as denominational schools do. Middle class parents, confident that their daughters' social lives would still be more than adequate, would choose single sex schools within the state sector. An ideology of parental choice would permit it. The remaining mixed schools would be unbalanced in both class and sex terms - indeed 'boys' schools with a minority of working class girls in them. Heads would have to be given a greater say in who attended and both the idea and the practice of comprehensive education would be undermined. It could well be the thin end of the wedge. For this reason, if no other, those in favour of single sex education must tread warily.

The fact that the two issues have become politically entangled in a backlash is evidence of the extent to which in general class and sexual divisions have become intertwined. Inevitably, as these social divisions are embodied in educational organisations commitments to any particular change reflects more basic commitments to preserving or removing class or sexual divisions. Progress is rarely made on two fronts simultaneously despite the modified and moderate interest shown in remedies for gender inequality, e.g. in single sex setting. The cause of reducing class inequality in education is unlikely to be sacrificed to the cause of reducing gender or racial inequality. Already, there is more than a suggestion of pulling back from the brink with some of those most involved in single sex setting being hesitant to recommend its wider application.[27]

This could stem either from a fear that the results of single sex setting are more apparent than real, a sort of 'Hawthorne effect'[28] or fear of following the implications of such research through into policy proposals. Despite an increase in general sympathy for feminist concerns it still takes some nerve to stick out for feminist causes in education and the eclipse of sex by class as a public issue is almost an exact reflection of what happens socially in most mixed secondary schools.

In the final section I speculate that this might be explained, at both levels, as a sign that the balance in maintaining educational inequality has shifted from system integration to social integration. A consequence of this is that discrimination lodged at the informal or social level is harder to remove.

In practical terms the move from formal to informal discrimination is represented by the shift from the explicitly selective and class based grammar/secondary modern arrangement to the only implicitly selective mixed comprehensive pattern. The overall result has been a much closer interplay between class and sexual divisions in mixed comprehensives, making it hard to distinguish their separate effects.

Social and system integration: a theory of educational change

To move from the detail of everyday life in schools to structural features of a society at the broadest level is always a tricky enterprise. Paradoxically it is the personal processes that always impress us most and, as Edwards observes, it is always easier to grasp the nature and direction of roles and role conflict than the structures which stand behind and generate them.[29] As he puts it,

> social integration has a tendency to eclipse system integration, making it possible only with difficulty to show how a particular form of system integration is reflected in or reproduced by a particular form of social integration.[30]

The terms social and system integration, introduced by Lockwood, represent two levels at which society can be integrated. The distinction between what binds, or separates, individuals or groups (social) may seem arbitrary, but it rests, ultimately, on the sorts of mechanisms used. Ideology figures largely to integrate individuals whilst the cement for the institutions tends to be other institutional means such as the market.

Writing in distinctly theoretical terms Lockwood offered a hypothesis about social change. It was simply that social change would only occur if a disjunction or contradiction arising at the level of system integration was accompanied by conflict at the level of social integration. More precisely

> since the only systematically differentiated parts of a society are its institutional patterns the only source of social disorder arising from system disorder is that which takes the form of incompatible institutional patterns.

In other words role conflict which occurs at the level of social integration is a necessary but not sufficient condition for change at the system level too. More important for the argument of this paper is the implciation that if role conflict is avoided it may act as a brake on social change. This might be exactly what happened with coeducation.

The type of social relations that flourish in mixed schools seem to discourage both sexes, but especially girls, from stepping outside traditional gender stereotypes of themselves and of subjects. Gender based role conflict, which is always uncomfortable, is thus avoided. An unmeetable demand for facilities was also avoided. Thus the failure of coeducation to alter the opportunity structure of boys and girls stems from the effect it had in permitting gender to be deployed to defuse endemic tensions arising from the competition for resources within education. Gender was indirectly reinforced as a condition of access by the removal of the formal barriers (exemplified by single sex schools) between the sexes.

In principle the market has decreased as a means of allocating educational resources yet market type relations endure and have effectively reappeared in mixed schools. To grasp this fact we need, as Edwards suggests, to look behind the behaviour of individual girls and boys to the structures, in this case to the 'interests' of boys and girls and the different forms of educational organisation which promote or obstruct them.

The argument is one of functionalist effects, not intentions. The comprehensive/coeducational reorganisation depended upon more or less the same levels of demand being maintained. It was accompanied by growth but not by massive investment. Nevertheless the system integration between economic institutions and educational ones was put under political pressure and the post-war consensus over education broken[31]; not least was the strain between local and central government that this issue exposed.

Perhaps the most well-known systemic adjustment has been what Dore has called the 'diploma disease' or educational inflation.[32] Comprehensives have justified themselves in part by pride in the increase in numbers entering examinations and getting certificates.[33] Yet this increase in the supply of qualified school leavers could not, on its own, create appropriate employment for them. The other adjustment, serving the same function, has been subject of this paper and is the perpetuation of gender as a condition of access in education.

NOTES

1. Lockwood, D. Social and System Integration, in Zollschan, G.K. and Hirsch, H.N. (eds.) Explorations in Social Change, Boston, 1964, Routledge and Kegan Paul.
2. For a thorough and recent review of research into coeducation see Bone, A. Girls and Girls Only Schools: A Review of the Evidence Equal Opportunities Commission, Manchester 1983.
3. Byrne, E. Women and Education Tavistock, London 1978.
4. I am grateful to my colleague, Carol Dyhouse, for bringing this to my attention and for telling me how forward thinking and perceptive this union had been. See her forthcoming Feminism and the debate over coeducation/ single sex schooling: some historical perspectives History of Education Society Conference Papers, Dec. 1984.
5. Weinberg, A. (1979) An Analysis of the Persistence of the Single Sex School in the English Education System Unpublished Ph.D. thesis, University of Sussex.
6. DES/HMI Curricular Differences for Boys and Girls Education Survey 21, 1975.
7. Shipman, M. 'The Limits of Positive Discrination' in Marland, M. (ed.) Education for the Inner City, London, Heinemann Educational Books 1980.
8. There are many accounts but see Spender, D. and Sarah, E. Learning to Lose: Sexism and Education, London, The Women's Press 1980, and Deem, R. (ed.) Coeducation Reconsidered, Open University Press, Milton Keynes, 1984.

9. Spender, D. 'The role of teachers: what choice do they have?' in Council of Europe (ed.) Sex Stereotyping in Schools Swets and Zeitlinger 1982.
10. Duxbury, J. 'Girls and Physics - the role of a Head of Science' School Science Review, Vol. 65, 1984.
11. Kelly, A. 'The Construction of Masculine Science', forthcoming in British Journal of Sociology of Education.
12. Kelly, Ibid.
13. Legrand, J. The Strategy of Equality, London, Allen and Unwin 1982.
14. ILEA Analysis of Differences in Staying On Rates between Girls and Boys and Different Divisions, 1981.
15. Byrne, D., Williamson, B. and Fletcher, B. The Poverty of Education, Robertson, London 1975.
16. Byrne, E. Planning and Educational Inequality NFER, Slough 1974.
17. Pyle, D. 'The demand for education' in Bernbaum, G. (ed.) Schooling in Decline London Macmillan, 1979.
18. Willis, P. Learning to Labour, Saxon House, London, 1977.
19. TES 22.7.83, TES 16.9.83.
20. Development and Change Vol. VI, No.2, April 1975. Institute of Social Studies, The Hague.
21. Schaffer, B. and Huang Wen Lsien 'Distribution and the Theory of Access' in Development and Change Vol. VI, No. 2, April 1975.
22. Lamb, G. 'Marxism, Access and the State' in Development and Change, Vo,. VI, No. 2, April 1975.
23. What might be effective in terms of positive discrimination is not fixed: it depends totally on the context. Social solidarity based on class or sex can be an extremely strong resource and should be available to individuals. For a suggestive argument about the costs of undermining it in class terms, see Young, D.A. and Brandis, W. 'Two Types of Streaming and their Probable Application in Comprehensive Schools' in Cosin, B. (ed.) School and Society: a Sociological Reader Open University, Routledge and Kegan Paul, London, 1971.
24. Smith, S. 'single Sex Setting' in Deem, R. (ed.) Coeducation Reconsidered Open University Press, Milton Keynes, 1984.

25. Pratt, J. et al. 'Girl Friendly Schooling' Attitudes of Teachers. Paper given to Girl Friendly Conference, Manchester, September 1984.
26. Parkin, F. Marxism and Class Theory: a bourgeois critique Tavistock, London, 1979.
27. TES 17.2.84.
28. A 'Hawthorne effect' is where a subject(s) of an experiment improve their performance, whatever factor is manipulated. It is usally assumed that this is because people actually like the importance or attention of belonging to an experiment.
29. Edwards, T. 'Schooling for change. Function, correspondence and cause' in Dale, R. (ed.) Education and the State: Schooling and the National Interest Falmer Press, 1981.
30. Ibid.
31. Centre for Contemporary Cultural Studies, Unpopular Education, Schooling and Social Democracy in England Since 1944 Hutchinson, London 1981.
32. Dore, R. The Diploma Disease: Education, Qualification and Development London, Allen and Unwin.
33. Steedman, J. Progress in Secondary Schools, National Children's Bureau, London 1980.

SCHOOLS, DISCIPLINE AND SOCIAL CONTROL

Ann-Marie Wolpe

Control over pupils in schools is imposed by means of various instruments of power and a complex set of practices both of which have a long history. Some of these instruments and practices are overtly concerned with control, while some are identified in terms other than control. In effect, instruments and practices of control may be conceived as falling into two broad categories, beginning with disciplinary practices which establish in the first instance physical and bodily constraints over pupils, thereby creating the conditions in which other forms of control may be deployed. Although the constraint of pupils is a major concern of teachers in their daily practice it has been relatively neglected in sociological discussions which have focussed largely on the second form of control, that which is exercised through knowledge, ideology and the curriculum.

The paper firstly examines teachers' discourses about discipline and then locates these discourses in a more systematic framework drawing on the typology provided by Foucault on discipline. Secondly, it briefly discusses some aspects of the literature dealing with ideology, knowledge and the curriculum in education. This discussion reveals that the accounts produced of control through discipline on the one hand and control through ideology, knowledge and the curriculum on the other have been based on the assumption that these different modes can be adequately analysed in isolation from one another. The paper by drawing on Foucault's discussion of examinations, suggests that the processes of domination (and resistance to it) in the school can only be properly understood through analyses which draw out the relationship between the forms of discipline and the forms of control entailed in ideology, knowledge and the curriculum.[1]

DISCIPLINARY CONTROL

The problem of order is, and has always been, a major preoccupation of educationalists. The theme of the imminent breakdown of order within educational institutions is recurrent throughout the history of education. As Pearson (1983) says, '. . . the past, say the accumulated traditions of our national culture was a "golden age" of order and security'.

Within pedagogic discourse, discipline is conceptualised as the establishment and maintenance of control over the behaviour of pupils by means of physical constraints. In this sense, discipline has been, and is, exercised over all categories of pupils, irrespective of gender or class, although the form it takes may vary according to the category to which it is applied.

In the historical accounts of discipline within education there is a tendency to focus on specific means through which constraints on behaviour have been established and here the major preoccupation has been with corporal punishment and the historical changes which occurred in this mode of control.

The preoccupation with discipline in the sense of physical control has been well established in the literature. As Pincbeck and Hewitt (1973) tell us, the imposition and maintenance of disciplinary order were continuously referred to at the meetings of the Philanthropic Society dealing with their Reform Schools. Again, oral histories exemplify the continuous confrontations between teachers and pupils in working class schools where both boys and girls were subjected to physical punishments (Humphries, 1982). Indeed, girls have never been exempt from disciplinary measures which, although different to those applied to boys were, nevertheless, physically or mentally harsh. The early charity schools were very concerned with moral conduct but, according to Gardiner (1929) '. . . invented disciplinary methods to avoid excess of severity for girls'. Gardiner quotes from 'An Account of the Workhouse in 1732' where

. . . use was made of a board with seven holes and travelling peg against each child's name. For obstinate ill-doing a rod was pinned on

> the child; for 'high crimes' such as
> profanity, lying or pilfering, the culprit was
> dressed up in a fool's coat and made to sit in
> the middle of the schoolroom for an hour, a
> detested punishment. Pilferers were sent
> publicly in this unsightly garb to ask pardon
> of the person they had wronged
> (p.310-311)

In the 19th century the birch was commonly
used for both boys and girls and this was justified
on the grounds that original sin in children had to
be eradicated and this could be achieved through
beatings. Teachers, therefore, acting in loco
parentis could legitimately beat their charges,
although this often had tragic results. In a
famous case in 1860 - Regina v. Hopley - the
headmaster, Hopley, was charged following the death
of a 15 year old boy after 'excessive corporal
punishment'. Hopley's defence was based on the
Lockean principle of the need to beat obstinacy out
of the child, for which Hopley claimed he had
obtained permission from the boy's father
(Leinster-Mackay, 1977, p.2).

Such excessive practices no longer exist and
the changes may be partly attributed to the
formulation and acceptance of child-centred
approaches in which, after World War 1

> . . . getting children free was seen as a
> political and moral imperative. German
> militarism was taken to be founded in
> 'discipline' and the 'grotesque tragedy' of a
> German subservience
> (Walkerdine, 1983, p.81)

Although a child-centred ideology has been
dominant in educational practice, its application
has been neither uniform nor unequivocal.
Furthermore, it has not succeeded in eradicating
corporal punishment although it has, no doubt
contributed to the transformation of its use. In
the contemporary discussions, state schools tend to
be characterised as falling at one or other end of
a disciplinary continuum. On the one hand, these
schools are seen as havens of disciplinary harmony.
Thus, the Chief Inspector of Education in Surrey,
writing in 1979, stated:

> If one reads the right-wing press and never
> visits a school, one might be forgiven for

thinking that all our schools were blackboard
jungles and that the entire system was
breaking down. This is not the case. One can
visit school after school and meet polite,
hard-working and orderly pupils: go into
classroom after classroom and see teachers
teaching and children learning. The vast
majority of our schools are orderly and
disciplined places where the teacher is in
control.
(Dean, 1979, p.24)

At the other extreme is Dawson's account
(1981) of the state of Eltham Green School before
he took over - a school in which, as one teacher
said in a television interview 'life has been very
difficult'. There was no quiet in the classrooms,
children rushed through the corridors pushing aside
the teachers, desks and chairs were thrown out of
the windows five floors up - chaos seemed to reign.

While such manifestations of 'resistance' by
pupils dramatizes the problem of order, the
question of discipline is, nonetheless, just as
immediately present in situations of harmony as the
quotation from the Chief Inspector makes clear.
Even in the latter type of case teachers are aware
that the cooperation of the pupils is by no means
automatic or axiomatic. Discipline is high on the
list of teachers' priorities. In 1975, a teachers'
journal, Comprehensive Education, found that its
readers ranked discipline as 'the subject they
would like most the journal to discuss'. In an
article in that journal, M.J. Smith (1975), then
head of modern languages at a comprehensive school,
quoted young teachers as saying 'they could not do
the job they were trained for because of the lack
of discipline in the schools'.

Teachers see themselves as the sole agents of
control over pupils. The problematic nature of
this role is posed for the teacher from the
beginning of his or her training in the course of
teaching practice. Practical advice from
supervisors constitutes an important element in the
acquisition of skills pertinent to the maintenance
of discipline. Nonetheless, in their first jobs
teachers experience the problem of discipline as
traumatic, as the following illustrates.

Specially depressed about tomorrow as I have
all my worst classes. Today ended in a riot.
We did nothing last class. Everyone shouted

> . . . hitting each other. Spitting at each
> other. One whose book was spat on threw the
> book away. Said it was spoilt. He would
> 'catch disease . . . V.D. off it'. He said
> he'd go tell the head.
> (Hannam et al, 1976, p.77)

This exemplifies the everyday experience of young
teachers. Terms such as 'fear', 'loneliness', and
'isolation' are commonly used by teachers to
describe their classroom situations.

The response to this in the teachers'
discourse and practices is to emphasize the
necessity to make pupils obey instructions. The
capacity to achieve this is conceived of as
directly related to qualities and skills of the
individual teacher. The successful teacher is one
who exercises successful classroom control and this
depends on disciplinary techniques, not only on
well prepared lessons.

The acquisition of the necessary skills is
seen to be the result of practical experience in
the employment of disciplinary techniques and
recipes handed down by experienced teachers. These
disciplinary strategies vary enormously and in ways
which may reflect the social conditions of the
school - physical location, class composition,
gender and so forth.

The recipes for the maintenance of classroom
control are essentially pragmatic and appear to
have little to do with their training which
includes psychology of learning and social
psychology. Generally, the advice of experienced
teachers to new colleagues is that by some specific
act immediate ascendancy may be established in the
classroom. This may be achieved by a range of
strategies from the infliction of petty
humiliations to corporal punishment. One teacher
recalled how his headmaster had solemnly advised
him to knock onto the floor the first boy he set
eyes on - this would have an immediate and
desirable effect on the whole class. Another
teacher related how he had been advised to
humiliate and marginalise, preferably, the meekest
and most innocuous person in the classroom through
verbal abuse.

Whatever the strategies advocated, there was a
common objective - the immediate assertion, whether
by verbal or physcial means, of control. The
classroom is represented as a site of potential
warfare which only the teacher deploying his or her

skills, can subdue.

And yet these practices appear to be divested of disciplinary content in so far as they are defined and seen in terms relating to abilities vested in the teachers themselves, that is an integral part of individual teachers' personal qualities, abilities and experience.

This does not preclude the operation of other practices which are located in discourses dealing with the psychology of the individual pupil and consequently which focus on the pupil as the subject. These discourses are largely influenced by 'progressive ideas' which gained popularity in the 1920s and 1930s, as already mentioned in relation to corporal punishment.

> [Here] educational methods based on creative effort, self-regulated learning and a variety of informal techniques seemed more and more to fit both the well-publicized theories of psychologists and the possibilities of the elementary school.
> (Lawson and Silver, 1973, p.401)

The notion of freeing the individual pupils from the rigour of authority appears to be fairly widely held, although the practical measures adopted in order to attain this state varies considerably, with the greatest input at infant and junior school levels. Many proponents, including the 'New Romantics', appear to believe that 'motivation to learn is an inherent part of the human condition', and that failure to learn may well be the 'loss of motivation' or similar physiological state which could well be induced by the

> . . . lack of freedom in the classroom [which] creates a threatening environment in which the learners experience so much fear . . . that learning is impeded
> (Hargreaves, 1974, p.1999)

Such discourses result in the recommendation of various strategies including the establishment of 'trust' between teacher and pupil, a discourse which, on the surface, appears at variance with that of classroom control, and yet these two discourses co-exist and are not questioned by the teachers.

A further element which tends to lead to

differential conceptions and practices of control
is gender. There is a widely held view that men,
by virtue of their masculinity, can achieve
discipline far more easily than women. In an
interview, a young woman teacher spoke about a
sports master whom, she said, related to girls
'very much half-way between the older boy-friend
and the caring father, depending on which way he
comes across', while, at the same time maintaining
control over the boys as well. This she saw as
linked to his masculinity and physical presence.

> He's the absolute archetype - your blond 6'2"
> sports master, a really beautiful bloke. All
> the boys in the form admired him, because he
> was the kind of good-looking athletic bloke
> they wanted to become and he was twice as big
> as most of them anyway. Even though the
> mildest, kindest person, nobody dared say
> anything. He didn't even have to threaten
> them. There was this kind of assumption there
> all the time. All the girls were in love with
> him, because he was everybody's idea of the
> perfect dreamboat who would take them to the
> altar one day. I mean that he had it both
> ways in that sense.[2]

Whilst it would be interesting to analyse this
statement in detail, suffice to say that this
description of the sports teacher directly involved
the sexuality of the teacher.

Ideas about gender relations are expressed in
other ways as well. A science teacher, of large
stature, argued that men with big voices had
distinct advantages over women whom, because of
feminine dress and high-pitched voices, he though
would be unable to maintain control. He suggested
that women science teachers were the worst off
because they taught in a man's world and had to
'try much harder to set the class to listen'. In
his experience, the only successful woman science
teacher had a 'sergeant major manner' and was not
'trampled upon' like other women.

But quite clearly, women teachers, like their
male counterparts, do employ a range of
disciplinary instruments, strategies and tactics
and do, to a greater or lesser extent, succeed in
imposing a measure of control. Women's sexuality
and femininity is one such strategy of control.

The following is merely one illustration of
this. As one woman said, it is possible to exploit

being female through the presentation of self to a classroom of boys as a woman in need of protection. She said

> One of the sort of responses . . . is to get boys to develop protectiveness towards you so that they are not going to mess around in your classroom because, poor miss, we feel sorry for her, we feel protective, we don't want to make her life a misery. . . . There's a fairly direct sexuality that operates, and it's not just me. I have attempted to talk about it with other woman friends. There is some sort of direct level of sexuality between a woman teacher and boys as pupils and there is some kind of appeal to that used in discipline. I don't know exactly how it works . . . I have been in situations where it almost started to get out of hand, to get suggestive remarks, that sort of thing. I think that was one of the things that started getting me aware of the fact that it was going on at all.

Interestingly this teacher confined her remarks to the relationship between women teachers and boys - as she presented it boys constituted the problems in classroom control. Although clearly she exercised disciplinary control over girls, presumably employing other than sexual strategies, she did not recognise this as part of the disciplinary procedures.

The necessity of 'custodial constraints', the 'limitations upon the freedom of the immature in their own best interests', the need to establish and maintain physical control over pupils presents itself almost exclusively as a problem of disciplinary strategies or recipes. The relationship between the modes of control on the one hand, and, on the other hand, the social environment - both internal to the school and in the society at large - of disciplinary practices and the relationship of these to ideological positions, cultural practices and the teaching of the curriculum, appears not to arise as a problem. The exclusive focus on modes of discipline mirrors, as will be shown below, the neglect of discipline in the work on ideology, culture and the curriculum.

Before attempting to point the way to a linkage between disciplinary and ideological/

cultural/knowledge control, it may be worthwhile systematizing teachers' discourses and practices of disciplinary control through a brief discussion of Foucault's typology.

INSTRUMENTS OF DISCIPLINE

In Discipline and Punish (1982) Foucault provides a basis for analysing the emergence of disciplinary procedures and the forms they take. One of his main concerns is with the problem of power and how the form of punishment which he describes as 'coercive, corporal, solitary, secret' came to replace the 'representative form' of the classical period in which the 'objective of punishment' was the body and not the 'soul'. He sets out to examine how 'compliant' subjects, not en masse, but as individuals, may be contained, how 'docile bodies' are created.

Foucault argues that there is a need for the production of docile people with specific qualities or 'utilities' if factories and armies as well as prisons and schools are to operate successfully. All these organisations or institutions are dependent on the availability of subjects with these qualities. Such subjects can only be produced through the utilization of disciplinary power, a power 'expressed' in various processes and rooted in particular conditions.

> These methods which make possible the meticulous control of the operations of the body, which assured the constant subjection of its forces and imposed upon them a relation of docility-utility, might be called 'disciplines'.
> (Foucault, 1982, p.137)

Discipline is embodied in methods involving 'constant surveillance' and 'subtle coercion'.

Elsewhere referring specifically to the change in the nature of punishment Foucault says that the transition from 'inflicting of penalties' to the 'imposition of surveillance' occurs at 'the moment when it became understood that it was more efficient and profitable in terms of the economy of power to place people under surveillance than to subject them to some exemplary penalty' (Gordon, 1980, p.38).

Surveillance becomes a more effective method for achieving particular ends. The production of the 'subjected and practised bodies', 'docile bodies' occurs through discipline, which itself

> increases the forces of the body in economic terms of utility and diminishes these same forces in political terms of obedience
> (Foucault, 1982, p.138)

Foucault confronts the inevitable contradictions that must develop out of a system which both increases individuals' abilities and yet, simultaneously, denies them access to power and the right to resist their own economic exploitation. There is always the danger that with access to knowledge, subjects may gain access to power. But as a result of disciplinary procedures these routes to power are curbed. The increase in abilities and aptitudes could create a revolutionary situation but this development is prevented, he argues, through the application of disciplinary power.

> [Discipline] dissociates power from the body; on the one hand it turns it into an 'aptitude', a 'capacity', which it seeks to increase; on the other hand, it reverses the course of energy, the power that might result from it, and turns it into a relation of strict subjection. If economic exploitation separates the force and the product of labour, let us say that disciplinary coercion establishes in the body the constricting link between an increased aptitude and an increased domination.
> (1982, p.138)

These conditions occur in schools, workshops and in military organizations. They are throughout history, 'adopted in response to particular needs'. In other words these practices arise out of developments which generate contradictions which require some resolution. Foucault here invokes a functionalism to explain the emergence of disciplinary methods.

Foucault then sets out the processes of discipline which range from the use of what he terms 'the simple instrument' of disciplinary control to the more complex forms of normalizing judgements culminating in examinations through which the docile subjects are created by the schools, or army or places of work.

CONTROL IN SCHOOLS

Foucault's discussion may be utilized to indicate in a more systematic way, the discourses and practices of disciplinary control which exist in the school.

According to Foucault, surveillance is a necessary condition which 'presupposes a mechanism that coerces by means of observation'. In order to make observations possible a construction is required that makes 'visible those who are inside it' and as a result the design of the buildings becomes important. Although schools have their origin in the monastic order, the design of 19th century schoolroom buildings provide the opportunity for a particular form of surveillance. Illustrations of the 19th century show how the monitorial system developed by Dr. Andrew Bell and which 'dominated popular education for half a century' was employed in classrooms in which the teacher had a clear view of all pupils sitting on raised platforms or in circular rooms with the master surrounded by the pupils, very much in the style of the Panopticon.

Dawson (1981) highlights the relevance of building design for the observation of discipline in the present day formal disciplinary control. He asserts that the 'architecture of many large and expensively built schools' is dysfunctional. One of his first acts, on taking control of Eltham Green School, was to fill in the ornamental ponds which he said led pupils to push each other in constantly, put a window in his study and purchase binoculars. With insight he said:

> If a little more attention were given to school design a great many disciplinary problems could be eliminated. Along with the window I had installed went a pair of high-powered binoculars. These enabled me to identify the local villains hanging about the gate. Knowing who is to invade you is a fairly sure way of knowing what sort of trouble to expect. The binoculars were also ueful for determining which of our boys were going into the neighbouring girls' school by climbing the fence in the park on the other side of the road.
> (Dawson, 1981, pp.18-19)[3]

Dawson's comments express the sentiments of many

school authorities concerning the increasing difficulties they experience maintaining surveillance over pupils. Factors relating to size, split site occupancy, complexities generated by the wide range of options on the time table resulting in a great deal of movement within the school buildings - which may be further complicated by streaming or setting procedures - all contribute to a weakening of surveillance.

It is significant that this has led to a different form of surveillance - the pastoral system. A discourse of welfare - 'caring for the individual pupil', 'the individual pupil's best interests at heart' - which is central to the pastoral system in schools entails practices which constitutes new forms of surveillance and disciplinary control. As Sarap put it:

> It is often said that teachers are working for the children's best interests, but usually pastoral care directly supports the structure, discipline and values of the school. There is now a move towards having a welfare officer based at the school. Lateness and attendance patterns are investigated by educational psychologists, as they may reveal an underlying 'problem'. Other social services are brought in. There are tutorial classes at home, sanctuaries, 'sin-bins', remedial centres. With the increasing intervention of the state, there is growth in the ideology of pastoral care, involviang teachers, social workers, police and doctors in this problem, the problem of youth, 'discipline' and 'order'.
>   (Sarap, 1982, p.14)

Teachers can, therefore, under the pastoral care system initiate a set of procedures which may lead to the worst miscreants being withdrawn from, or at least contained within, the school system by means other than the more usual forms of disciplinary power. The role of specialists - doctors, psychiatrists, social workers, and so on - may be decisive here since their views on how the pupil is to be handled is not open to question. In effect a system has developed with a complicated communication network, linked to specialists all of whom are engaged in controlling particular groups of pupils. This network may also involve the whole family since familial relations are often seen to be part of the process of pastoral care.

Surveillance is, inter alia, concerned with the temporal control of pupils. This is achieved through the timetable which establishes 'rhythms', 'particular occupations' and 'regulates the cycle of repetition' to be performed and adopted by the pupils. The timetable which has evolved gradually has direct consequences for pedagogic practice, and is

> . . . specializing the time of training and detaching it from the adult time, from the time of mastery, arranging different stages, separated from one another by graded examination, drawing up programmes, each of which involves exercises of increasing difficulty; qualifying individuals according to the ways in which they progress through these series.
>
> (Foucault, 1982, p.159)

The timetable 'partitions as closely as possible time pace and movement'. Examining the schedules of schools in the 19th century demonstrates the manner in which pupils' every activity was regulated from early morning until bedtime, starting at 5 a.m. and ending at 10 p.m. at night. Manuals were produced detailing not only the time table to be adopted but also the form the commands should take to direct the activity of each period (Lawson and Silver, 1973).

This rigidity of control no longer exists. Indeed the rhythm of schools may often be interrupted, as Dawson woefully points out, through a number of bureaucratic procedures such as health inspection, vaccinations, visits by specialists, questionnaires and so on. Furthermore, other conditions have developed which make it much more difficult to enforce the timetable and to regulate the pupils' activities. The fragmentation of the timetable referred to above, the considerable movement of pupils demanded by large, sprawling schools, the sheer size of the student body and the accompanying anonymity, provide pupils with the opportunity to adopt a range of strategies to avoid attending particular lessons and to escape the regulation and timetabling of other activities.

These measures are accompanied by the 'simple instruments of control' which include corporal punishment, humiliations and ritual. Mention has already been made in the earlier section of this paper to corporal punishment and the strategies adopted by teachers to establish control. Ritual forms of control are evident in the wearing of school uniform, morning assembly and similar activities. All these 'simple instruments of control' operate differentially according to the nature of the school. However, these practices do not constitute the full picture of disciplinary control. As mentioned above, Foucault draws attention to the consequence of the timetable which 'involves exercises of increasing difficulty'. It is at this point that he introduces the concept of 'normalizing judgements' which he says are concerned with non-conformity, and the reduction of gaps between the subjects. Before discussing this, however, it is necessary to turn briefly to the literature dealing with ideological, cultural and knowledge control.

CONTROL AND RESISTANCE:
IDEOLOGY, CULTURE AND KNOWLEDGE

Thus far I have outlined modes of control which depend for their operation on surveillance and physical constraint and regulation. By contrast, as is well known, a body of literature has emerged which focuses exclusively on the control of pupils which purports to be established through culture, ideology and knowledge. Since the attempt to impose such control frequently meets with resistance, culture, ideology and knowledge are conceived of as sites of struggle. Indeed, the analysis of resistance in these spheres illustrates the preoccupation with forms of control which are assumed to be unrelated to the modes of disciplinary control discussed above, although there is an implied recognition that the latter are not sufficient to produce the 'model pupils' demanded of the educational system. There is a consistent view held that where forms of control are imposed there will always be some form of resistance. Foucault pointed out, what is generally accepted, that prisons fail to 'transform criminals into honest citizens' and serve 'to manufacture new criminals and to drive existing criminals into criminality'. Similarly schools fail to transform all children into model pupils via the processes of disciplinary power, and its various instruments. The extent of this failure may be gauged by examination results. For example in 1981 of all school leavers, 11% failed to get any qualification, and 36% failed to get any higher grade qualifications in O or CSE examinations.

This failure has been conceived of as resistance to a dominant culture and has become a central issue in recent work concerned with education and control.

Informed by the analyses of cultural formations, in which the role of culture is privileged, Willis (1977) in what has become a classical text, provided an account of why working class young males voluntarily and knowingly, through their rejection of the whole process of certification and hence the goals of the educational system, collude in their own failure to achieve within that system. Likewise Apple (1982) invokes the notion of cultural formations to argue that students are able

> . . . to develop within their own day to day lives in school an array of working class themes and attitudes which give them strength and can act against the ideological values represented by the school.
> (1982, p.101)

Resistance is seen as a group rather than an individual response to an educational system which is alienating and whose values and products are outside the lived experience of the youth. The resistance is defined in terms of cultural practices as an opposition to a supposedly ideologically integrated system expressing the values and ideologies of the ruling classes with the curriculum reproducing the hegemonic relations of the society.

While Willis and Apple analysed control in terms of 'cultural formations' and stressed resistance by working-class male pupils to the dominant culture, thereby emphasizing the active role of pupils, earlier work (M.F.D. Young, 1971; Bowles and Gintis, 1976), by contrast, highlighted the imposition of control through the ideological content of knowledge. In this approach the curriculum was given priority and pupils conceived of as the passive recipients of the teachers' ideologically constructed knowledge. What these writers suggested, was that the school transmits, or attempts to transmit, to successive generations of pupils, through the taught curriculum, those ideologies which enable the transition from school to work to be achieved with minimal problems and difficulties.

What is of considerable interest is the fact that whereas Willis and Apple define cultural formations as sites of resistance and Young and Bowles and Gintis analyse the school as a mechanism of the transmission of ideologically structured knowledge to passive subjects, in neither approach is the question posed as to the relationship between modes of disciplinary control and the imposition of culture or knowledge on active resisters to, or passive recipients of, culture and/or knowledge.

Clearly, although not recognised by these writers, in both cases, the attempt to discuss cultural, ideological and knowledge control outside of and external to disciplinary control is problematized. It is precisely here that Foucault's conception of normalizing judgements becomes relevant.

DISCIPLINARY CONTROL AND KNOWLEDGE, CULTURE AND IDEOLOGY

In Foucault's terms, normalizing judgement involves ranking and grading which in effect 'marks the gaps, hierarchizes qualities, skills and aptitudes but it also punishes and rewards' (Foucault, 1982, p.181). At one level Foucault's discussion of normalizing judgements appears to parallel the work discussed in the previous section since the writers referred to are concerned with the outcome of 'hierarchizing qualities'. In this sense, normalizing judgements have an effect on pedagogical practices: streaming, setting, and so on, all of which are subjected to constant revisions and change depending on current ideas. What these practices achieve is the classification of pupils according to so-called objective criteria.

This may also be seen, by way of illustration, in some of the differences which operate between boys and girls. Boys, for example, may be rewarded for pursuing certain subjects such as chemistry or physics whilst girls may be punished - in this case through petty humiliations - for attempting such courses. In other words normalizing judgements are invoked in the course of maintaining the physical sciences as the suitable courses for boys and not for girls. Furthermore similar judgements may be made by the boys themselves who may exert control over girls who do well in their school subjects by

a system of penalties which they apply to such
girls, penalties which relate to interpersonal
relationships[4].

Of greater importance in the present context,
however, is Foucault's contention that normalizing
judgements occur in the examination which is

> at the centre of the procedures that
> constitute the individual as effect and object
> of power, as effect and object of knowledge.
> It is the examination which by containing
> hierarchical surveillance and normalizing
> judgements assures the great disciplinary
> functions of distribution and classification.
>
> With it are ritualized those disciplines that
> . . . are a modality of power for which
> individual difference is relevant.
> (Foucault, 1982, p.192)

Not all pupils are subjected to such forms of
control. There are those who never intend to sit
any examinations at all and who are therefore
outside the forces of control operating through the
normalizing judgements and examinations. The
numbers so affected are greater than the 11% who
never attain any qualifications and must include
those who obtain very poor results in the few
examinations they do sit.

Such groups of pupils may constitute the
'disaffected pupils' for whom the pastoral system
has been developed in an attempt to contain them
within the confines of the school, whatever form
that containment may take. The extent of the
success of such strategies in terms of exerting
disciplinary power has yet to be assessed but
clearly such a system has not obliterated the
problems that such pupils may generate.

It would appear to be the case that it is at
the point of the final school leaving examination
system that the lacunae in the system occur, most
particularly in regard to this group of disaffected
pupils. One could argue that in order to
understand fully the processes involved in the
'failure' of schooling amongst such a group one
needs to consider not only the role of their own
cultural formation, but further the relationship of
all the forms of disciplinary control which this
paper has attempted to set out.

If examinations are the 'centre of
disciplinary procedures, as Foucault claims, and

there seems little reason to doubt this, then their role in the educational system is of extreme importance. The controlling mechanisms of the examination system are directly and indirectly apparent, and include the control over those who may present themselves for an examination, the form and content of the curriculum, and the whole certification process.

Schools determine who may or may not sit examinations. It is generally the case that only those who are thought likely to pass the more prestigious examinations - G.C.E. - are allowed by the schools to enter these. Potential failures are channelled into C.S.E. classes, thereby not jeopardising the school's examination record: it is better to have C.S.E. passes than G.C.E. failures. The form the control takes in such circumstances is double - punishment can be the barring of pupils committed to the whole process of certification from sitting the examinations, as well as control over which syllabus the pupils may follow.

The curriculum the schools follow is determined in the first instance by the G.C.E. examinations which in turn are specified by the universities. Because of a set of historical circumstances, the Universities established their control over what constitutes legitimate knowledge. This in turn is directed at the schools and determines what the schools should teach; school syllabuses are largely guided by what is decreed for them. In this way hegemonic control over knowledge is maintained.

The examination system therefore not only controls pupils through the constraints imposed by the system itself, but also sets the seal on the content of the knowledge the pupils receive. Control, therefore, is both of physical and mental forms.

Yet another form of control is vested in the whole process of examination. Certification has become increasingly important for pupils not only in the course of pursuing higher and further education - with ever increasing high standards being demanded and more and more qualifications - but also in the search for jobs. In order to gain the necessary qualifications examinations have to be written with all the attendant conformity to disciplinary measures.

The examination system highlights the ways in which the two areas of control - that is both physical and mental - can be scrutinised. In raising this issue, other problems clearly do emerge.

This paper has hinted at the different forms of control which are contained within progressive forms of education. It has not been possible to consider these at all. But clearly methods adopted by people like A.S. Neill were of a different order and imposed a different set of controls. In such cases the pupil was seen as an active actor very different from the pupils who were considered as entering with a tabula rasa and on whom the knowledge to be imparted is to be imprinted through different strategies.

Now all these processes themselves may be related to external structures in the society which include economic and familial areas. As already mentioned the labour market has close links with the process of certification in that it may create a set of demands which are transmitted to the educational system. The responses to these demands by the educational system have repercussions in terms not only in regard to content but also in regard to the disciplinary procedures and hence disciplinary power.

By drawing attention to these two modes of control - physical and mental - a whole set of questions about both internal and external connections are raised. With education at the crossroads it would appear to be an appropriate occasion to examine these forces of control and their interrelationships. It is only with a fuller understanding of these procedures that effective changes may be introduced into the educational system.

NOTES

1. A version of this paper was given at the International Sociology of Education Conference, Birmingham, 1984 and at a staff seminar at Hull University. I am indebted to all those who commented on the paper. I would also like to thank in particular Annette Kuhn, Harold Wolpe, Steve Walker and Len Barton for their detailed and helpful comments on this paper.

2. The evidence quoted from interviews with teachers is from my unpublished research material.

3. This school has again been in the news and the

focus of public confrontation between Mr.
Dawson (no longer the head) and a famous ex-
pupil, pop star Boy George. Mr. Dawson
publicly referred to Boy George's schooling as
a 'waste of time'. In response to this the
singer wrote: 'The teaching methods used at
Eltham Green School were not special in any
way, they were standard methods. The only
real power Peter Dawson wielded was because of
the existence of corporal punishment and his
visual similarity to a well known dictator'
(Times Educational Supplement, 4.5.84).
4.	I am indebted to Tanya Baker who suggested
this line of analysis at a seminar.

REFERENCES

Apple, M.W. (1982) Education and Power, Routledge
    and Kegan Paul.
Bowles, S. and Curtis, H. (1976) Schooling in
    Capitalist America, London, Routledge & Kegan
    Paul.
Dawson, P. (1981) Making a Comprehensive Work,
    Blackwell.
Dean, J. (1979) 'An Inspector Calls' in Discipline
    in Primary and Secondary Schools Today,
    Jennings, A. (ed.), Ward Lock.
Foucault, M. (1982) Discipline and Punish,
    Peregrine Books.
Gardiner, D. (1929) English Girlhood at School
Gordon, C. (1980) Michael Foucault Power/Knowledge,
    The Harvester Press.
Hannam, C., Smyth, P. and Stephenson, N. (1976) The
    First Year of Teaching, Penguin Books.
Hargreaves, D.H. (1974) 'Deschoolers and New
    Romantics' in Educability, Schools and
    Ideology, Flude M. and Ahier, J. (eds.), Croom
    Helm.
Humphries, S. (1981) Hooligans and Rebels,
    Blackwell.
Lawson, J. and Silver, H. (1973) A Social History
    of England, Methuen & Co.
Leinster-Mackay, D.P. (1977), 'Regina v. Hopley:
    Some Historical Reflections on Corporal
    Punishment' in Journal of Educational Adminis-
    tration and History, Vol. 9, No. 1.
Sarup, M. (1982) Education, State and Crisis, Rout-
    ledge & Kegan Paul.
Smith, M.J. (1975) 'Discipline in the Classroom'in
    Comprehensive Education, No. 30, Summer.
Walkerdine, V. (1983) 'It's only natural:

rethinking child-centred pedagogy' in _Is there anyone here from Education?_, Wolpe, A.M. and Donald, J. (eds.) Pluto Press.

Willis, P. (1977) _Learning to Labour_, Saxon House.

Young, M.F.D. (1971) _Knowledge and Control_, Collier MacMillan.

THE COMPLIANT-CREATIVE WORKER: THE IDEOLOGICAL RECONSTRUCTION OF THE SCHOOL LEAVER

Heather Cathcart and Geoff Esland

Our purpose in this paper is to examine some of the more recent developments in the education of 14-16 year olds, and in particular certain curriculum initiatives in the areas of industrial awareness and preparation for work. We shall be concerned both with the ideological substance of these initiatives and with the centralist-corporatist political structures which are being brought into play to legitimate and strengthen their adoption, recognizing that they represent a major departure from what had previously been regarded as the constitutional basis on which the state, LEAs and teaching profession had co-existed (Lawton 1980, Kogan 1983). We recognize, too, that the commitment of the present Thatcher government to an authoritarian mode of curriculum regulation at all levels of education and its expanding use of the apparatus of the state for this purpose should caution us against being over-sanguine about the capacity of teachers and educational administrators to debate and confront the implications of these new developments. The use of expenditure cuts in education to create space for political intervention in the internal activities of educational institutions, as, for example, in the case of the Technical and Vocational Education Initiative (TVEI) and the transfer from the LEAs to the MSC of 25% of the funding for non-advanced further education have shown that the Thatcher administration feels little necessity for restraint in the setting up of machinery for extending its political control over educational policy. Combined with the creation of the NAB and the Council for the Accreditation of Teacher Education, which is to review the balance and content of teacher education, and with the movement towards national and local corporatism in curriculum planning, this policy has tightened by several notches the ratchets of political control and ideological pressure on educational practice.

It would be mistaken to assume that these and other assaults on existing educational structures will generate anything like a unified reaction, either from teacher organizations or from the various consumer groups within education.[1] Interests around specific issues are inevitably fragmented and usually give rise only to limited and disparate forms of resistance. One of the clear sources of this fragmentation is the disjunction which exists between resource issues ('fighting the cuts') and ideological issues relating to the implementation of policy. As Cawson and Saunders have pointed out, local resistance in particular tends to be characterized by the competitive politics of consumerist interest groups which may not necessarily coalesce on other issues (Cawson and Saunders, 1983). These groups are often middle class and tend to mobilise most readily around questions of resource provision (hospitals, schools, transport, etc.). On these grounds, of course, there is strong likelihood of convergence with professional interests, but on ideological issues relating, for instance, to the relevance of technical and vocational curricula, political reactions are likely to be less uniform. This is further underlined by the ambivalence and separation of identity which exists within teacher organizations between their function as professional associations and as trade unions. As recent political events have demonstrated, it is this ambivalence and diffusion of focus which has rendered them ineffective in the forming of a collective response to the curricular and training initiatives taken by the state in the transition from school to work .

Another important conditioner of professional and consumer responses is the depoliticisation of issues which might be expected to generate resistance. It is clear that the ideological parameters which prefigure and legitimate many of the initiatives currently being taken have been so thoroughly prepared, constructed and transmitted during the past decade that they effectively depoliticise the content which is prescribed within them. A significant feature of the Conservative administration since 1979 has, for example, been its relative success in sustaining the

depoliticisation of its economic policy. Such a
statement, of course, ought to be a contradiction
in terms but it is the case that in spite of the
depth of the recession, the deindustrialisation of
manufacturing centres and the massive increase in
youth unemployment, the Thatcher administration has
managed to sustain the belief among a substantial
proportion of the electorate that structural
changes in the economy on the scale which we have
witnessed are not only inevitable but in some
senses desirable, and only insignificantly
connected with political choices. As Hall has
argued, the durability of the government's economic
policy ultimately rests on its apparent success in
making sense of the perceptions and material
conditions of large sections of the working class
(Hall, 1983). The view that the processes of
industrial decline and recomposition are the
unpalatable but necessary preconditions for
industrial revival ultimately has to win acceptance
from those who have most to lose by it. That it
has done so for the past five years is due in no
small measure to the proclaiming of economic and
political nationalism and to the mobilisation of a
large-scale and broad-fronted ideological onslaught
on the social democratic, liberal humanist
philosophies which had underpinned social policy
since 1945.

Using Gramsci's distinction between the
'organic' and the 'conjunctural' elements of
crisis, Stuart Hall has argued that the move to the
right in Britain constitutes 'an "organic"
phenomenon', in which efforts by the right to
conserve and defend the existing economic and
political structure

> cannot be merely defensive. They will be
> formative: aiming at a new balance of forces,
> the emergence of new elements, the attempt to
> put together a new 'historic bloc', new
> political configurations and 'philosophies', a
> profound restructuring of the state and the
> ideological discourses which construct the
> crisis and represent it as it is 'lived' as a
> practical reality: new programmes and
> policies, pointing to a new result, a new sort
> of 'settlement' . . . Political and
> ideological work is required to disarticulate
> old formations, and to rework their elements
> into new ones.
> Hall, 1983

175

Education has borne as much of the brunt of
this disarticulation and restructuring as any other
area of national policy. The message by now is
familiar: Britain's economic decline and
uncompetitiveness are due on the one hand to the
efficiency and innovativeness of other national
economies, which are reducing Britain's share of
world markets, and, on the other, to the legacy of
social democratic consensus politics and labour
practices, which have led to British industry
becoming overmanned and burdened with restrictive
practices. Add to this the putative failure of the
British education system to give support to the
'wealth-creation' process, and to produce
adequately-prepared school leavers and graduates,
and almost the entire case is seen to rest on the
lack of national resolve, the narrow self-interest
of the unionised working class, the perpetuation of
outworn practices and institutions and the self-
indulgence of an education system which over-values
its academic and liberal humanist traditions.
Thus, the restoration of the interests of capital
and the conditions of expanded accumulation are
represented in a form which scapegoats the trade
unions, the education system and the public service
sector generally, while the consequences of
monetarist policies and political choices favouring
defence, law and order, privatisation and the free
movement of capital are ignored. By screening off
these and similar issues and by substantially
moving the terrain of debate from the social
democratic position which had prevailed since the
1950s, this ideological package has, in Hall's
phrase, 'shifted the parameters of common sense',
and now constitutes the framework within which new
agendas for policy are constructed (Hall 1982).

As far as educational policy is concerned,
this shift had led to fundamental reappraisals by
the state both of the purpose and content of
education as well as of the political structures
through which resources for education are
'delivered'. Ideologies of educational content and
practice have become increasingly fashioned around
the view that the liberal humanist emphasis of
British education has somehow failed the nation. A
recent influence in this development has been
Martin Wiener's book 'English Culture and the
Decline of the Industrial Spirit' which has been
much quoted in business and political circles
(Wiener, M. 1981). Wiener's argument that the

tradition of liberal education in Britain has played a significant part in the creation of negative attitudes towards industrial capitalism has been cited by many as evidence for the need for a major shift in national values towards a greater recognition and support of 'enterprise'. As part of the belief that liberal education has promoted anti- or non-capitalist attitudes, it is claimed that it does little for the average and lower achiever in providing a relevant basis for work, and for higher achievers it provides a curriculum which is too academically specialized and, therefore, inappropriate for industrial regeneration. This is in spite of the fact that substantial numbers of large employers persist in favouring academic over applied degrees, and university graduates over polytechnic graduates (Boys, C. 1984). The conclusion is unmistakable that through a variety of interventions the Thatcher government has set out to destabilize the curriculum and the teaching profession and to further the delegitimation of liberal education, while promoting a curriculum whose concerns are instrumental and skill-led and predicated on 'capability' and 'enterprise' rather than on critical understanding.

What we are witnessing is, in Wexler's terms, a process of 'deschooling by default' in which curriculum subjects are 'decomposed' into skills, and alternative (non-school) sources of education and training are increasingly looked upon as providing the appropriate models of learning. Although the extensive cuts in resources experienced by education fall ostensibly within the government's policy for the control of the money supply, they also betoken a political resolve to weaken the capacity which liberal education has for promoting social and political dissent and intellectual critique. The problem for the New Right lies, in Wexler's terms, in education's potential for 'truth-seeking': 'Teaching in the name of truth may include critical evaluation of the capitalist version of reality, or even the demand and right to realise possibilities that capitalism would deny' (Wexler et al, 1981). The growing emphasis in teacher education on subject specialism and the downgrading of educational theory, the repeated searches for and accusations of 'Marxist bias' in higher education, and the vociferous attack from the right on peace studies are merely the most obvious manifestations of a political project which has as its objective the political and moral transformation of education.

The attack on liberal education from the New Right is in some senses a mirror image of the critique mounted by the left during the mid-seventies. At the heart of that critique was the concern that liberal humanist ideology while proclaiming the importance of individual self-development was lending legitimacy to the requirement of the capitalist economy for a stratified and attitudinally attuned labour force. What this critique underestimated was the degree to which the curricular and pedagogical reforms of the late sixties and early seventies had actually led to the creation of an educational agenda which could be represented by the right as undermining the nation's economic future. The compromises within liberal-humanist education which for the left could be portrayed as inadequately facing up to the capitalist reality underlying it could be attacked by the right for promoting values antithetical to industry and the national economy and to the standards required of young people. Thus, in spite of the rapid rise in youth unemployment since 1976, the right has succeeded in retaining the offensive against liberal education, has continued to promulgate the myth that young people (and their teachers) are responsible for their own unemployment, and, largely through the invoking of economic survival, has begun the process of decomposition of elements of liberal education.

This process draws much of its impetus from a revival of economic nationalism and a rampant technological determinism, in which the main burden of responsibility for industrial decline in the past and economic regeneration in the future is laid on institutions of education and training. The other potential partners in this undertaking are on the whole sleeping ones, immutable within the monetarist ideological universe: the export of capital and the transfer by multinationals to overseas sites of production, the favoured treatment of agriculture and the dominance of defence contracts within the electronics industry are typically set aside, as is the responsibility of high interest rates and crippling exchange rates between 1979 and 1982 for Britain's unprecedented deindustrialization. In a political economy where these factors are seen as imperatives, the liberal humanist goals of social justice and personal

development have been severely attenuated in favour
of those emphasizing vocational preparation and a
technically-oriented curriculum. The pressure on
education to deliver technical competences, skills
and respect for workplace disciplines has,
outwardly at least, transformed professional
concerns and vocabularies as can be seen from the
current range of DES in-service and ESRC research
priorities. Clearly, for liberal humanism is being
substituted a version of social and economic
Darwinism where enterprise and the possession of
skills for 'technological capability' have become
the dominant values.

This reappraisal of the nature, purpose and
content of education has, of course, been fuelled
by the dilemmas of educators facing disappearing
employment opportunities for their school leavers.
But, more significantly, the reappraisal has drawn
some of its strength from a readiness in some
(largely Conservative) quarters to exploit the
unresolved contradictions which lay behind the
comprehensivization settlement during the 1960s.
Throughout the development of the comprehensive
school policy the concern has been largely with the
form of comprehensivization rather than its
substance. The primary issue has always been one
of access to educational resources and the location
of the individual pupil in an ostensibly non-
selective system rather than the class-cultural
basis of the curriculum and examination system
which have continued to perpetuate the class
divisions of the tripartite system. The disguised
nature of the selection process in the
comprehensive school was, of course, at the heart
of the attack on reformist policies by the so-
called 'new' sociology of education of the early
1970s, but recognition of this contradiction has
re-emerged in the education policy of the
Conservative government in quite a new guise. We
now find that the 'irrelevance' of education for
the lower-achieving 40% of school leavers is used
to legitimate the strengthening of selection and
the allocation to this band of young people of a
more 'relevant' technical and vocationally-oriented
curriculum. In view of the continuing low
probability of employment for this group of school
leavers it is difficult to escape Gleeson's
conclusion that

> the plethora of curriculum guidelines
> emanating from the MSC and the DES at the

present time may obscure a related and perhaps
more pressing political problem: namely the
effect a fall in demand for labour has on the
principles of authority and discipline in
society. Work preparation for non-existent
jobs, therefore, takes on a 'new' connotation;
one less concerned with training for
particular technical skills and one more
concerned with 'educating' young people for
the social order.
Gleeson, D. (1983)

That this policy has not produced the wholehearted
condemnation from the liberal wing of the
educational community that might have been expected
is a measure both of the ambivalence towards
educational ends which currently prevails and of
the difficulty which liberal educators have in
defending comprehensives against the charge of
failing the low achievers. Perhaps the clearest
demonstration of this has been the public
commitment of a number of prominent 'liberal'
members of the educational establishment to the
RSA's project 'Education for Capability' with its
very clear espousal of technical values.

Although schools have yet to move some way
before this technicist ideology becomes practice,
the revival of an aggressive form of technological
determinism within the state departments
responsible for industry and employment has led to
the clear prescription for education to service the
technological future rather than to engage
critically with it. This applies particularly to
further education, where social education has been
largely displaced by courses in social and life
skills (Moore, 1983), and to some extent to higher
education where the hostility shown to sociology
and the attempts to reduce the social science input
to teacher education give fairly convincing
indications of the wish to curtail the critical
study of policy and social institutions.
Predictably, in much of the literature available
for 'awareness of industry' courses in schools, it
is an idealised view of industry which is
presented. Teachers are enjoined to foster an
understanding (i.e. an acceptance) of the 'wealth
creation' process and a recognition that industrial
growth, consumerism and new technology are
synonymous with progress. In outlining the
education and training aims of his Department to
the House of Lords Select Committee on Science and

Technology, the Chief Engineer and Scientist at the Department of Trade and Industry made the statement that

> These aims reflect the two sides of the education process: first getting youngsters to see education as a preparation for a productive life contributing to the wealth on which our Society (sic) and its values depend; and second to try and match the content of education to the future needs of employers so that it lays the foundation of understanding on which specific skills can be built through occupational training and the continuing education which will be an increasing feature of working life.
>
> House of Lords Select Committee on Science and Technology, 1984.

The Industry-Education Unit at the DTI which was established in 1978 sets out to promote and fund a range of activities in the education system which embody the aims outlined above. These include the Micro Electronics Project, the SATROs – Science and Technology Regional Organisations – the Information Technology Centres and the CNC equipment in further education college programmes.

The unproblematised view of industry which the DTI takes as part of its aim of changing the attitudes and culture of young people can be seen in the booklet entitled 'Industry in Perspective' (B.P. et al, 1983). Published in conjunction with a number of large companies it is intended as a briefing document for teachers and senior pupils. Although there is a passing mention of some of the social costs associated with industrialisation it is most striking that almost all of the problematic issues are ignored. In an important sense, the fostering of an unproblematic 'awareness of industry' as understood by the protagonists of this view is a serious political intervention in the curriculum but one which is largely unrecognized as such. So 'naturalized' has this view of industrial capitalism become that any questioning of it would in all probability be attacked as 'Marxist bias'. That it has survived with relatively little debate is an indication of the hegemonic power of the current wave of economic nationalism and the technological determinism which goes with it.

After James Callaghan's Ruskin College speech in October 1976 had launched the so-called 'Great

Debate', a number of initiatives were begun which attempted to implement the new commitment to developing in schools a positive view of industry. One of the more well-known was the Schools Council Industry Project (SCIP) which had originated in 1975 with an approach to the Schools Council by the TUC requesting curricular materials which would counter the negative attitudes of school leavers to trade unions. But the Schools Council felt that there were advantages in including the CBI in a wider scheme to improve young people's understanding of industry, and it was on this basis that the 'Industry Project' was planned. The SCIP was the only initiative to emerge during the late seventies which formally built in a trade union perspective. Others such as the CBI-sponsored Understanding British Industry, Project Trident, Young Enterprise, Understanding Industry, and the Industrial Society's Challenge of Industry Conferences identified specific tasks and modes of operation and became part of the repertoire available to the Schools Industry Liaison Officers who were appointed in increasing numbers by LEAs from the late seventies onwards. The main concern shared by each of them was the development of a greater awareness of industrial processes and practice. Some UBI schemes, for example, have concentrated on promoting teacher secondments into industry. Project Trident's school-industry work is concerned with the development of work experience schemes for young people and the Young Enterprise Scheme provides encouragement to sixth-formers to set up and run their own 'scale-model' companies on commercial lines with their own working capital and management structures.

For the six-year period after the start of the Great Debate 'awareness of industry' curricula in schools were extremely variable and dependent on the energies and availability of staff attached to the various national projects. Since the introduction of TVEI in November 1982, the piecemeal nature of this provision has begun to give way to more coherent strategies within LEAs in which industrial practice is seen in relation to systematic programmes of technical and vocational education.

A new feature in this development and a direct outcome of New Right ideology is a growing emphasis on 'education for enterprise'. This encouragement of school leavers to consider setting up their own businesses, ostensibly promoted as a means of creating jobs, also clearly carries within it the essence of competitiveness and possessive individualism. A particularly notable example of the importance currently attached to 'education for enterprise' is a discussion paper from the Society of Education Officers which takes as its starting point the view that

> The economic, cultural and social future of the United Kingdom rests on our ability to exploit the new technologies in competition with other advanced nations. Without the contribution of education in developing the attitudes and skills which make up technological capability, the economic future must be in serious doubt. The slow response in this country to opportunities which have already appeared and been lost can be attributed in a large part to deeply inbuilt social forces and to the shortcomings of education itself. Weaknesses in technological capability point inevitably to a decline in material standards and, in important respects, in the quality of life.
> Society of Education Officers, 1983.

In order to overcome what the SEO identifies as the shortcomings of education in this regard, the paper proposes that the

> long-term objectives of the education service ought to include the following:
> 1. To emphasize publicly the value of a systematic approach to teaching the individual and collective skills and attitudes which are associated with enterprise; such teaching to be through the existing curricular structures wherever possible, in business-related contexts and at all stages of education - beginning at the most general level in primary schools and stretching through advanced academic research.
> 2. To encourage a more closely co-ordinated national strategy towards Education for Enterprise.
> 3. To reorient and co-ordinate the use of project work in secondary schools, further and higher education, such as to draw more effectively on opportunities for commercially viable service or product innovation and development.

4. To examine the contribution of further
    and higher education in meeting the
    special needs of small businesses and to
    encourage a more effective use of the
    resources available in education.

    Ibid.

The arguments adduced for the strategies
proposed are predicated on a vision of the new
industrialism in which information technology
becomes the 'meta-technology' which is 'energising
a new phase in the economy and culture'. It
subscribes to a computer utopianism with global
implications and, ironically, draws the conclusion
that 'Education must be much more strongly oriented
towards giving individuals the capacity to be
autonomous, self-supporting and self-directing'.
What is absent from arguments such as these is any
concept of education doing anything other than
passively accepting this process with all its
implications for deskilled and fragmented work
roles and the concentration of control in the hands
of companies and organizations whose task is to
manage information. The notion that one of the
major purposes of education is to enable the
critical understanding and evaluation of social
futures is entirely absent.
    The new educational principles being called
for to support the new industrialism are epitomised
in the concept of the compliant - creative worker.
Constructed during the course of the attack on
progressive education in the 1970s by the right in
Britain, this concept encapsulates much that has
followed in education and training policy since
that time. The apparently contradictory
characteristics it implies are highly functional to
the working experience which has given rise to it
and consistent with much of the criticism which has
been made of the preparedness of school leavers for
work and the unsatisfactory nature of the
transition from school to work. In short, it
defines the ideal worker of the future.
    The creativity envisaged bears little
relationship, of course, to the concept of
creativity which flourished in the educational
theories of the sixties. That creativity which
drew its sustenance from the psychological theories
of Piaget and existential philosophy was founded on
an open-ended concept of cognition and an expanding
consciousness in which the concrete and the

abstract were seen in a continuing dialectical
relationship. The ideal pedagogical mode, in the
phrase of the time, was 'learning by discovery'.
By contrast, the innovation, initiative and
enterprise called for in the current discourse are
entirely instrumental. They are directed at
practical or technical rather than intellectual
development, at information rather than knowledge,
at syncretism rather than criticism and at skills
rather than understanding. Above all, the
initiative and enterprise thought to be needed by
current conditions of work are not expected to be
directed towards those conditions themselves. The
expectation is that workers will be creative in the
furthering of capitalist goals but compliant
towards the social relations and structures they
find in the workplace, including the need to adapt
to the consequences of the introduction of new
technology.

Wexler et al have argued that schools are now
being asked to satisfy fundamentally contradictory
demands of the production process:

> When the skills needed for job performance
> come to include the ability to understand and
> respond creatively to the changing needs of
> the overall process and to participate
> actively in coordination and innovation, then
> it is more difficult to maintain the attitudes
> and dispositions necessary for a willing
> submission to an hierarchical organisation of
> that production process . . . The concrete
> expression of these contradications is the
> simultaneous demand for workers who have broad
> general competencies (smart workers) but who
> have also internalised the model of
> hierarchical social relations as personal
> dispositions (docile workers). Without these
> general competencies, the competitive,
> adaptive development of production is
> inhibited. But if they are in fact developed,
> they threaten to disrupt the existing social
> relations of production.
> Wexler, P. et al, 1981

Wexler et al go on to suggest that to achieve this
contradiction, curriculum subjects are undergoing
'decomposition' – English into communication
skills, social education into social and life
skills – thereby reducing their potential for
promoting critical understanding. This point is

also made by Moore in his analysis of further
education curricula in Britain, in which he argues
that the emphasis on skills within the FE
curriculum

> effectively cuts young people off from bodies
> of abstract theoretical knowledge through
> which they could elaborate structural and
> collective understandings of their situation.
> Moore, R. 1983

In tandem with this ideological attack on
liberal education has been a substantial shift
within the political structures used in the
delivery of these new curricula. The hitherto
decentralized nature of the British education
system and teacher autonomy have represented a
fairly substantial buttress against political
control of the curriculum. In Kogan's term, the
'socio-technology of education' makes it inherently
impossible for the state to control the curriculum
in any direct sense. And further, as he points
out, the current international consensus is that
the top-down strategies of curriculum change do not
generally work because teachers' attitudes to the
cumulative impact of such innovation are
unfavourable. For this reason, he suggests that
even where there are strong policy directives from
the centre they 'have probably generally been
followed by empirical-rational strategies of
information, dissemination and training' (Kogan
1983). Citing the growth of progressive education
as an example, he argues that 'the most important
changes in British education have been bottom-up'
and that 'on the larger social objectives endorsed
and pushed by central government, such as . . .
education as a way to economic change, there has
been virtually complete failure' (Ibid). The
failure of the top-down model of educational
innovation is also a factor in the development of
the Schools Council Industry Project which is
discussed below.

But if we look at the actual operation of the
policy to strengthen the industrial orientation of
schools, the picture is considerably more complex
than Kogan's analysis would imply. The two state
departments most conspicuously involved in this
activity - the MSC and the Department of Industry -
combine a top-down policy of selective funding and
ultimate control of content with the exploitation
of locally-generated curricula and pedagogical

approaches. Quite clearly, since the start of the Great Debate there has been a considerable extension of the role of the state in curriculum regulation at all levels of education.

It is openly acknowledged by the Departments of Industry and of Education that the Industry-Education Unit of the DOI was set up in 1978 to facilitate the influence of industry on the education system and to provide direct funding of school-industry initiatives in a way in which the DES was constitutionally unable to do. The primacy of the DES within education has, of course, been further substantially diminished by the large-scale involvement of the MSC in education and training - most recently in the setting up of the TVEI. Part of the response of the DES can be seen in the increasingly directive stance of HMI with regard to vocationally-relevant curricula both within schools and initial teacher training. A recently published HMI Discussion Paper entitled Teacher Training and Preparation for Working Life contains the recommendation that

> No student preparing for secondary school teaching should complete a course of initial training without a clear idea of how to help pupils prepare for their adult working life. This idea should include some specific understanding of the needs of industry; the personal as well as academic qualities needed for the school leaver; some knowledge of careers education, and the channels of information open to young people in their choice of career or, increasingly, their search for alternatives to immediate employment.
> DES/HMI, 1982

The existence of two state departments in this field as well as the MSC, each with a distinct budget, constitutional status, ideological stance and mode of operation underlines the necessity for a disaggregated theory of the state in the empirical investigation of this policy area. It is also necessary to recognize both the corporatist and pluralist tendencies which are apparent in the operations of state departments in interactions with their interest groups. As a recent article by Streeck has argued, neither corporatist nor pluralist theories are adequate in themselves for explaining the complexities of such relationships,

187

and he suggests that they should be seen in combination (Streeck, 1983). The Department of Industry's role, for example, in promoting industry-education liaison demonstrates elements of both corporatism and pluralism. Its main function is to act as financial provider for the approved activities of a wide range of interest groups, such as the Science and Technology Regional Organisations (SATROs), the 'Opening Windows on Engineering' Project and the Microelectronics Project, which determine their own agendas and forms of local practice but also constitute part of the consultative process operated by the Department.

The MSC, on the other hand, can be seen as a more thoroughgoing corporatist structure with a composition at national, regional and, in the case of TVEI, local levels, which includes unions, employers, representatives from education and departmental staff. Perhaps the most significant aspect of this in the case of the TVEI is that it uses financial provision to allow the formal involvement of non-educational bodies in the determination of LEA policy. As Streeck has argued, the price of incorporation in a corporatist structure is the requirement for self-regulation in the implementation of policy outcomes, and the control of dissent among rank and file members. The trade-off of advantage to the participating group is very finely balanced. The ambivalence of the TUC and its member unions towards the introduction of the YTS scheme is a clear example of the tension which can arise between the leadership and rank and file in a corporatist context.

The Schools Council Industry Project (SCIP) which has been one of the principal recent initiatives in school-industry collaboration exemplifies corporatism at both national and local levels. The Project took as its starting point the view that there was little to be gained from the provision of centrally-prepared teaching materials. 'The Council's experience has led it towards the view that locally-based curriculum development was markedly more effective than what is known in the jargon as "centre-periphery" models . . .' (SCIP Interim Report, 1979). The Project chose rather to adopt a localized mode of operation in which SCIP co-ordinators in five contrasting LEAs were 'to work with the teachers in the process of forging links with the local employment environment in order to develop the curriculum' (Jamieson and Lightfoot, 1982). Local groups of teachers, employers and trade unionists were asked to draw up proposals for introducing 'industrial awareness' into the curriculum, with a strong emphasis being placed on the use of 'adults other than teachers' in educational roles, non-vocational work experience for pupils, as well as problem-solving techniques, group work, simulation and role playing.

The corporatism which characterized the initiation of the Project by the TUC and CBI therefore came to be superseded by a form of 'local' corporatism. Although the central organizations of both the TUC and CBI had envisaged the Project in terms of a top-down, centralized provision of materials, the Project team decided to opt for a bottom-up model - a devolved pattern of development which relied almost wholly on local collaboration. In this it can be contrasted with the mode of operation adopted by the MSC and DOI in which, as was argued above, locally-generated curricula are used within a top-down model ensuring ultimate control.

This reliance on local collaboration, and its attendant emphasis on <u>processes</u>, means that responsibility for <u>content</u> has been left to local decision-making. The implications of this policy for the content of industrial awareness initiatives in schools have been documented by Jamieson and Lightfoot in their account of the first phase of the SCIP Project. They argue that because the imprimatur of the CBI and TUC as joint partners in the project was thought by teachers to ensure balance, teaching material on the subject of industry and society was almost always seen as uncontroversial. They point out that teachers tend not to handle many of the fundamental issues which tend to be controversial (the distribution of rewards in society, the causes of unemployment, ownership and control of industry) although they add that 'There was considerable treatment of what might be called "lower level" controversy (strikes, media coverage, picketing)' (Jamieson and Lightfoot 1982). Teachers tended to concentrate on the reactions of individuals to economic processes rather than on the causes of those processes and to transmit essentially technical information about industry. In the light of this it is not surprising to find the statement that 'it is difficult to find many examples of employers indicating displeasure at syllabus content on the grounds that it did not show industry in a good light' (Ibid).

The involvement of adults other than teachers in the classroom also increases the likelihood of depoliticisation, as there is an imbalance between the involvement of employers and trade unionists in industrial awareness activity in schools. It appears that employers and industrial managers argue for the inclusion of their contributions across a broad range of the curriculum, while trade unionists habitually take a narrower view, restricting themselves to such areas as health and safety at work. Schools mirror these judgements, calling on employers and managers to fulfil a number of functions while viewing trade unionists as having a narrower brief. Although this imbalance has become apparent to those within the project, it is difficult to see how it could be remedied with such an extensively devolved system.

The Schools Council Industry Project is important for a number of reasons. It demonstrates how a bottom-up model of educational innovation can result in the depoliticisation of contentious material through its own organizational structure. In addition, its supposedly liberative pedagogy, in the use of adults other than teachers, can be seen as a strengthening of hegemonic control and 'commonsense attitudes', particularly when this is reinforced by a local corporatist structure. This local corporatism is legitimating intervention by industrialists in curriculum planning in ways which until recently were seen as inappropriate by industrialists themselves, and which are still not wholly espoused in formal statements by employers. This is a significant extension of the long-standing role of companies in producing subject-based curriculum materials for use in schools. Employer participation characterizes most of the local committees which have come into being in the industry-education area, but it is particularly significant in the case of SCIP which presents itself as liberative pedagogy offering a non-partisan view of industrial practice. It is partly because of this status that SCIP local projects have been able to provide the blueprint, in pedagogy, subject matter and use of personnel, for a number of TVEI schemes.

We have attempted in this paper to review the ideological substance of educational initiatives taken for the social and political education of 14-

16 year olds, particularly under the Conservative government since 1979. We have also considered some of the political structures created to secure changes in the behaviour and attitudes of teachers, which have been characterized by an emphasis on national and local corporatism, the use of adults other than teachers in the educational process, and the mobilization of local resources for the development of relevant curricula. But this appears to have taken place in a way which has squeezed out the trade union contribution and perspective and offered an inherently conservative and non-critical view of industry. We would argue that the content of this industrially-oriented curricula requires fuller discussion in the context of a more rigorous and less biased social and political education.

NOTE

1.   A possible exception to this is the rejection by a number of parent groups of proposals for a return to grammar schools which some Conservative-led education committees have put forward. See Simon, B. 1984.

REFERENCES

Apple, M. (1980) 'Curricular Form and the Logic of Technical Control: Building the Possessive Individual' in Barton , L., Meighan, R. and Walker, S. (eds.) Schooling, Ideology and the Curriculum, Sussex, Falmer Press.

Boys, C. (1984) 'Are Employers Making the Most of Higher Education?' Personnel Management, August 1984.

BP et al (1983) Industry in Perspective published by a consortium of companies with the support of the DOI.

Cawson, A. and Saunders, P. (1983) 'Corporatism, Competitive Politics and Class Struggle' in King, R. (ed.) Capital and Politics, London, Routledge.

Department of Education and Science (1982) Teacher Training and Preparation for Working Life: an HMI Discussion Paper, London, HMSO.

Gleeson, D. (1983) General Introduction in Gleeson, D. (ed.) Youth Training and the Search for Work, London, Routledge.

Hall, S. (1982) 'The Battle for Socialist Ideas in the 1980s' in The Socialist Register 1982, London, Merlin.

Hall, S. (1983) 'The Great Moving Right Show' in Hall, S. and Jacques, M. (eds.) The Politics of Thatcherism, London, Lawrence and Wishart.

Hill, S. (1981) Competition and Control at Work, London, Heinemann Education.

House of Lords Select Committee on Science and Technology: Minutes of Evidence taken 16th February, 1984, Department of Trade and Industry, London, HMSO.

Jamieson, I. and Lightfoot, M. (1982) Schools and Industry: Derivations from the Schools Council Industry Project, Schools Council Working Paper 73, London, Methuen.

Kogan, M. (1983) 'The Case of Education' in Young, K. (ed.) National Interests and Local Government, London, Heinemann.

Lawton, D. (1980) The Politics of the School Curriculum, London, Routledge.

Moore, R. (1983) 'Further Education, Pedagogy and Production in Gleeson, D. (ed.) Youth Training and the Search for Work, London, Routledge.

Schools Council Industry Project (1979) Interim Report, London, Schools Council.

Simon, B. (1984) 'Breaking School Rules' in Marxism Today, September.

Society of Education Officers (1983) Key Issues for Industry and Education, Society of Education Officers Occasional Paper, Number Three.

Streeck, W. (1983) 'Between Pluralism and Corporatism: German Business Associations and the State, Journal of Public Policy, Vol. 3, No. 3.

Weiner, M.J. (1981) English Culture and the Decline of the Industrial Spirit 1850-1980, Cambridge University Press.

Wexler, P., Whitson, T. and Moskowitz, E.J. (1981) 'Deschooling by Default: The Changing Social Functions of Public Schooling', Interchange, Vol. 12, Nos. 2-3.

ON THE 'RELATIVE AUTONOMY' OF EDUCATION: MICRO - AND MACRO - STRUCTURES

Ronald King

This paper takes up one of the concerns of the first Westhill Conference of 1978; the relationships between education and other social structures, and those between the different so-called 'levels' of education, classrooms, schools and systems[1]. I believe these are perennial concerns, and assumptions about these relationships are present in most discussions in the sociology of education, even if they are not actually mentioned. As time-markers in the sociology of education I will refer to two commentaries on the state of the subject: the earlier one by Basil Bernstein (1972) and the recent related pair by Brian Davies (1982,1983). From the first I take the metaphor of the sociological 'news'; from the second the metaphors of 'story' and 'poetry'.[2]

I begin with a consideration of what we mean by education and other structures, by levels of education, and by those two faces of human social behaviour, autonomy and constraint. This leads to an evaluation of three sets of approaches to investigating and explaining the autonomy and constraint of education; these I roughly categorise as, correspondence, codes and coping.

MICRO - AND MACRO - STRUCTURES: AUTONOMY AND CONSTRAINT

My starting point is a definition of social structure which I think is unexceptional. 'Structure in so far as it really occurs . . . can be found in the real behaviour of everyday life, primarily in repetitive encounters'. Although Randall Collins (1975) writes as a neo-Weberian, with a little selectivity and varying amounts of generosity this concept can be found in Durkheim,

Marx, Parsons and Schutz.[3] This definition does not present the image of people 'inside' a social structure; the pattern of their behaviour towards one another, their social relationships, is the structure. Individuals may feel themselves to be inside a structure, such as a 'school' or 'education system', because the other individuals with whom they relate, directly or indirectly, are physically external to them. This understandably leads to the reification of social structures, where the set of social relationships is regarded as a non - or extra - human thing. A second point is again unexceptional in being present to varying degrees in many sociological perspectives; that in relating to one another in patterned or structured ways, people do not simply behave - they act. They have subjective meanings and purposes in so behaving. We can therefore classify social structures in two ways; according to the purposes of the acting individuals, and according to the number of individuals relating directly or indirectly to one another. Classification by purpose means we can refer to economic structures, educational structures, and so on; the social institutions of the old terminology.[4] Classification by the number of individuals in the relationship means we can refer to the social structure of a classroom, a school or an educational system, using the same concept of structure. Since structures are the repeated actions of individuals, they are not static but continuously created. If you wait in an empty classroom for the teacher and children to arrive you can see the process of structure as they relate to one another in patterned ways. As the repeated relationships between people, it is not difficult to see how some degree of change is inherent in any structure. 'Everything is in a state of flux' (Heraclitus, 480BC). This points to the other dimension of structures - time. The structure created in making a lesson happen, as described by George Payne (1976), lasts less than a minute; that of a school class, lasts for about a year, on and off.

The number and time dimensions of structure have been presented graphically by Collins (1981a) and I make use of a modified version here. Collins' version uses a space scale to subsume the number of persons, which draws attention to the way all human interaction takes place in material locations, such as classrooms and playgrounds. We can plot any sociological investigation on the diagram. Wallerstein's (1980) world system would be up at the top right hand side involving millions of people over hundreds of years, and the exchange between one woman and one boy analysed by Speier (1971), which lasted a minute or so, would be in the bottom left hand side. In our field, Margaret Archer on The Origins of Educational Systems (1979) would be on the top right hand side; George Payne's (1976) 'Making a lesson happen' on the bottom left. Generally speaking, the larger the scale the longer the time considered.

Figure 9.1: Micro - and Macro - Structures

Number of people interacting

MACRO-STRUCTURES

(Aggregates of micro-structures)

'Education'   'Class'

MICRO-STRUCTURES

Classrooms
Workplaces
_____

Time over which they interact

What are the connections between micro-structures (few people - short time) and macro-structures (many people - long time)? In Collins' (1981b) view, macro-structures, such as class or education, consist of aggregates of micro-structures.[5] They do not exist in the here and now except as micro-experiences - being at work or school. Macro-concepts, he argues, are analysts' concepts, although typifications such as 'class' or 'education' may be part of an individual's subjectivity in micro-situations. Teachers have views on education but they (and researchers), never encounter education except in the micro-situations of schools and classrooms. Macro-sociological concepts can only be made fully empirical by grounding them in a sample of typical micro-events that make them up. My gloss on this would be, that to speak of a macro-structure, such as English primary education, is to make generalisations about the typical relationships between large numbers of teachers and pupils over a relatively long period of time. Most of these generalisations should also apply in the various micro-situations. For example, we can say that in most classrooms of English primary schools, children are taught by one teacher most of the time. But some of the typical relationships to be found in some classrooms are not to be found in all or most classrooms. Macro-structures are not empirically realised as the sum of micro-structures, but as a coding of typical relationships of micro-structures. However, particular micro-structures, such as individual classrooms, are not to be ignored if they contribute little to the analytical realisation of macro-structures. We have as much a theoretical problem in explaining the specific and atypical (in macro-terms) features of some micro-structures, as in explaining the widespread incidence (in space and time) of the typical features of micro-structures which constitute macro-structures.

There is not the time to deal with the methodological implications of these views. Suffice to say that it would take an army of ethnographers to study all the relevant classrooms that constitute even an element of the macro-structure of education for a given time and space. There should be a place for sampling procedures in the selection of micro-situations for study, and a place for the use of larger scale surveys involving interviews and questionnaires, to document the distribution of hypothesised typical relationships generated at the micro-level. This involves such old-fashioned often neglected concerns as sampling and statistical significance in pursuit of social significance.(6)

Where does the 'autonomy' of my title fit in with these considerations? The basis of the concept of structure as the repeated patterns of purposeful behaviour is in Weber's (1947) view of social action. The famous definition goes, 'Action is social in so far as, by virtue of the subjective meaning attached to it by the acting individual (or individuals), it takes into account the behaviour of others and is thereby orientated in its course'. Structures are the socially constituted behaviour of people. People are not constrained by structures. 'Structure' is a name we give to constrained, patterned behaviour. If we define autonomy as behaviour that is not constrained by an external agency, then fully autonomous behaviour is not social behaviour, and therefore social structure would not exist; there would be chaos or 'anarchy' in the popular use of the term.[7] As Davies (1976) puts it, in a slightly different context, 'the social is control'. Autonomy is commonly used in discussing the relationships between structures of different purposes, usually at the macro-level. This is the principal domain of neo-Marxist studies of education.

NEO-MARXISTS' CORRESPONDENCE AND 'RELATIVE AUTONOMY'

It is not my intention to make yet another critique of the growing body of different kinds of neo-Marxist analyses of education, except in placing some of them in the micro-macro framework I have outlined, and to look at Bernstein's phrase, at the 'news' they have delivered, as he suggests, at the conceptual and empirical levels.[8] In doing so I will refer to the recent commentary on the relative autonomy thesis by David Reynolds (1984), whose analysis I find much to agree with.

In the days of the 'orthodox' sociology of education we used to talk about education and 'society' a great deal, as shown in the books of the period, such as, Society and the Teacher's Role, Society and the Education of Teachers.[9] In this context 'society' refers to all the other relationships occurring between people over a given time and in a general space (usually one country), apart from those defined as educational; a usage of which implies that education is not a part of society. 'Society' has been replaced by 'capitalism' in combination with 'education' or 'schooling'. How can we tell how one macro-structure relates to another, such as capitalism and education? Let us see what answers we get from some neo-Marxists.

Bowles and Gintis' (1976) analysis of Schooling in Capitalist America is made at the macro-level of their title. Their 'correspondence' thesis concerns only the structure of the relationships of education and production; both

197

are hierarchical, selective and specialised. These structural features certainly exist at the micro levels of school and workplace, although Bowles and Gintis make few references to the available evidence. One way to show how the macro-structures of education and capitalism relate to one another is to demonstrate continuity of relationships between the constituent micro-structures. Relationships between businessmen and superintendents on school boards in the 1880s have been clearly shown in Katz's (1971) study of Boston, but such direct relationships are not so easily demonstrated in either modern America or Britain. Another way is to use the general method of comparison. The proposition that certain structural features are characteristic of capitalist education can be tested by comparison with non-capitalist societies. There are no ethnographies of Soviet classrooms that I know of, but in the available accounts of education at the macro-level we find descriptions of the hierarchy and specialisation of knowledge and of pupils, and evidence of social selectivity (see, for example, Grant 1979). Zajada (1980) has shown how in the option system, it is the children of the 'intelligencia' who predominate in the high status subjects leading to higher education. Unfortunately, we have no Cicourel and Kitsuse (1963) to analyse the micro-events concerned. However, it is clear that these structural features are not a characteristic of a particular kind of economic 'base' - capitalism. This is confirmed in the wide-ranging historical analysis of Ramirez (1981), which showed, in Reynolds' (1984) summary, that, 'The specific links between capitalism and schooling appeared unproven and unclear . . .'

If it is argued that the economy of the Soviet Union is a form of state capitalism, then we must make our comparisons with an industrial society where profit is not a purpose. Does one exist? I've not seen a reference to an example in the neo-Marxist literature. In so far as they make comparisons, Bowles and Gintis (and other neo-Marxists) compare capitalist schooling with that of a society they would like to see exist. Reality, of a kind, is compared with a political dream. Part of their sociological news is from nowhere.

Another method of showing how one macro-structure may relate to another is by demonstrating continuity of subjectivity or purpose. This is an element in Althusser's (1972) macro-level speculative analysis of education in unspecified 'mature capitalist formations', as being an ideological state apparatus in the production of the social relations of production. However, it is clear that one purpose of those people who constitute any state, is that the mass education they control should create certain forms of consciousness. To this degree, ISA's are commonplace, although their nature and purpose varies. In post-revolutionary, pre-industrial France it was 'education by state, for the state' (Vaughan and Archer 1971). This was an element in the 200 word Imperial Rescript memorised and recited daily by Japanese schoolchildren from 1890 until 1945, proclaiming the divinity of the emperor and the supremacy of Japan (Brameld 1968). In both countries, one of the purposes of education was the creation of a mass conscript army for colonial conquest and control. In neither case did mass education accompany or follow the growth of industrial capitalism. Gellner (1983) has suggested that modern political movements are more concerned with the generation of the consciousness of nationhood, than that of a new economic order, such as socialism. Such evidence as we have suggests that education, as some kind of ISA, may be part of this generation of national consciousness, most purposefully in post-colonial states, as shown in Foster's (1967) study of Ghana.

Althusser's proposition of the 'relative autonomy' of education from production in 'mature capitalist formations' is too vague to be very useful. The condition of full autonomy for education is not easily imaginable; this would mean that the relationships of those concerned with what is defined as education were totally unconstrained by any other structures or agencies. Nil autonomy would mean that those people whose relationships constitute the structure of education would be only and totally constrained by non-educational structures or agencies. This is fairly close to Bowles and Gintis' (1976) analysis. But empirical reality strongly suggests that relative autonomy is the condition of all structures, both micro and macro, if only through people's consciousness of other structures (a point I will return to later). As Reynolds (1984) puts it '(relative autonomy) suggests not that humans are either free or determined but that there are both determinations and freedoms'.

The general, but often unstated, assumption of false consciousness in capitalist societies allows many neo-Marxists to ignore the subjectivities of people, even when they are studied in micro-situations. The basic micro-situations studied by Sharp and Green (1976) were not the classrooms of the infants' department they studied, but those of the probing interviews with the headteacher and three teachers, talking about nine children and about education in general. As Davies (1983) puts it, 'Their jumps from thier little bits of here and now to their big story leaves some of their actors . . . pretty trampled'[10] Their macro-level 'big story' is that 'progressive' education is effectively conservative in preserving the existing (capitalist) social order; a truism that applies to the official purpose of almost any mass educational system, and ignores what might be special about infant education either at the macro-level, or at the micro-level of the school they studied.

There is a 'big story' in Paul Willis's Learning to Labour (1977) but its macro-sociological propositions are grounded in some micro-events. 'Education' is that of the 'lads' he studied, to some extent, in classrooms, and 'production' is based upon the micro-situation of their work. Thus he gives some empirical precision to Athusser's proposition of the 'relative autonomy' of education in relation to production, in considering the 'teaching paradigm' to be 'relatively autonomous'. This is in part a consequence of taking into account the subjectivities of the lads, their teachers and their parents, so that, in Weber's (1947) terms, the explanations have some adequacy at the level of meaning. For example, we have some understanding of the typical lad's actions in leaving school to take up an unskilled or semi-skilled job like his father's. As Parkin (1979) observes, 'Inside every neo-Marxist there seems to be a Weberian struggling to get out'. (Regrettably, it isn't every one; only some). Willis's conclusions concerning the importance of the lads' families in occupational placement would have been greatly strengthened had comparisons been made with the 'ear 'oles' in the micro-situations of school, work and family.[11] Perhaps we would also have a better idea of how some working class 'kids' get middle class jobs.

The degree of Willis's intellectual honesty stands in contrast to the work of some other neo-Marxists. Their failure is, in Weber's (1948) terms, to recognise 'inconvenient facts', 'facts that are inconvenient for their party opinions'. The more they ignore the existence of Eastern bloc countries, and the existence of forms of consciousness that they do not approve, the more their 'news' must be regarded as 'stories'.[12]

CODES, CLASSIFICATION AND 'RELATIVE AUTONOMY'

In Olive Banks' (1978) discussion of the relationship of micro - and macro - approaches at the first Westhill conference, she posed Basil Bernstein as making the most important attempt to construct a model for the sociology of education. I propose to look, in his own terms, at the 'news' he has delivered, as he suggests, at the conceptual and empirical level. In doing so I make a sharp distinction between his work on language and his anthologised writings in <u>Class, Codes and Control Volume 3;</u> between linguistic codes and knowledge codes.[13]

His work on language represents one of the biggest sociological research enterprises in this country, and presents a good example of the aggregation of micro-situations to make generalizations at the macro-structural level. The micro-situations of the research are not the classrooms and homes of the children in the sample, but researcher-interview situations. The speech samples obtained are aggregated mainly according to the concepts of class and codes. In this, social class does not refer directly to the work situation of the parents, but to a quantification of their combined occupational and educational status - a common enough approximation, but one that leaves the hypothesis of the association between language and social class <u>per se</u> untested. Despite the important criticisms of the research processes by Rosen (1972), Labov (1972), Dittmar (1976) and others, its seminal importance in stimulating interest in the importance of language in education is undeniable. The reporting of sex differences in language usage is honest in view of the absence of gender in the original theoretical proposi- tions.[14]

There are, however, considerable conceptual problems with the hypothesised language codes. As Tony Edwards (1976) points out, it is not clear whether these refer to the structure of the language used or to the organising principles of the language. In all the tables of results, codes do not appear, only linguistical elements

hypothesised to be the constituents of an
elaborated code, such as the number of verb-forms.
Jackson (1974) has concluded that the results can
be interpreted without the use of the concept of
code at all. Ethnomethodology was invented after
this language research was under way. The
demonstration of the embeddedness of speech and the
use of glossing in the accomplishment of the
sharing of meanings (see, for example, Cicourel
1973), suggests the possible real existence of
something like restricted codes. The irony is that
the research has been the search for the
hypothesised elaborated code, whose context-free
quality is even denied by the very methods used to
demonstrate its existence. You can't help but talk
about <u>something</u> if you wish to be understood by
somebody else. The meanings transmitted by speech
are of little interest to Bernstein. Jackson quotes
Bernstein as saying, 'the conceptual exploration of
the codes has ended'. Let it be.

The essays which make up <u>Class, Codes and
Controls Vol. 3</u> have a different, and in my view,
inferior status to the pioneering and substantial
work on language. None of the essays is based on
original research, and references to other people's
research are few. If I were to give time in
proportion to the importance of this collection I
would stop now, but that would be intellectually
dishonest. On the other hand I am reluctant to go
over in any detail the criticisms I and others have
made before. In an unsatisfactory compromise I
will make a brief summary.(15)

Bernstein's explanations are of a presumed
social reality, described as 'idealised' or
'ideational', which does not correspond
satisfactorily to empirical reality.(16) There is
little evidence to show that secondary schools are
becoming more 'open' or that infant education is
characterised by an 'invisible' pedagogy (King
1976, 1979a, 1981). Classification and frame
explain nothing when applied to real cases; they
are new names, not new concepts (see Pring 1975,
Gibson 1977). Educational knowledge codes,
classification and framing are tautologically
defined (Pring 1975, Gibson 1977, King 1979). The
real existence of these codes is at best dubious,
and their location with human agents is never
explained; they could not be satisfactorily placed
on the number/time schema I outlined earlier. They
are used hypostatically. 'Underneath' or 'below'
the educational process lies the determining code.

On The 'Relative Autonomy' of Education

The connection between language and educational codes is not conceptually or empirically justified - they are similar only in name (Hargreaves 1977, King 1979a and b).

To be slightly more specific in relation to my title, I will deal in a little more detail with the essay 'Aspects of the relations between education and production'. As the title suggests this speculative analysis is mainly at the macro-structure level, but with some reference to the micro-structures of schools and work. 'Classification' was originally used in connection with educational knowledge, but here it is extended to include relationships between teachers and pupils, and those between education and production. Framing too, is extended to include the relationships of production. Bernstein points out that academically able pupils, whose education is, in his terms, strongly classified and framed by examinations and syllabuses, are likely to have access to positions in the production process where they have power (tautologically equated with weak classification) and the control of subordinates (tautologically, weak framing). In his formulation +C+F in school leads to -C-F at work. Conversely, less able, non-examinees are taught in conditions of -C-F (a reference to 'Newsom' type provision), and enter work under conditions of +C+F, that is, with little power and under strong control. As Bernstein points out this is a denial of the simple correspondence thesis of Bowles and Gintis (1976), and indicates that education is not dependent on the mode of production but is 'relatively autonomous'.

The validity of this analysis is clear, but it can be accomplished without the use of the terms classification and framing. Willis (1977) reaches a similar conclusion with respect to the transition of his non-examinee lads from school to low skill occupations, suggesting that the ideological socialisation into the acceptance of capitalism of such pupils in school is unnecessary, since they are adequately controlled through the material and economic relations of work. ('Wage slaves' of classic Marxism). Bernstein, Willis (1977) and Althusser (1972) basically agree that only those who have power in the capitalist production process are required to believe in the system, and that this acceptance may be acquired through extended formal education of a competitive kind.

This 'relative autonomy' thesis weakens if not

contradicts that of the earlier 'Classification and Framing' paper, where a move towards weak classification and framing was posed to be happening in response to increased specialisation of the industrial work force. However, Bernstein had, in this earlier paper, acknowledged what was obviously happening in schools; that subject 'boundaries' were being 'broken' for, and pupil choice was being extended to, 'the less "able" children whom we have given up educating', but without explaining why. It was quite clear from my study of secondary schools that the headteachers of modern and comprehensive schools had introduced special schemes for non-examined pupils in response to what they defined as a problem of the control of such pupils, whose education received little legitimacy from their parents or their potential employers (King 1973). In these circumstances the pupils themselves were sought as sources of legitimacy, through courses celebrating choice, interest and relevance. White (1968), no Marxist, suggested that these schemes were covertly intended to produce a docile, local-orientated workforce of semi and unskilled manual workers. However, as Bernstein points out, the British workforce is not particularly docile, as evidenced in strikes and working to rule – again a contradiction of the Bowles and Gintis thesis, although for a Marxist anything short of revolution is probably docility.

The 'relative autonomy' thesis potentially undermines much of Bernstein's earlier theorising. It questions the simple adaptive relationshp posed between education and 'external', systems in the 'Ritual in Education' the 'Open Schools: Open Society?' and in the 'Classification and Framing' papers. It also renders less problematic the 'interruptions' and 'contradictions' of the 'Pedagogies' paper. Effectively the whole structuralist element of Bernstein's analysis, that the structure of social relationships tend to a similar form, is weakened, and the explanation in terms of patterns of codes or classification and framing invalidated.

Given all these reservations, the various explanatory schema on the levels of education and the relationship between education and other macro-structures are of limited worth.[17] These criticisms are not to be mitigated by Bernstein's own admission that some of his ideas are metaphorical, 'strange' and 'underdeveloped'. In his own imagery these essays are not 'news'. In

Davies' (1982) view, 'All sociologies . . . are empirical and positivist if they collect and generalise about data', 'The alternative is poetry'. Bernstein is our best poet.

COPING STRATEGIES: CONSTRAINT AND AUTONOMY

It is with some relief that I come to the third rough category of approaches - that of 'coping' as used by Andy Hargreaves (1978) and Andrew Pollard (1982), which, with some reservations, show a measure of compatibility with the presentation I made at the start of this paper. The acknowledged origin of this concept applied to education, is the article by Westbury (1973). In this prescriptive and evaluative piece he refers to such pedagogical methods as 'chalk and talk' as examples of 'coping strategies', which permit teachers 'given their resources, to cope with the demands of the classroom setting'. Westbury assumes that limited material resources prevent teachers from engaging in an ill-defined 'open-education'.

Hargreaves uses 'coping strategies' as a key concept in a 'framework' linking 'structural questions to interactionist concerns'. The structural questions he takes from Marxism, on the implicit assumption that it offers the only or best analysis of class and capitalism. In his more recent writings I think we have evidence that at this stage, here was another 'Weberian struggling to get out' (see Hargreaves 1980, 1981). There is no need to attempt to combine 'interactionist concerns' with any structuralist theory. As with the concept of social structure already used in this paper, the principal Weberian concepts of action, power, authority and bureaucracy, all combine structure (the patterns of relationships between people) and subjectivity (their meanings in so doing) (King 1980, 1983).

Unfortunately, my understanding of his framework is not helped by Hargreaves' use of figurative and metaphorical language, starting with 'coping strategy'. 'Coping strategies are the product of constructive and creative activity on the part of the teachers'. This seems to mean that coping strategies are classroom-based micro-structures, created by the purposeful behaviour of teachers. (By my dictionary, 'tactics' might be the better military metaphor - strategy precedes action). Since coping is 'contending successfully'

205

(Concise Oxford Dictionary), if a teacher defines the outcome of her actions as 'successful', she will try the same again, that is, create a stable classroom structure. That coping strategies are 'adaptive' says nothing more than teaching is a <u>social</u> action, which 'takes into account the behaviour of others and is thereby orientated in its course'. (Weber's (1974) definition again).

Hargreaves makes a distinction between 'institutional' and 'societal' constraints on coping strategies. Institutional constraints are those of the micro-situation of school and classroom. He gives particular attention to material 'pressures', which is a recognition that all human interaction, including teaching, takes place in material spaces which put limits on actions. The question is, how can we demonstrate the nature of these constraints? Hargreaves gives examples from his own research in two middle schools which show how <u>subjectively</u> defined material limitations have real consequences. Teachers reported that they could not use certain methods because of lack of facilities. Westbury (1973) is referred to in this connection, and Sharp and Green's (1976) suggestion that infants' teachers' use of so-called 'busyness' is a response to large class sizes and building restrictions. In both cases it is the authors who define the material conditions as constraints, not the teachers. How could these suggested consequences be demonstrated? Westbury actually had the data to do so, from a survey of provision and pedagogical practices in Canadian schools. It would have been simple for his hypothesis to have been tested by correlating the incidence of 'chalk and talk' with class size. Sharp and Green's hypothesis could be similarly tested.

The electricism of Pollard's (1982) 'revised model of coping strategies' obscures rather than clarifies the concept for me, especially his use of that favourite sociological metaphor of 'role'. The concept of role is a redundant reification (see Coulson 1972 and Cicourel 1973). Actors on the stage play roles, but people in other real-life micro-situations, whilst acting in the sense of pursuing purposeful behaviour, do not have roles. The metaphor of role is sometimes widened so that the social world is a stage, as in Shakespeare and in Goffman's (1969) 'dramaturgical' sociology. As Mennell (1980) concludes, 'the concept of role is certainly one which virtually all sociologists find useful, as far as it goes. But it does not go very far'.

Pollard's equivalent to Hargreaves' (1978) 'institutional constraints' is the 'classroom micro-social structure', and between them they provide a number of examples of possible sources of constraint; subjective, structural, as well as material, including, relations with other teachers, the age and social origins of pupils, the subject taught and professional socialisation. All of these are testable using the comparative method, as in an example of professional socialisation in my own research (King 1978). A few infants' teachers were defined by their headmistresses as not being 'proper infants' teachers'. They did do things differently to their colleagues (had different 'coping strategies' - if you like), for example, using direct control ('don't do that') rather than oblique control ('someone's being silly'). They were aware of their being different, and they and their headmistresses attributed this to their not being 'infant trained'. This example contradicts Green's (1977) view that the constraints of material conditions, rather than ideology, accounts for infants' teachers' practices. These teachers worked in the same material conditions as their colleagues, but taught differently because of their non-acceptance of elements of the ideology of infants' teaching.

'Societal constraints' for Hargreaves (1978) are those which are extra-educational in origin, but as he points out these are 'institutionally mediated'. In the terms I used earlier, teachers may have concepts of non-educational macro-structures, like the occupational structure, which constrain the micro-structure of classrooms. Hargreaves' own rather slender example is a recording of teachers talking, showing how their consciousness of the macro-occupational structure, may constrain the micro-structure of pupils' so-called 'guided' choice of learning method. Both he and Pollard make use of the Gramscian[18] concept of hegemony, to pose the existence of similar kinds of subjectivity in many micro-structures, (that is, in macro-structures which are the aggregates of micro-structures), and in macro-structures of different purposes. (In old-fashioned terms; in society in general including education). My more limited but specific example of the continuity of subjectivities is that of the ideology of educational meritocracy, based upon a study of

organisational change in secondary schools (King
1982). At the school level, politically willed and
resourced meritocracy is one purpose behind
comprehensive reorganisation and reduced sex-
differentiation. It is realised in the expansion
of exam opportunities and changed grouping
practices, and the consequent close monitoring of
pupils' learning progress. At the level of the
occupational structure, meritocracy is related to
credentialism; the use of increased educational
qualifications for social closure purposes by
specific occupational groups, in competition for
power, status and economic resources (Collins 1978,
Parkin 1979). The relative autonomy thesis places
education somewhere between being 'determined' by
external structures and 'determining' those
structures. This particular analysis, showing
educational meritocracy 'feeding' credentialism,
suggests that, to a degree, education has been more
'determining' than 'determined'. The
organisational changes are not simply outcomes of
this school-work relationship, but an integral part
of it.

Hargreaves (1978) subsumes the elements of his
analysis into a simile of a bicycle wheel, which
becomes a metaphor of a 'cycle of causality' in
which the teacher is the 'linch pin'. Pollard's
'model' is less poetically introduced, but the
merit of both is that they confirm that education
is only experienced in the micro-situations of
school and classroom, and that like all social
processes it is subject to multiple constraints,
and therefore with respect to any one constraint,
relatively autonomous. The three aspects of social
constraint, structure, subjective and material,
always operate together. As Collins (1976) puts
it, 'The subjective idealist, materialist, and
structural levels of analysis are not only not
rivals, but none of them is an adequate explanation
without the others'. Headteachers of British
maintained schools have legal, that is
bureaucratic, authority, in organising 'their'
schools. They (usually) have autonomy in this
structural respect to the extent that they can make
decisions about the organization without
necessarily referring to other people. However, in
the material conditions of large secondary schools,
headteachers subjectively define their having a
problem in organising the structure of
relationships of staff and children, to realise the
taken-for-granted ideology of the school as a

community (King 1983). They experience the material conditions as constraining. Their autonomy is exercised in organising pastoral care structures which are intended (among other things) to create feelings of belonging, but this ideological element is not necessarily felt to be constraining.

Material and structural constraints are the more likely to be experienced as limiting autonomy, because a person's subjective reality is part of his or her notion of individuality. However, it is the sociologist's task to examine the social as constraining, whether it is so defined by the acting individuals or not. This sometimes makes the sociological news rather discomforting, but as Berger and Kellner (1981) point out, 'Freedom cannot be disclosed by the method of any empirical science; sociology most emphatically included'. People (and sociologists studying them) are most aware of the limitation on their autonomy and the nature of social constraints, when their autonomy is reduced. As Leiter's (1981) study suggests, teachers feel most constrained by organisational structures which they subjectively define not to be in their interests. If individual teachers have any autonomy it is because they are teachers not particular individuals. This can be seen when the actions of a particular teacher are defined as transcending those of teachers. Berger and Berger (1978) give the example of a teacher who took off all his clothes in a sex education lesson: he was sacked. The limitations on a maintained school headteacher's autonomy is shown in the rare cases of schools being closed by local authorities because the organisation is judged to be unacceptable, as with the William Tyndale School, where, according to some accounts, the organisation, celebrating pupil autonomy, allowed some to play football in the playground all day (Auld 1976).

POETRY, STORIES AND NEWS

In this paper I have tried to show that the solution to the problem of the relationship between macro - and micro - levels of analysis is in recognising macro-structures as being aggregates of micro-structures. 'Education' is all the purposeful interactions in every school and classroom, in a given space and for a certain time. In every micro-situation, people's actions are constrained, because they are social. None of the three kinds of constraint, structural (relations with other people), subjective (purposes, beliefs, ideologies), and material, is ever totally constraining, because they always occur together. Determinisms, whether structural, ideological or material, are always partial. Relative autonomy is the common state of existence, and it is remarkable that this sociological truism has taken so long to be applied to education.

Reynolds (1984) is probably right in suggesting that its recent popularity is due to its being seen as 'a simple way of reviving rather dashed liberal hopes'. However the generation by sociologists of education of 'transformative practice' to realise these hopes 'is clearly not one that is shared by all members of the discipline, many of whom would regard political commitment of this kind as intellectually undesirable in its effects on scholarship'; myself included, and not only because of the parlous state of the subject since the neo-Marxist incursion.

Although, apart from a few liberal sentiments, Bernstein, quite properly, has never made his political disposition clear, his theoretical position does resemble that of the neo-Marxists. Whereas theirs 'owe(s) more to a commitment to a certain theoretical view of what empirical reality ought to be' (Reynolds 1984), his is based upon false assumptions of empirical reality. But like theirs, his theories are not based on 'a sensitively grounded appreciation of what empirical reality actually is' (Reynolds 1984). Their 'stories' and 'poetry' are not sociological 'news'.

We are never going to generate a conceptual scheme which will enable us to make definitive explanations of educational processes. Education, at the macro and especially micro - structural levels, is too varied and variable for us to ever sample much more than reltively small spaces and short times of empirical reality. In Weberian terms, the empirical task is to establish the patterns of behaviour between teachers and pupils, at particular times and in particular places, which constitute the structure of education at both the micro - and macro - levels, in terms of their subjective meanings in pursuit of economic, status and power interests, and of the resources available to them. It is the availability of the resources, both within the relationships and from extra-educational structures, that allow degrees of autonomy. What I hope we can do in the sociology of education is to make our 'news' delivery as honest as we can, even if, like all news, it is of necessity incomplete: and leave the 'poetry' and 'big stories' to others.

NOTES

1. See the contributions by Hargreaves, D., Banks and Hargreaves, A. to Barton and Meighan (1978).
2. Metaphors lose their effect in transcription. However, I take Bernstein's 'news' to refer to empirical realisations of education. Davies' (1983) 'big story' refers to highly generalised explanations generated independently of empirical studies; what Weber called 'emanationist theories'. (See Freund 1968). His 'poetry' (Davies 1982) has a similar meaning, referring to speculative 'theorising'. Theories should be explanations of empirical reality; that is, the explanatory element of Bernstein's news.
3. It is at least implied in Durkheim's (1936, 1951) social facts and in his anomie, in Marx's alienation (see Jordan 1971), in Parsons et al's (1953) social system, and in Schutz's (1972) primacy of 'everyday life'.
4. Individuals may of course have more than one purpose in their behaving, and may not legitimate those purposes. This classification is of the prime and common purpose.
5. This proposition follows from Weber's (1968) view of 'collectivities'. '. . . for the subjective interpretation of action in sociological work these collectivities (i.e. state, associations, business corporations, foundations) must be treated solely as the resultants of individual persons, since these alone can be treated as agents in the course of subjectively understandable action'. (Vol. 1, p.13). For a discussion of the problems of aggregation in educational research see King (1980a).
6. As in my own attempt, King (1982).
7. This concept of autonomy is taken from Katz (1965, 1968).
8. Recent critiques include O'Keefe (1979), Demaine (1981) and Hargreaves (1982).
9. Musgrove and Taylor (1969), and Taylor (1969), respectively.

10. Davies includes Keddie (1971) and Willis (1977) in this category.
11. This point is also made by Evans (1983).
12. Bottomore (1975) puts the first point very clearly '. . . a Marxist sociology at the present time would have to be capable of providing not only a 'real' analysis of capitalist society, but also a 'real' analysis of those forms of society which have emerged from revolutions inspired by Marxism itself, but which display many features that are problematic from the standpoint of Marxist theory' (p.22). It must be acknowledged that Bellaby (1977) is a rare exception in referring to Eastern Bloc education.
13. The language work is reported mainly in the volumes of the series edited by Bernstein Primary Specialization, Language and Education London: Routledge and Kegan Paul.
14. For example Hawkins (1971).
15. For a more extended treatment see King (1983).
16. Attempts to operationalise Bernstein's concepts include King (1976, 1979, 1981), Hannam (1975), Hamilton (1976), and Adelman (1977).
17. See his Introduction to Bernstein (1975) and Bernstein (1982).
18. See Entwistle (1978).

REFERENCES

Adelman, C. (1977) 'Sociological Constructions: Teachers' Categories' in Woods, P. and Hammersley, M. (eds.) School Experience, Beckenham: Croom Helm.
Althusser, L. (1972) 'Ideology and Ideological State Apparatuses' in Cosin, B.R. (ed.) Education, Structure and Society, Harmondsworth: Penguin.
Archer, M. (1979) Social Origins of Educational Systems, London: Sage.
Auld, R. (1976) William Tyndale Junior and Infants' Schools, London: Inner London Education Authority.
Banks, O. (1978) 'School and Society' in Barton, L. and Meighan, R. (eds.) op cit.
Barton, L. and Meighan, R. (eds.) (1978) Sociological Interpretations of Schooling and Classrooms : A Reappraisal, Driffield: Nafferton.

Bellaby, P. (1977) The Sociology of Comprehensive Schooling, London: Methuen.

Berger, P.L. and Berger, B. (1976) Sociology: A Biographical Approach, Harmondsworth: Penguin.

Berger, P.L. and Kellner, H. (1981) Sociology Reinterpreted, Harmondsworth: Penguin.

Bernstein, B.B. (1972) 'Sociology and the Sociology of Education: A Brief Account' in Eighteen Plus, Milton Keynes: Open University.

Bernstein, B.B. (1975) Class Codes and Control Vol. III, London: Routledge and Kegan Paul.

Bernstein, B.B. (1982) 'Codes, Modalities and the Process of Cultural Reproduction - A Model' in Apple, M.W. (ed.) Cultural and Economic Reproduction in Education, London: Routledge and Kegan Paul.

Bottomore, T. (1975) Marxist Sociology, London: Macmillan.

Bowles, S. and Gintis, H. (1976) Schooling in Capitalist America, London: Routledge and Kegan Paul.

Brameld, T. (1968) Japan - Culture, Education and Change, New York: Holt, Rinehart and Winston.

Cicourel, A.V. (1973) Cognitive Sociology Harmondsworth: Penguin.

Cicourel, A.V. and Kitsuse, J.I. (1963) The Educational Decision Makers, Indianapolis: Bobbs-Merrill.

Collins, R. (1975) Conflict Sociology, London: Academic Press.

Collins, R. (1978) The Credential Society, New York: Academic Press.

Collins, R. (1981a) 'The Micro-foundations of Macro-sociology' American Journal of Sociology 86 (March).

Collins, R. (1981b) 'Micro-translation as a Theory Building Strategy, Time, Space and Number as Pure Macro-Variables' in Knorr-Cetina, K. and Cicourel, A.V. (eds.) Advances in Social Theory and Methodology, London: Routledge and Kegan Paul.

Coulson, M. (1972) 'Role a Redundant Concept' in Jackson, J.A. (ed.) Role, Cambridge: Cambridge University Press.

Davies, B. (1976) Social Control and Education, London: Methuen.

Davies, B. (1982) 'Sociology and the Sociology of Education' in Hartnett, A. (ed.) The Social Sciences in Educational Studies, London: Heinemann.

Davies, B. (1983) 'The Sociology of Education' in

Hirst, P.H. (ed.) Educational Theory and its Foundation Disciplines, London: Routledge and Kegan Paul.

Demaine, J. (1981) Contemporary Theories in the Sociology of Education, London: Macmillan.

Dittmar, N. Sociolinguistics, London: Arnold.

Durkheim, E. (1938) The Rules of Sociological Method, Chicago: University of Chicago Press.

Durkheim, E. (1951) Suicide, Glencoe: Free Press.

Edwards, A.D. (1976) Language in Culture and Class, London: Heinemann.

Entwistle, H. (1978) Antonio Gramsci, London: Routledge and Kegan Paul.

Evans, J. (1983) 'Critique of Validity in Social Research' in Hammersley, M. (ed.) The Ethnography of Schooling, Driffield: Nafferton.

Foster, P.J. (1967) Education and Social Change in Ghana, London: Routledge and Kegan Paul.

Freund, N. (1968) The Sociology of Max Weber, London: Allen Lane.

Gellner, E. (1983) Nations and Nationalism, Oxford: Blackwell.

Gibson, R. (1977) 'Bernstein's Classification and Framing' Higher Education Review, 9.

Goffman, E. (1969) The Presentation of Self in Everyday Life, Harmondsworth: Penguin.

Grant, N. (1979) Soviet Education, Harmondsworth: Penguin.

Green, A.G. (1977) 'Structural Features of the Classroom' in Woods, P. and Hammersley, M. (eds.) School Experience, London: Croom Helm.

Hamilton, D. (1976) 'The Advent of Curriculum Integration: Paradigm Lost or Paradigm Regained' in Stubbs, M. and Delamont, S. (eds.) Explorations in Classroom Observation, Chichester: Wiley.

Hannan, A. (1975) 'The Problem of the "Unmotivated" in an Open School' in Channan, G. and Delamont, S. (eds.) Fronteers of Classroom Research, Slough: NFER.

Hargreaves, A. (1977) 'Progressivism and Pupil Autonomy' Sociological Review, 25.

Hargreaves, A. (1978) 'The Significance of Classroom Coping Strategies' in Barton and Meighan op cit.

Hargreaves, A. (1980) 'Synthesis and the Study of Strategies: A Project for the Sociological Imagination', in Woods, P. (ed.) Pupil Strategies. Explorations in the Sociology of the School, Croom Helm 1980.

Hargreaves, A. (1981) 'Contrastive Rhetoric and

Extremist Talk: Teachers, Hegemony and the Educationalist Context', in Barton, L. and Walker, S. (ed.) Schools, Teachers and Teaching, Lewes: Falmer Press.

Hargreaves, D.H. (1978) 'Whatever Happened to Symbolic Interactionism?' in Barton and Meighan op cit.

Hawkins, P.R. (1975) 'The Influence of Sex, Social Class and Pause Location in the Hesitation Phenomena of 7 year Old Children', in Bernstein, B.B. (ed.) Class Codes and Control Vol. 2, London: Routledge and Kegan Paul.

Jackson, L.A. (1977) 'The Myth of Elaborated and Restricted Codes' in Cosin, B.R. et al (eds.) School and Society, London: Routledge and Kegan Paul.

Jordan, Z.A. (1971) Karl Marx, London: Joseph.

Katz, F.E. (1965) 'The School as A Complex Social Organisation - A Consideration of Patterns of Autonomy' Harvard Educational Review, 34.

Katz, F.E. (1968) Autonomy and Organisation, New York: Random House.

Katz, M.B. (1971) Class, Bureaucracy and Schools, New York, Praeger.

Keddie, N. (1971) 'Classroom Knowledge' in Young, M.F.D. (ed.) Knowledge and Control, London: Macmillan.

King, R.A. (1973) School Organisation and Pupil Involvement, London: Routledge and Kegan Paul.

King, R.A. (1976) 'Bernstein's Sociology of the School - Some Propositions Tested' British Journal of Sociology, 27, 4.

King, R.A. (1978) All Things Bright and Beautiful? Chichester: Wiley.

King, R.A. (1979a) '"Someone's being Silly". Language and Social Control in Infants' Classrooms', Language for Learning, 1, 1.

King, R.A. (1979b) 'The Search for the "Invisible" Pedagogy', Sociology, 13, 3.

King, R.A. (1980a) 'Real Groups and False Aggregates in Educational Research', Educational Studies, 6, 3.

King, R.A. (1980b) 'Weberian Perspectives and the Study of Education', British Journal of the Sociology of Education, 1, 1,

King, R.A. (1981) 'Bernstein's Sociology of the School: a Further Testing', British Journal of Sociology, 32, 2.

King, R.A. (1982) 'Organisation Change in Secondary Schools: an Action Approach', British Journal of Sociology of Education, 3, 1.

King, R.A. (1983) The Sociology of School Organization, London: Methuen.

Labov, W. (1972) 'The Logic of Non-Standard English' in Giglioli, P. (ed.) Language and Social Context, Harmondsworth: Penguin.

Leiter, J. (1981) 'Perceived Teacher Autonomy and the Meaning of Organisational Control' Sociological Quarterly, 22.

Mennell, S.J. (1980), Sociological Theory, London: Nelson.

Musgrove, F. and Taylor, P. (1969) Society and the Teacher's Role, London: Routledge and Kegan Paul.

O'Keefe, D.J. (1979) 'Capitalism and Correspondence', Higher Education Review, 12.

Parkin, F. (1979) Marxism and Class Theory - a Bourgeois Critique, London: Tavistock.

Parsons, T., Bales, R.F. and Shils, E.A. (1953) Working Papers on the Theory of Action, New York: Free Press.

Payne, G. (1976) 'Making a Lesson Happen' in Hammersley, M. et al (eds.) The Process of Schooling, London: Routledge and Kegan Paul.

Pollard, A. (1982) 'A Model of Classroom Coping Strategies' British Journal of Sociology of Education, 3, 1.

Pring, R. (1975) 'Bernstein's Classification and Framing of Educational Knowledge' Scottish Educational Studies, 7.

Ramirez, F.O. (1981) 'Comparative Education: Synthesis and Agenda', in Short, J.F. (ed.) The State of Sociology, London: Sage.

Reynolds, D. (1984) 'Relative Autonomy reconstructed' in Barton, L. and Walker, S. (eds.) Social Crisis and Educational Research London: Croom Helm.

Rosen, H. (1972) Language and Class - A Critical Look at the Theories of Basil Bernstein London Facing Wall Press.

Schutz, A. (1972) The Phenomenology of the Social World, London: Heinemann.

Sharp, R. and Green, A. (1976) Education and Social Control, London: Routledge and Kegan Paul.

Speier, M. (1970) 'The Everyday World of the Child' in Douglas, J.D. (ed.) Understanding Everyday Life, London: Routledge and Kegan Paul.

Taylor, W. (1969), Society and the Education of Teachers, London: Faber.

Vaughan, M. and Archer, M.S. (1971) Social Conflict and Educational Change in England and France, Oxford: OUP.

Wallerstein, I. (1980) The Modern World System, Vol. 2. New York: Academic Press.

Weber, M. (1947) The Theory of Social and Economic Organisation, New York: Free Press.

Weber, M. (1948) From Max Weber:Essays in Sociology London: Routledge and Kegan Paul.

Weber, M. (1968) Economy and Society: An Outline of Interpretive Sociology, New York: Bedminster.

Westbury, I. (1973) 'Conventional Classrooms, Open Classrooms and the Technology of Teaching' Journal of Curriculum Studies, 5.

White, J. (1968) 'Instruction for Obedience?' New Society, 292.

Willis, P. (1977) Learning to Labour, London: Saxon House.

Zajada, J. (1980) 'Educational and Social Stratification in the Soviet Union' Comparative Education, 16, 1.

ORGANISING THE UNCONSCIOUS:
TOWARDS A SOCIAL PSYCHOLOGY OF EDUCATION

Philip Wexler

INTRODUCTION

My aim is to try to bring together historical developments in work in the social analysis of education, the changing social context in which it takes place, and the possibilities for practical transformative activity. I am going to talk about changes in the field, about more general social changes and about education.

A centre which held together for the past ten years has split apart. Work that announced itself as 'new sociology of education', has splintered into several evidently different paths. The view that social commitment should park itself at the door of good value-free, useful science expressed by A. Hargreaves (1982) is only one instance of a much more general reassertion of scientistic ideology in social studies. The theoretical renaissance in which atheoretical liberal empiricism was once replaced by a vigorous Marxist theory, has devolved toward a fashion-seeking theoreticism, that follows the Parisian style no less closely than the couturiers. The practical interest in education has become shrill, a ritualized and an ahistorical incantation toward a static essence, that is ironically called 'social change'.

The dynamism of the new sociology of education was that it was theory and research for practice, where practice was a concretely specifiable social project. What we have now is the separation of theoretical, empirical, and practical aspects of this intellectual movement and their separate but cumulative emptying and purposeless ritualization. I think that the so-called 'new sociology of education' is finished.

218

The end of the new sociology of education is in part a result of the depression in the academic industries, and increases in the exploitation, immiseration, and general limitations in the conditions of academic work. But it is also responsive to the latest general crisis of capitalism and its socioeconomic, cultural and educational aspects. Not only the unemployment and the massive suffering of industrial wage workers in the older mechanical industries, like steel and autos, but the entire backward movement of cultural expression, the 'restoration', about an earlier time, of which Marx wrote (1959):

> . . . society now seems to have fallen back behind its point of departure . . . and in order that no doubt as to the relapse may be possible, the old dates arise again, the old chronology, the old edicts . . . Easy come, easy go.

In the U.S., we have seen how efforts to reassert and extend the market, at the same time as reviving the forms and attachments of organicism - in fundamentalist religion, patriarchal family, and militarist patriotism - have led to the emergence of corporatist social arrangements. This social model is hailed on Wall Street as a social restructuring, new industrialization, and so on. In American education it has meant not simply a reorientation of curriculum toward corporate needs, but an institutional reorganization, and refinancing, which like corporatism generally, is unmaking the long American republican crusade to create public education (Wexler and Grabiner, 1984).

The defense against these onslaughts have, at least in the U.S., so far, while they are occasionally remarkable, like the women's encampment for peace in upstate New York, the electoral campaign of Jesse Jackson - remained uninspired by any historically innovative forms of practice.

The theory of education, as a theory of practice, has remained, during this time, defensive, without daring, and fearful of engaging unfamiliar aspects of historical social change. Instead of rethinking its theoretical and practical programs HISTORICALLY, it has remained static, even while talking about education and change.

Current radical theory does not look toward

an emergent social future. It relies, rather, upon various calls for cultural resistance in the discovery and valuation of relatively autonomous, unmassified forms of cultures of exploited groups. Its understanding of the operation of 'culture' is ordinarily limited to the stereotyped reproduction/ resistance pair. It does not explain what the analysis of culture could mean for radical political practice, beyond the glorification of traditional organicist cultures. Like the right-wing reaction that it opposes it looks historically backward. What then are the present historical directions and possibilities for a radical social theory of education?

SOCIAL THEORY AND SOCIETY

The basis of an historically appropriate radical theory of education already exists. It is represented, though not obviously, in social theory, and its less immediate basis is the current transformation of society, especially in the change in the social forces of production.

The social and theoretical bases of a radical social theory of education have themselves changed. One reason that it is so difficult to make explicit the social theoretic context of educational theory is that social theory, especially radical or critical theory, is becoming less visible. The primary change in modern social theory is a change in its very form of appearance, its medium. Critical social theory, as we have known and used it as a point of departure for understanding education in society, appears to have given way to museumization and bibliophile scholarship. But critical social theory is accessible albeit in hiding. It is increasingly embedded in literary theory and apparently replaced by the rise of textualism. The American philosopher Rorty (1982: 155), in observing this tendency, wrote of

> . . . the plausible claim that literature has now displaced religion, science, and philosophy as the presiding discipline of our culture.

Rorty attributes this general highbrow cultural change to the resurgence of Romanticism, in post-structuralism, not only as intellectual movement, but also as a form of life. The anthropologist Geertz (1980) also asserts the

ascendance of what he calls the text analogy,
explaining it as part of a cultural shift in which
boundaries, or genres, become blurred. We could, I
think, find a political explanation for the
interest of radical social theorists in various
forms of literary theory by extending Perry
Anderson's (1976) thesis that western Marxism is 'a
product of defeat' and its history, since 1918 has
been one of the divorce of Marxism from political
practice, and its swing to bourgeois culture, as
represented in 'successive types of European
idealism'.

A much less popular explanation for this shift
is the very unfashionable Marxist one, that is
nowadays derided as crude, mechanical and vulgar.
That is to suggest that the rise of literary theory
- as the displacement and hiding place of social
theory - is occurring because literary theory is an
aspect of the particular social formation.
Literary or symbolic theories are important because
they express changes in social life.

A main change in social life is that
signification has itself become a force of
production to unprecedented degree. The basic
productive energy or force of production in
capitalist society is becoming information. There
is occurring a <u>revolution in the forces of produc-
tion</u>, from industrial to informational production.
The centrality of information in basic production,
distribution and communication, and services,
represents a basic shift in the quality or
character of the productive basis of society.

In his overview of research on these changes,
Timothy Luke wrote (1983: 61-64):

> American producers increasingly are engaged
> either directly in the production of
> information or indirectly in the informationa-
> lization of goods-production and services
> provision . . . industrial capitalism has been
> greatly augmented if not nearly displaced by
> American informational capitalism . . .
> informational capital has not eliminated
> industrial or agricultural capital. Rather,
> it has begun to informationalize industrial
> production . . . just as industrial capital
> industrialized agriculture . . .

The current highbrow, academic emphasis on the
study of signification and semiosis appear as <u>de-
productionized versions of actual changes in social</u>

organization. As always, bourgeois theory abstracts from specific historical changes in the mode of production, represses the historically changing drama of class conflict, and gives us the shell of change in the guise of a universalized theoretical 'discovery'. Structuralism and post-structuralism, despite their refusal for themselves of any social basis, any sociology of knowledge, are not, as Foucault (1973) says, asocial. Rather, they state, in highbrow language, abstracted from production or from class conflict, (the repressed scene and drama of capitalism), an emergent, changed society.

EDUCATION AND THE UNCONSCIOUS

What is coming to constitute education in such a society? Currently, even the education that works for social class domination, may be contained in organizational forms, social relations, that are inappropriate or unsuited to them.

The ruling class, at such times, cannot understand why school-education does not work, and why, even among the most privileged youths, it is only instrumental rewards that provide a basis for conformity to the social routines of schools.

What we are seeing in our study of identity and disaffection among socially diverse youths, is that school-education is not engaging their energies and attentions. I suggest that one main reason for this is that the school's organization of pedagogy, its actual mode of immediate social relations, is modelled on the older mode of production and organization, while the youths are already relating to future organizational and productive forms through which they do their collective self-production, for identity-work.

To put it in very traditional terms, one could say that the conflict of generations that characterizes the schools that we are studying is the result of a structural contradiction between the forces and relations of production. Educators are imposing on youths a mode of social relations that is contradictory to the forces of interactional technology through which they are doing their 'work' - becoming somebody.

To understand not only how the form and medium of social theory is changing with the informational revolution in the forces of production, but also how education works, I think we have to understand the relation between mass communications and the lives of individual youths. Aside from their current effect, mass communications are ANTICIPATORY of formal or structural changes in education. This anticipatory educational medium, which already occupies as much time as the school in the U.S. (a conservative estimate is that the t.v. is on about seven hours each day), is now more organized, and more effectively penetrates the individual's unconscious structure of cognition and motivation. Mass communication researchers report (Roberts and Bachen, 1981)

> In all cases, the responses of heavy viewers revealed a conception of the world that differs from reality but that is characteristic of television's world.

When the literary theorists speak (or write) about 'discourse forming the subject', they are not describing a purely theoretical discovery, but a real historic change in the mode of production and education. The relation between mass discourse and individual formation and motivation is the emergent educational relation. Education follows the forces of production. Where they become informational/communicational, semiotic, and the formation of the subject occurs significantly through mass discourse, then it is that relation which is the educational one. The mass communications/individual relation now already better exemplifies the educational relation than does the school, which as we know it, with all its structural limitations of industrial and, later, corporate productive organization, is being surpassed, as new modes of education develop.

The change in the content and social form of education, where mass communications are seen as the foreshadowing or anticipation of emergent education, is the basis for thinking about what would a transformative, counter-hegemonic education be up against in such a society. Organizing the unconscious is a way of underlining some aspects of a counter-hegemonic education in a semiotic, oppressive, class society.

This will require not only a more specific understanding of the operation of the mass text, but also of the dynamics of the individual in relation to it. It is not surprising, however, that until now, radical education theory has refused to have any dealings with the question of 'psychology and education'.

Academic educational psychology ignores the collective discursive formation of the individual to focus instead on more refined forms of organizational stratification by measuring 'individual differences'. Its most recent advance, so-called 'cognitive science', acknowledges the changing forces of information production, but removes them from social relations and mystifies them in the typical way; making them into individual attributes.

Academic social psychology of education remains the last bastion of functionalist sociology: socialization, roles, influence, group dynamics, leadership in the classroom.

Similar ideologizing of social change occurs in depth psychology. The unconscious formation of the individual that was once described as universal instincts or better, libido, which is to say mechanical energy. Now, the unconscious formation of the individual takes account of and deflects understanding of social changes by saying that 'the unconscious is structured like a language'. Information replaces mechanism, but in an individualized and universalized form - the double device of capitalist ideology. I want to suggest, in a partial and preliminary way, some of the relations of collective symbolic operation at the individual level that I think educational practice is going to have to take account of, if it is to work as a radical practice.

NOTES ON A THEORY OF THE UNCONSCIOUS

The 'text' is not a metaphor, but the real collective symbolic structure through which individuals are formed. The content of this individualized appropriation of the collective symbolism is, as Deleuze and Guattari (1977) have understood, not a simple oedipal myth, but, increasingly, newer myths of late capitalism.

These myths are sexual and domestic myths. This does not mean that sexuality and domesticity are not activities, but only points toward the current centrality of their ideological role, and the subjective denial of production. 'Penthouse' and 'Harlequin' romances are the most popular mass exteriorisation of the sexual wishes, and 'Good Housekeeping' or 'Better Homes and Gardens' present collective domestic fantasy. These impersonally retold sagas, or modern mythologies, are structured, in both the form of their presentation and reception, not like a bourgeois novel, but like a soap-opera. Everyday realism, false concreteness, is the ideological form of the organization of mythic contents which constitute the formally-fragmented serial appropriation of a collective text.

These pseudo-realistically structured scenes are the ideology of the unconscious. Its motives, drives or energy are not simply abstract 'libido'. They are the drives of the subjective aspect of the mode of production; specific fears and hopes of particular kinds of labour-power. Let me indicate two examples of a wide array of processes: a central dynamic for the individual is the tension between these two levels. The ideological work of unconscious subjectivity is encoding or translating of drives of psychologies of labour power into serialized scenes of sex/domesticity: de-productionizing individual desire.

A second central dynamic, one which operates the relation between individual functioning and the collective cultural text is IDENTIFICATION.

Identification is an ideology of individualism. It is the desire to be like the other. What is called 'desire' is the path of identification. In a capitalist society that path is either through 'possession' or 'death'. Incorporation is the compensatory reaction to the drive for excessive difference.

Identification is the key concept not simply of bourgeois psychological theory; in the vaunted teacher-student relation, it is also seen as the central mechanism of education.

One accomplishment of successful identification is to replicate in the individual the tension of symbolic disjunction between labour-power and myth, which enables the continuous activity of the unconscious: it moves interpretation away from production, and the fears and needs it generates, into serialized mythologies of domesticity and sexuality. Identification is still an educational ideal - although it is a basic ground for the working of bourgeois ideology.

In our research, we see concrete examples of how the failures and successes of identification in schools work. With disaffction, for example, the student moves identity-work into the mythological realm, and seeks to blot out the actual conditions of identity production in the school. This is not 'resistance', but self-mythologising, facing the student away from the conditions of her/his own self-production. The identifying student becomes like the teacher, torn, always hopeful of self-realization in social production in the shcoolplace, yet ready for a more displaced, symbolic expression of self-realization through 'consumption'.

TOWARD A SOCIAL PSYCHOLOGY OF EDUCATION

What are the educational possibilities in this society of mass mythology and denial of social production, where both educational failures and successes both lead to ideological subjects, though of different sorts?

A central ANALYTICAL RESOURCE for developing an historically specific, counter-hegemonic education is in bourgeois social theory and practice. Just as literary theory is the deproductionized and de-classed theory of a class, semiotic or informational society, so too, its practice, literary criticism, is a starting point for developing an appropriate counterpractice.

In the transformed society, an alternative, radical education will require knowledge of the practices of re-appropriation. An active 'criticism' means, first, reversing the current mythological translation of everyday life into pseudo-concrete, serialized realism. Making the unconscious translation of the psychology of labour-power into the myths of personal sexual and domestic life a conscious interpretive practice of the organized re-theft of mass communications is a necessary modern form of literacy.

The educational principle of identification will be replaced with a struggle for expression. Expression means, in a signified society, not simply writing, or interpretation. It certainly does not mean substituting what Jameson (1981) calls a positive or utopian hermeneutic for a negative, critical one. It means changing the mode of individual-discourse relation. Writing becomes 'writing over'.

The counterhegemonic education I am suggesting is the transformation of bourgeois literary criticism, which is becoming the dominant intellectual practice. Some move away from a purely contemplative criticism has already begun. There are moves toward understanding criticism more actively and collectively, as reader-response, interpretive communities, and criticism as an institution.

I am talking about education as expanded literacy and criticism. In the semiotized, signified society, self-formation means the ability to write-over, to express, the process of collective or group formation, in which criticism is the interpretive/expressive moment. This points toward a new literacy, and a new meaning of reading and writing, for which the extreme example is graffiti. It is, for many of the NYC subway writers, a collective production of group identity through collective 'writing over'.

What precisely re-appropriation, expression, writing-over, literacy and criticism will mean in the emerging society are the questions for trying to develop an historically meaningful educational practice.

CONCLUSION

That work will require giving up backward-looking radical romanticism; overcoming the fear of communications technology; and beginning to understand that education is education in the process of creative, active symbolic appropriation, through active criticism, which is expression.

I believe that the accomplishment of this goal will require immersion in the collective symbolic text, and a systematic understanding of its relation to both the forces of production and the individual unconscious. That is just part of the intellectual work which lies ahead after the new sociology of education.

REFERENCES

Anderson, Perry (1976) Considerations on Western Marxism, London: NLB.

Deleuze, G. and Guattari, F. (1977) Anti-Oedipus: Capitalism and Schizophrenia, New York: Viking.

Foucault, Michel (1973) The Order of Things: An Archaeology of the Human Sciences, New York: Vintage.

Geertz, Clifford (1980) 'Blurred Genres: The Refiguration of Social Thought'. The American Scholar, Spring (165-179).

Hargreaves, Andy (1982) 'Resistance and Relative Autonomy Theories: Problems of Distortion and Incoherence in Recent Marxist Analyses of Education'. British Journal of Sociology of Education, Vol. 3, No. 2, 1982 (pp. 107-126).

Jameson, Frederic (1981) The Political Unconscious:
    Narrative as a Socially Symbolic Act, Ithaca,
    New York: Cornell.
Luke, Timothy (1983) Telos, No. 56 (Summer)
    'Informationalism and Ecology', pp. 59-77.
Marx, Karl (1959) 'The Eighteenth Brumaire of Louis
    Bonaparte', pp. 318-348 in Lewes Feuer (ed.)
    Marx and Engels: Basic Writings on Politics
    and Philosophy, New York: Anchor.
Roberts, Donald F. and Christine M. Bachen (1981)
    'Mass Communication Effects' pp. 309-356 in
    Annual Review of Psychology, 32, 1981, Annual
    Reviews Inc.
Rorty, Richard (1982) Consequences of Pragmatism,
    Sussex: Harvester Press.
Wexler, Philip and Gene Grabiner (1984 - in press)
    'The Education Question: American During the
    Crisis' in Rachel Sharp (ed.) Capitalist
    Crisis, the State and Education: A Comparative
    Politics of Education.

EDUCATION AND SOCIAL CHANGE - AUTHOR INDEX

Adelman, C. 202 n16
Allport, K. 3
Althusser, L. 198-9, 200, 203
Amarel, M., with A. Bussis 4
Anderson, P. 221
Apple, M.W. 166, 167
Applegate, J., with K. Newman 5
Archer, M.S. 195
Archer, M.S., with M. Vaughan 199
Arfwedson, G. 39
Arnold, M. 120-1
Auld, R. 209

Bacharach, S.B. 54, 58
Bachen, C.M., with D.F. Roberts 223
Bailey, A.J. 30, 44, 55-6
Bailey, F.G. 58
Baker, T. 168 n4
Baldridge, V.J. 58
Bales, R.F., with T. Parsons 193-4
Ball, S.J. 30
Ballard, P. 116 n6
Banks, O. 193 n1, 201
Becker, H. 12, 33
Bellaby, P. 201 n12
Bennett, C. 22
Bereiter, C. 93 n8
Berger, B., with P.L. Berger 209
Berger, P.L. 209
Bernbaum, G. 141 n17
Bernstein, B. 111-12, 127, 193, 201, 202, 203-5,
   210
Berube, M. 95, 96
Bethell, P. 21
Beynon, T. 67

Blackie, J. 124
Blase, J. 14
Boissevain, J. 58
Bone, A. 138 n2
Bottomore, T. 201 n12
Bowles, S. 112, 166, 167, 197-8, 199, 203, 204
Boys, C. 177
Boyson, R. 19, 68, 122
Brameld, T. 199
Brandis, W., with D.A. Young 23, 145
Braun, R.J. 99
Braverman, H. 58
Briggs, A. 64
B.P. 181
Broadfoot, P. 112
Brown, J.B., with S.S. Fergusson 68
Brown, O., with F. Fuller 6-7, 14
Brown, P.J.B. 68, 70
Burden, P., with K. Newman 5
Burke, P., with J. Christensen 5; with R. Fessler 5
Burns, T. 45
Bussis, A. 4
Byrne, D. 141 n15
Byrne, E. 138 n3, 141 n16

Carrier, C., with R. McNergner 4-5
Carspeken, P. 71, 85
Castells, M. 63, 83
Cawson, A. 174
Centre for Contemporary Cultural Studies 68, 149 n32
Chittenden, E., with A. Bussis 4
Christensen, J. 5; with R. Fessler 5
Cicourel, A.V. 198, 202, 206
Clegg, S. 58
Cockburn, C. 63, 68
Collins, R. 58, 193-5, 208
Cosin, B. 145 n23
Coulson, M. 206
Coulter, F. 5
Crick, M. 65
Cuban, L. 91, 95, 100, 101
Cyert, R.M. 30, 39

Dale, R. 147 n30
Davies, B. 193, 197, 200, 205
Dawson, P. 155, 162-3, 164
Dean, J. 154-5
Deem, R. 140 n8, 145 n24
Deleuze, G. 224

Gittell, M. 91, 95-6, 98, 99, 100; with M. Berube 95, 96
Gleeson, D. 179-80
Goffman, E. 206
Goldthorpe, J. 22
Gordon, C. 160
Gould, R. 62-3
Gouldner, A. 93
Grabiner, G., with P. Wexler 219
Grace, G. 113 n4, 116 n7, 120, 127 n15
Gramsci, A. 64, 175, 207
Grant, N. 198
Gray, A. 57
Green, A., with R. Sharp 200, 206
Green, A.G. 207
Green, C., with A. Gartner 100 n12
Greenfield, W., with J. Blase 14
Gross, R. 99 n11
Guattari, F., with G. Deleuze 224

Hall, S. 175, 176
Hamilton, D. 202 n16
Hammersley, M. 30
Hannam, A. 202 n16
Hannam, C. 155-6
Hargreaves, A. 77, 193 n1, 197 n8, 203, 205, 206, 207, 208, 218
Hargreaves, D.H. 31, 33, 88, 157, 193 n1
Harnett, P. 96, 105
Havinghurst, R. 4
Hawkins, P.R. 201 n14
Hentoff, N. 92
Hevesi, A.G., with M. Gittell 91, 95-6, 99, 100
Hewitt, M., with I. Pinchbeck 153
Hextall, I. 112
Holly, M.L. 6
Holmes, E. 116 n7, 120
Holt, J. 93 n7
Howe, L. with M. Lauter 96
Howey, K. 5
Howey, K., with R. Willie 3-4
Hoyle, E. 29-30, 43-4, 57
Huang Wen Lsien, with B. Schaffer 143
Huberman, M. 4
Hudak, G., with B. Tabachnik 7
Humphries, S. 153
Hunt, O. 4
Hunter, C. 30, 79

Lockwood, D. 137, 147-8
Loevinger, J. 4
Lortie, D. 14, 90, 102
Lowe, R. 118
Luke, T. 221

McNergney, R. 4-5
March, J.G. 58; with R.M. Cyert 30, 39
Marland, M. 46, 140 n7
Martin, D. 112 n1
Marx, K. 193-4, 219
Mathieson, M. 121 n11
Mayer, M. 101
Mennell, S.J. 206-7
Merseyside Socialist Research Group 65, 69
Miller, H.D.R., with P. Carspeken 71, 85; with G.
  Wallace 68
Moskowitz, E.J., with P. Wexler 177, 185
Moore, R. 180, 186
Musgrave, P. 128 n16
Musgrove, F. 30, 122, 197 n9
Myers, D.A. 104 n13

Neill, A.S. 19
Newcastle Commission (1861) 115-16
Newman, K. 5
Nias, J. 5, 6, 7, 8, 9, 12, 14, 15-16, 17
Nickson, A., with F. Gaffiken 67

Oja, S. 4-5
O'Keefe, D.J. 197 n8
Olsen, J., with J.G. March 58
O'Neill, E. 116 n7
Osterman, P., with R. Gross 99 n11
Ozga, J. 120

Parkin, F. 145, 200, 208
Parsons, J., with F. Fuller 6-7
Parsons, T. 193-4
Partridge, J. 34
Passow, A.H. 102
Payne, G. 194, 195
Pearl, A. 102, 104
Pearson, L. 153
Peters, D., with R. Sutton 5
Peterson, A. 5
Piaget, J. 4, 184

EDUCATION AND SOCIAL CHANGE - GENERAL INDEX

Callaghan, James 68, 181-2
Cambridgeshire 112 nl
Canada 88, 89 n5
capitalism
  and belief 203
  crisis of 219
  see also cuts
  and education 177-9, 181, 182-6, 197-9, 203
  informational 221-2
  international 68, 83, 178
  'myths of' 224-5
  and social division 142
  state 198
'Casterbridge High School' 31-3, 38-57
  headmaster of 35-7, 41-2, 46, 49-54
  staff discussion day at 46-8
Catholic Party 65
Catholic schools 67
  reorganisation 70, 77, 81
  unions in 72
Catholic Teachers' Association 72
catholics 65, 82
Centre Party 65
Certificate of Secondary Education 34, 169
  'Mode III' 35, 52
Christians see catholics and protestants
class see social class
co-education 78, 137-46, 148, 208
  arguments for 79, 80-1, 145, 146
  and educational demands 148
  see also single-sex schools
Communist Party 67, 72
community
  control of education, proposals for, in USA 89,
    91, 95, 99, 101
  meaning of 78-9
comprehensive schools 30-57
  acceptability 144
  assessment in 126
  formation 31-49, 50, 76-82, 140-2
  'mixed economy' 77
  philosophies 35-6, 41, 47-8, 51, 56, 58, 80,
    140-2, 144
  political costs 138
  politics in 54, 56, 58
  public policy and 56
  and social divisions 139-41, 144, 147, 179
  types 29, 76-7
  see also co-education and under reorganisation
computers in schools 142-3
Confederation of British Industry 182, 189

240

schools (continued)
  life-cycles 62
  occupation 70-1
  power in 29-30, 54, 55, 56-8, 125
  reorganisation see under reorganisation
  ritual in 165
  selective 80, 141-2, 144, 145-6
  see also co-education, comprehensive schools,
    curriculum, grammar schools, pupils, secondary
    modern schools, single-sex schools and
    teachers
Schools Council Industry Project 182, 186, 188-91
science teaching
  gender and 138, 140, 142-3, 145, 158, 167
  and industry 180-1, 188
secondary modern schools 33-8
self see identity
setting 167
  single-sex 145, 146
  see also streaming
sex discrimination see under girls and women
Sex Discrimination Act 144, 145
sex education 209
sexuality see heterosexuality
Shanker, Albert 91
'Shottsford Road School' 31-3, 35-6, 40-1, 44
single-sex schools 79
  arguments for 80-1, 137, 145
  benefits for boys 145
  benefits for girls 137, 140, 145
  and catholicism 67
  and feminism 80, 81, 139, 145-7
  parents and 76
  resistance to 144, 145
  SDA and 144
  see also co-education
'situational self' 8, 15-16, 23, 24
sixth forms 45, 79
social class
  and blame 93, 94, 96-8, 104-6
  and consumer interests 174
  definitions 201
  and discipline 156
  and education 81, 113-23, 128, 138, 139-41, 144,
    166, 179, 200, 222
  and educational spending 141
  and sexual division 138, 141, 144, 145-7
  teachers', in USA 93, 94-8
  and values 96, 105